Culture and Project Management

A very useful insight and guide to handling a challenging aspect of group activity. Omar has distilled the best of theory and approach on the subject. More importantly by using examples and anecdotes, non-specialists like me can better grasp the issues and solutions in my own professional context.

Chou Chong, Investment Director,
Aberdeen Asset Management Asia Limited

In Culture and Project Management *Omar Zein offers a masterful review of well-known and accepted theories related to how different types of cultures may look at the same event or experience and why this matters when doing business together. What sets this book apart, however, is that Zein also explains why typical approaches to developing rapport for a multicultural team over the long term are quite different from managing short-term projects where time is of the essence. Best of all, he offers clear strategies for short-term managers on what to consider as they assess the international makeup of their team and how then to work with this diversity to achieve the successful and timely completion of their projects.*

Ruth E. Van Reken,
co-author, *Third Culture Kids: Growing Up Among Worlds*;
co-founder, Families in Global Transition

A very understandable and approachable description with great examples of the concrete impact culture has in one of the work-life areas, the area of project management. A must read for every international project manager, with examples relating to both short-term projects and long-term programs.

Egbert Schram, Managing Director,
Itim International and the Hofstede Centre

Culture and Project Management

Managing Diversity in Multicultural Projects

OMAR ZEIN

For Michel & Manon

With much love & affection

30/7/2017

GOWER

Published by
Gower Publishing Limited
Wey Court East
Union Road
Farnham
Surrey, GU9 7PT
England

Gower Publishing Company
110 Cherry Street
Suite 3-1
Burlington, VT 05401-3818
USA

www.gowerpublishing.com

British Library Cataloguing in Publication Data
A catalogue record for this book is available from the British Library

Library of Congress Cataloging-in-Publication Data
Zein, Omar.
  Culture and project management : managing diversity in multicultural projects / by Omar Zein.
    pages cm
  Includes bibliographical references and index.
  ISBN 978-1-4724-1382-6 (hardback) -- ISBN 978-1-4724-1383-3 (ebook) -- ISBN 978-1-4724-1384-0 (epub) 1. Project management. 2. Organizational culture. I. Title.
  HD69.P75Z447 2015
  658.4'04--dc23
                                                                                    2014044632

ISBN 9781472413826 (hbk)
ISBN 9781472413833 (ebk – PDF)
ISBN 9781472413840 (ebk – ePUB)

Reprinted 2015

Printed in the United Kingdom by Henry Ling Limited, at the Dorset Press, Dorchester, DT1 1HD

Contents

List of Figures

List of Tables

Foreword

Omar is a first-generation British citizen born to Syrian parents in Saudi Arabia where he spent his childhood years. He was educated in the UK where he went to an international school prior to university and lives and works in the UK and Italy; frequently travelling all over the world to meet and work with international clients. He is the perfect example of the modern multicultural manager and, because he has enormous emotional intelligence, he is capable of understanding other people's issues. So, who else could have written this book?

I have seen Omar present at conferences, read some of his articles and his book is very much an extension of this work. It is organised in a very logical and elegant way, bringing us slowly but surely to understand culture and human nature, and finally, its effect on our practices.

What makes this book eminently readable is that it is full of stories, anecdotes and real-life examples that Omar has collected over years of practice. They are all useful and help weave the context and practice of project and programme management in a multicultural project environment. He helps make the unfamiliar and often scary environment of a team composed of people coming from different racial, national, social and religious backgrounds familiar and reassuring.

In Part I, Omar clarifies what culture means and how it is developed, demystifying the mysterious and magical aura that often surrounds discussion on culture; he makes it real and tangible. He does not fear to tackle the bull by the horns, which is refreshing in a world where political correctness often hides deep cultural conflicts and value anxieties. He then describes practical project situations and outlines issues found in real-life multinational projects. Anybody who has worked on such projects will relate to Omar's examples. Again he brings in his own personal experience into the writing and makes it real by telling stories of real people in real situations. You can feel for them and therefore it is very effective in making the reader understand how to prepare for these multicultural situations.

In Chapter 2 in Part II, Omar looks at the research that has underpinned our knowledge of culture, and particularly national culture. It is refreshing to see that he goes beyond the seminal, but too often exclusively cited, Hofstede four dimension's study to look at other research. This broadens our perspective and makes us understand what some of the wider world issues are. He then selects, among all these dimensions, those that best apply to project management and explains them both simply and eloquently.

In the rest of Part II and using a cross-cultural project management scenario, Omar reviews the cultural orientations that he has selected in detail and provides a wealth of examples about the society, family, government and the workplace, as well as easy-to-read tables. These allow the reader to truly grasp the meaning behind each orientation and to relate it to their own experience. Part III is the one you will read through quickly the first time and come back to over and over as you start applying Omar's recommendations and need to ground them.

Chapter 10 in Part III sets the context in which multicultural projects will flourish. Although one could challenge the types of organisations Omar describes as reductionist, there is validity in describing the classic types of organisations from a project point of view. It is a simple black and white approach that keeps the reader focused on the core subject of the book and avoids shifting into a discussion on organisational structures. The same applies to the discussion on roles and responsibilities in Chapter 11 and their main project tasks. In each case, the actual description is kept to its simplest in order to be able to focus on the influence of cultural dimensions on the actions of different actors placed in this situation. In that sense, Omar has learned from the organisational psychologists, by keeping the variables at a minimum to be able to focus on the core elements of the discussion. Throughout the rest of Part III, Omar illustrates the effect of the earlier elaborated cultural orientations on specific project management practices covering both the hard and soft aspects.

In Part IV, Omar takes us through a project from a culturally aware perspective using six simple steps: awareness, observation, association, validation, strategy and action. He illustrates each step very effectively through a role-play example. This enables the reader to actually see a practical real-life application of the concepts outlined in the book.

Finally, in his conclusion, Omar outlines his vision for future elaboration of culture and project management and rightly warns us not to fall into complacency, but to continually challenge our own views and keep reflecting in order to stay culturally aware.

This book is a must for managers practicing in a multicultural and socially connected environment and I highly recommend it.

Michel Thiry, PhD, FAPM, PMI Fellow.
Managing Partner, Valense Ltd.
Author of *A Framework for Value Management Practice* and
Program Management

Preface

During 2003 and 2004, I was contracted by a major newspaper in Italy (*La Stampa*) to help set up the structure for the organisation and its support and reporting functions along with the governance and control standards for a major programme; changing the newspaper format from a broadsheet to a new tabloid format.

As one would expect, the impact of the programme went well beyond changing the rotary presses. It involved a complete change of the industrial machinery including the plate moulding machines, distribution and packaging, warehouse layout and movement, auxiliary and support infrastructure as well as of course, the massive printing presses. These elements were referred to as the *industrial projects* alongside which, a complete change of factory building layout was needed, the *construction project*.

The new newspaper format also meant that packaging dimensions would change and the distribution network needed to be guided to adapt their vehicles as well as the newspaper stands, to fit the new format.

There were also a number of ancillary IT projects; starting from the operating software of the new machinery, all the way to Material Resource Planning (MRP) and the desktop publishing software used by the journalists.

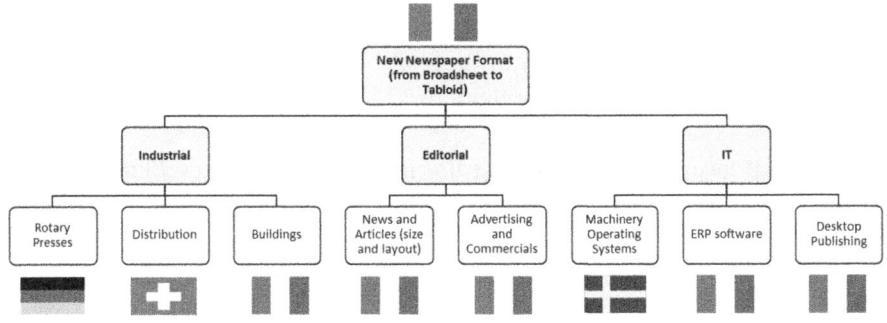

Figure P.1 **From broadsheet to tabloid**

Finally, the task of establishing the training needs for the various departments in *La Stampa* and structuring this training was a sizable project in itself.

Figure P1 illustrates a simplified breakdown of the programme:

At the top of the tree, we have the Italian Programme of *La Stampa* newspaper:

- change the newspaper format from broadsheet to tabloid.

At the next level we have the editorial projects involving:

- changing the size and layout of articles and news to fit the new format (performed by internal Italian staff with the aid of local sector consultants);

- changing the dimensions for page advertising, along with layout and pricing (performed by internal Italian staff in coordination with advertising clients and the aid of local sector consultants).

Industrial projects involving:

- replacing four rotary presses (German supplier);

- replacing an entire conveyor, distribution and packaging system (Swiss supplier);

- adapting the building layout (Italian supplier/architect).

IT projects involving:

- installation and configuration of the operating system for the rotary presses (Swedish supplier);

- updating and integrating the Enterprise Resource Planning (ERP) system (Italian supplier);

- updating the desktop publishing software (Italian suppliers).

These projects and their various sub-projects were all interdependent. From the starting point of selecting the supplier of the new presses, came various requirements for the layout, installation and commissioning of their machinery which included:

- the building layout to be prepared by the Italian architect (which had interdependencies with the entire factory functions);

- full specifications for the distribution system to be provided in advance by the Swiss supplier (which had interdependencies with the entire distribution network);

- full coordination with the Swedish supplier of the press operating systems (which had interdependencies with other IT systems including the ERP, MRP and desktop publishing software).

The list goes on for every major stakeholder.

At the heart of all this was the project manager. If we look at this example we can see four distinct national cultures present, each representing a different stakeholder and each with a different value contribution to the project:

Italian

The Italians tended to value public acknowledgement and respect for their work. Being in charge was also important for their self-esteem. They were willing to work the extra hours and weekends because of the prospects it offered to their career.

The Italians were uncomfortable with solutions that were untried and untested, preferring proven and stable technologies over newer technologies with useful but unproven functions.

German

As most evidently within the manufacturing sector, the Germans tended to be less concerned with acknowledgement or public esteem, pertaining a technical perspective towards their work and rejecting out of hours meetings and other activities if not absolutely necessary.

Although they had a preference to tried and tested solutions over newer but unproven ones, they were more willing to take chances than the Italians. As with most of the manufacturing sectors worldwide, they also favoured structure and respected hierarchy.

Swiss

Despite historical research providing data on the Swiss culture overall, my experience as well as that of my colleagues is that the Swiss culture is very varied depending on the region and cannot be generalised even for academic purposes. Not surprising given the country's geographical location and its three different national languages split over three distinct regions (Italian, French and German).

However, as for the supplier of the above distribution systems which was based in Zurich, the Swiss demonstrated a similarity to the Italians in that they also valued being acknowledged for their work and were willing to put in the extra hours and work weekends.

The Swiss did not avoid taking a calculated chance with newer technologies. However, unlike the Germans or the Italians, they were less rigid when it came to respecting hierarchy.

Swedish

The Swedes within the project were the exact opposite to the Italians. They were completely unconcerned with acknowledgement and even felt irritated or embarrassed whenever a well-meaning manager acknowledged their work publicly. They had a strong technical approach to their work and although they were happily willing to stay late hours and weekends, they only did so if meeting delivery deadline or if quality requirements demanded it; never for management meetings or team discussions.

They also favoured the latest available solutions and technologies even if untried. Their attitude was: it's better to try, fail, modify, try again and so on until the most effective possible solution works, rather than settle for any lesser but tried and tested one. They also had very little regard to hierarchy; be it at the technical or management levels.

I trust you agree that if the project management approach does not take into account the cultural differences between the stakeholders, then the project will not perform at its best. Even if project management best practices were perfectly implemented.

La Stampa was an eye opener for me as I witnessed conflicts that were not supported or addressed by the current project management standards and methodologies. For example, the Swedish supplier of the production operating system, and who is a world leader in their sector, wanted to deliver nothing less than a state of the art seamless and efficient solution and therefore proposed the latest and most innovative one they had recently developed. They then put themselves to the task of tweaking the various interfaces and integrations with other systems, and troubleshooting the resulting technical problems.

What the Swedes did not realise is that the Italians, being far less comfortable with uncertainty, would have much preferred a less recent version of their software that has already been tried and tested in the industry and can be implemented with minimum modification, even if that meant lesser functionality or automation. As a result, *La Stampa* managers were becoming anxious and uneasy each time the Swede's system conflicted with the hardware or interfacing software. They did not appreciate the Swedes' efforts towards innovation. Furthermore, as the interfacing systems including the desktop publishing and ERP were mainly selected and implemented by Italian suppliers who complained to *La Stampa* about the Swede's 'experimentation' at the project's cost, the conflict was becoming critical.

Other conflicts between the various stakeholders arose including communication (flat vs. hierarchical), working hours (late evening management meeting) and so on. Many, if not all, would have been easily avoided had culture been a part of the project management approach. Had the Swedes noted at the start that their Italian client and other interdependent suppliers did not share their approach to new solutions and preferred something tried and tested, they could have either proposed an earlier version of the system or elaborated clearly in their offer what implementing a new technology entails; therefore agreeing and effectively managing the stakeholders' expectations.

When we consider that *La Stampa's* example represents only European cultures and that many international projects have a mix of cultures from different continents and often sharing little in common, the importance of cultural consideration in international project management cannot be over-emphasised.

It is only fair having used my experience at *La Stampa* as an example that I should note that the programme was completed successfully; delivering expected value through the required specifications which were completed within budget and ahead of schedule. In this particular case, the various managements' maturity and dedication overrode the mild inter-European cultural conflicts. Numerous other examples were not so lucky.

Introduction

Globalisation, with all its economic and social effects, is a reality for most developed nations today. So much so that we often forget that not so long ago economies were independent and international travel was limited to the wealthy. When we further consider that there was no internet, cable television or international movie industry (or the movie industry altogether) we start to get a sense of how 'local' the local cultures were at the time. We needn't speculate so hard to imagine how it was, many movies have done a great job of portraying life in certain cultures at certain periods very well.

Hollywood movies set in the early 20th century and late 19th century often give a great insight into what 'local' culture meant at the time. *Gone With The Wind* or more recently Paul Thomas Anderson's *There Will Be Blood* are excellent portrayals. There are equivalent films from Germany, China, Egypt, Japan and almost all countries that have a movie industry.

Now let us consider how it was when the earliest multinationals started to operate in countries other than their own. Imagine an early last century's American oil baron (as played by Daniel Day Lewis in *There Will Be Blood*) travelling to China to establish a branch of his oil company in joint venture with a local Chinese business. The new company is not to be a mere importer of US oil, but will have its own operations in exploring and digging for local oil, all under the guidance of the well-experienced American baron of course, who have well-established and proven processes for all aspects of the business; be it logistics, legal, personnel, management, operations or finance.

Moving closer to our times, about a century ago, Management Consultancy was born as a discipline with the first firms operating in such a capacity being Arthur D. Little and Booz Allen Hamilton; helping organisations improve their operational and management practices.

Since then, the discipline grew rapidly and evolved to address a wide spectrum of needs that aimed at achieving higher efficiency and growth, which it went on to do successfully until globalisation started and large organisations began to expand overseas, just as in our imagined scenario of the oil baron above. They were hit by the first lessons of cultural impact on business practices. Not only did well-established management practices in the US fail to work abroad, they furthermore proved inimical and were detrimental to results.

The perceived virtues of 'getting down to business', 'openly addressing conflicts' and 'holding responsible persons accountable for their actions' were often seen as 'impolite and lacking in personal relation', 'rude and damaging to harmony' and 'improper attempts to signal out an individual rather than the group' respectively.

The results were astonishing; large joint ventures broke with ill feelings because the first management consultants failed to consider the impact that a different culture can have on their (very successful at home) theories. Thereafter, a number of studies and research were made by various experts to understand the cultural influence on management practices, and as a result, many international businesses have come to realise the need to adapt their practices to the hosting culture.

What is particularly pleasant and encouraging is that many businesses today also acknowledge that often the practices of the 'other' cultures, previously thought of as inferior from a management perspective, can often be more efficient and effective than their own. We are finally coming to the management realisation that our way is neither the 'only' way, nor the 'best' or 'better' way, but rather it is what we believe to works best for 'us'.

Notwithstanding the above, even the most culturally aware and prepared organisations do face a cyclical period of adjustment, learning and readjustment whenever they start operating in a new culture and prior to getting a locally efficient and effective working culture. This period of settling down is referred to as 'assimilation'.

Naturally, the shorter this 'assimilation' period is, the less 'suffering', costs and 'loss of business' the organisation has to face during its cross-cultural expansion. But what if no 'assimilation' period or a very minimal 'assimilation' period is available? What if our cross-cultural work has to start immediately?

This is exactly what we face in multicultural and cross-cultural projects and programmes.

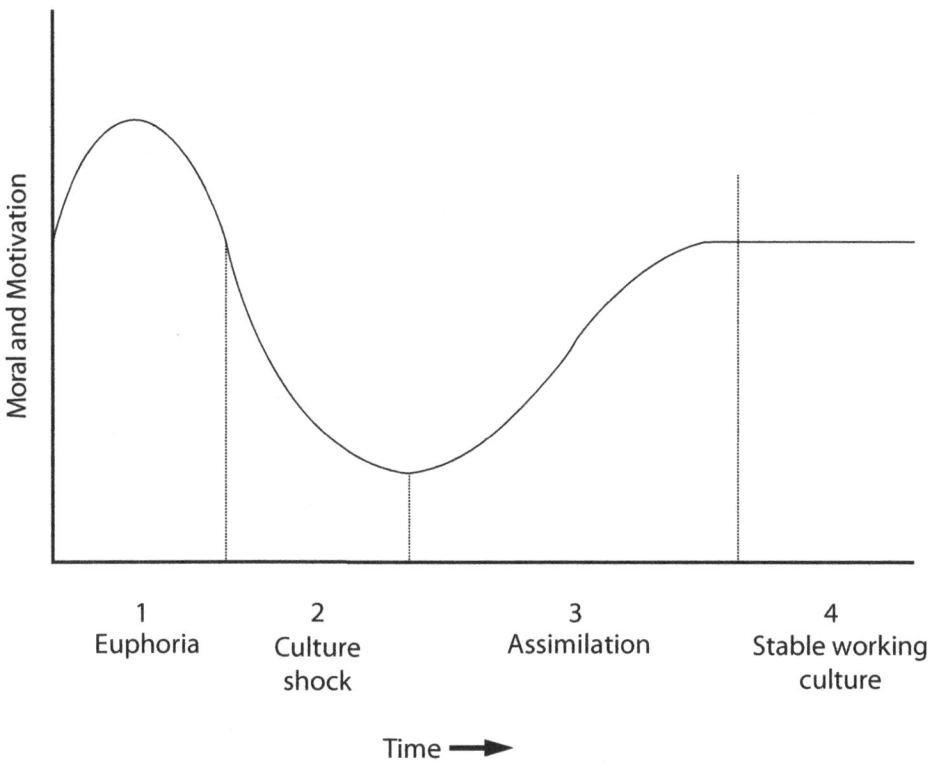

Figure I.1   Shock and assimilation

Projects, Processes and Cultural Assimilation

To date, most cultural research focuses on minimising conflict and making the best of the cultural mix when establishing a new business or operation overseas. This includes all aspects of the management, administrative, manufacturing, Human Resources and personnel processes.

Let us take a look at the experience of an American manufacturer that relocated and set up some of its production lines and related processes in Greece.

EUPHORIA

During the initial period after the establishment of the business overseas, following initial delays, cost overruns and various cultural, legal and logistical difficulties, everyone is happy and excited by the opportunities this new business will bring (see Figure I.1). Work has started with new colleagues in a new environment and culture, and the organisation as a whole wants to make the best of all the advantages this relocation gives (including lower labour, energy and distribution costs). The excitement of the Greek staff is no less than that of the Americans. They have the opportunity to work with a culture renowned for its business successes. They anticipate learning from their new colleagues and expect to enjoy the collaboration as much as the Americans. The motivation could not be higher.

SHOCK

A few months have passed and a number of serious issues between the Americans and the Greeks are starting to appear. From day one, the enthusiastic Americans wanted to get down to business straight away. The Greeks were taken aback. They needed some time to get to know their new colleagues; time for social activity and relationship building.

The Americans, on the other hand, were starting to feel hogtied and uneasy every time they needed to work through the hierarchy ladder just to address a work item with a Greek colleague, even for initial discussions and analytical purposes. The Greeks insisted that all communication be made through the right channels. Thus, a marketing manager should talk directly to the financial manager if he or she needed some information from the analysts or accountants, rather than talking to them directly. The analysts and accountants themselves were uncomfortable being approached directly by the marketing manager and insisted that they speak to their boss instead.

Every week or so, new scenario emerged that added to the gripes each of the national groups had about the management style of their counterparts.

Morale has fallen to an all-time low.

ASSIMILATION

Time passes and, slowly, each cultural group is now learning to reassess the situation; reflecting on the 'compromises' they would need to make, to enable the business work.

They slowly start to adjust, accepting part of the others' working practices and becoming more flexible in adapting their own practices. After six months, or perhaps a year, they settle into a new joint culture in which both groups are happy to work with each other (and even appreciate the other's practices and points of view). They have now assimilated.

Of course, there is another scenario in which each group simply sulks; in which case the new business is likely to experience significant ongoing problems.

STABLE STATE

By now a stable state has been established, involving a culture that is a mix of both organisational cultures and both national cultures.

How long does it take to reach this state? That depends on how much effort is put into it. Without sustained effort you may end up with a complete breakdown of working relations or, at the very least, an organic assimilation (if the organisation can afford it) that can take years. On the other hand, deliberate efforts involving the application of related cultural and management theory may resolve the matter in as short a period as six months.

Most projects simply do not have six months to spare.

By definition, projects are temporary and they are initiated in order to achieve predefined results. They have a defined start and an end which is unlikely to be flexible enough to allow sufficient 'assimilation' time. Indeed, in today's continually more competitive world, implementation times are getting stricter, giving less and less time to adjust to the new culture.

Furthermore, it is not only the local culture that will have an impact but also the project teams' mix of national cultures. With globalisation, increased numbers of multicultural teams have emerged, which may enjoy adjustment time to integrate as part of a business unit but for which no such luxury is possible as a project.

Multiculturalism then has a more profound effect on projects simply because projects involve multiple parties or organisations, requiring temporary working relationships with persons who may come from a different corporate culture. Add the national (or ethnic, or religious and so on) cultural aspect, and you have yourself a real challenge.

The Cost of Ignoring or Avoiding Culture

Given that cultural impact is well understood by international managers, it is unfortunate that it is still ignored or underplayed by the majority of organisations that could most benefit from understanding it.

The impact of failing to giving culture its due weight goes beyond the organisation and has a profound effect at a professional level, business level and even in terms of the national economy and income distribution. Please note that in referring to 'culture' I am implying both national and organisation cultures.

PROFESSIONAL LIMITATION

Any project manager who has to work within a multicultural environment, with stakeholders of varying cultures, will need to adjust their approach to communication, negotiation, governance and people management if they are to reduce conflict and increase harmony and efficiency.

While doing so comes naturally to anyone with good communication and people skills, there are times when the cultural diversity may take the manager well outside of their comfort zone when their natural skills as a good communicator are unlikely to suffice.

Given the increasing internationalisation of projects, the lack of cross-cultural skills will undoubtedly limit career prospects.

PREFERRING LARGER SUPPLIERS

I hope you wondered about my choice of the phrase 'avoiding culture' in the title. Ignoring culture may be an evident phenomenon but why would any organisation avoid culture? Simply because they can or think that they can afford to do so.

No seasoned project manager is unaware of the preference that larger organisations and government organisations have for larger suppliers. Be they material, professional services or HR suppliers. While the benefit of such a preference can be obvious in relation to specific needs of guaranteed higher supply capacity and lower levels of risk, there is often a second unconscious driver. Many larger organisations have adopted common standards and processes that are similar or familiar between them. The result of the standardised processes is better interface and communication between client and supplier specifically because they override cultural tendencies and therefore reduce or minimise the need to manage a client–supplier cultures.

The downsides of this practice can be:

- Risk of lower quality or higher prices for supplied products or services. Particularly in relation to professional services and especially management and business consulting, where it has been repeatedly demonstrated that smaller consultancies in comparison to the larger giants are often more flexible and better able to understand customer needs and integrate efficiently with their team.

- Client's expectations of their supplier can be exaggerated because they expect suppliers to take all the initiative to fit to their own culture. This is true not only for smaller but also for larger suppliers and while standardisation may reduce cultural conflicts, it does not eliminate it. The results are unmanaged client 'management' expectations and frustration, as well as under motivated suppliers and unhealthy working relationships.

- Higher dependency on large suppliers can render the client organisation less flexible to change. Should the need arise to work with smaller suppliers, the organisation will find itself at a disadvantage in being unable to manage the client–supplier interface. This often happens when a large organisation develops highly innovative new products for which the suppliers are relatively small. It also happens when an organisation operates in a country that does not have large suppliers. The failure of multinationals to work with local suppliers overseas is well documented and although part of the problem may relate to an unknown national culture, it is also often due to working with a small or medium-sized company culture.

- Rejecting smaller organisations due to their size reduces the distribution of wealth and hinders the growth of smaller businesses. While this may not fare as a priority for private organisations (as clients), it should be an issue for government and public administration.

MULTINATIONALS EXPECT THEIR BRANCHES AND SUBSIDIARIES TO ADOPT THEIR HEAD OFFICE CULTURE

Apart from seeming arrogant and disrespectful of local cultures, adopting a universal culture defined by head office is both inefficient and unrealistic; the results are alienation and demotivation. The only way a multinational can operate efficiently across its branches and subsidiaries is to embed cultural consideration in their growth. This we will discuss in later chapters.

Conclusion

Research into culture and management, continues with occasional socio-psychological perspectives identifying new cultural orientations that are significant to management practices. I have opted to make use of the established findings on culture and management and to adapt these to the specific needs of 'projects' and 'programmes' where they significantly differ from business processes.

For the purpose of simplicity, going forward, we will use the term 'project' to refer to both projects and programmes. And we will use the term 'project manager' to refer to any project or programme professional in charge of managing part of the project (project manager, project office manager, project executives and sponsors).

PART I
Understanding Culture

In Part I, we will explore culture in the various contexts in which it exists. We will explore how our culture comes to be and what factors play a part in shaping it. The aim is to gain a deeper understanding of the psychology of culture; an understanding that is essential to cross-cultural harmony and communication, and for the project manager to be properly equipped to address the cultural diversity within their own projects.

In the following Parts: 'Culture and the Project Environment' and 'Culture and the Project Team', we will look at specific tools that will allow the international project manager to best manage the cultural mix in their projects. However, please do not jump to those Parts without reading this one first. You may jump other chapters and come back to them when you need to, but not this one. Without a profound understanding of culture, its various elements and how it manifests in the group and the individual, jumping the gun will be like a non-project manager attempting to learn project management purely by learning how to use a project planning software.

Chapter 1

Elements of Culture

Defining Culture

It is worth taking a moment to be precise about the meaning of the term 'culture'.

> 'The ideas, customs, and social behaviour of a particular people or society.'
>
> *Oxford Dictionary*

> 'The way of life, especially the general customs and beliefs, of a particular group of people at a particular time.'
>
> *Cambridge Dictionary*

> 'The beliefs, customs, arts, etc., of a particular society, group, place, or time.'
>
> *Merriam-Webster Dictionary*

These dictionary definitions, which are largely in tune with one another, highlight the following:

- Culture is not born out of the individual. It is born out of the group.

- Culture encompasses a number of people who were conditioned by the same education and life experiences.

- Culture is the collective 'conditioning' of a given group, a tribe, a community or a nation which is different from that of other groups, tribes and communities.

Let's take a historical example: a simple agricultural society that once lived happily and peacefully until the arrival of invaders that repeatedly threatened their land, crops, livestock and their life. The members of this simple society started to explore ways to counter such threats, and came to structure themselves in a way that allowed them to fight off the invaders. They trained their men to become strong and learn the art of fighting. They gave more importance and respect to individuals who showed leadership and strategic vision. And soon, they developed a hierarchical structure of strong young men and wiser old men, who together established how to defend the society. The older men were the leaders, the younger strong men were the field fighters and defenders who underwent regular training.

One or two generations later, a whole new culture of hierarchy and masculinity has developed; valuing bravery, strength, strong leadership and respect for orders above other virtues, and assigning responsibilities for agricultural tasks, childcare and the home to the women and the elderly.

What is key to understand, is that these values of strength, bravery, autocracy and absolute respect for leadership are not perceived exclusively in the context of defence; these values are accepted and revered by the whole society as fundamental, including by the women and men who did not join the fighting force and continued to work on the farms. Consequently young women favoured more masculine and authoritative men to the humble hard-working farmer of a previous era.

As years and decades pass, and as the continent settles and the old threats are no more, the culture will still retain a strong bias towards hierarchy and masculinity. It will change now that the original driving forces have changed. But it will take long generations.

If a culture is born out of group's needs, is there any meaning to ask what is the culture of a certain individual? Does an individual have a culture?

Before we answer that question, ask yourself:

> *What are my beliefs and values in terms of family, politics, morality, religion, work practices, work ethic, leisure activities and friendship; and where did I learn these values from?*

You will find that you learned your values from various spheres of your life; your family, school, university, social circles, employer, workplace, sport club, travels, exposure to people from other nations and your very own interests that lead you to search for knowledge through books and experiences.

You will also find that not all the spheres that contributed to your values are necessarily related or connected, particularly those spheres that exist outside your society at large; yet each of these spheres represents a group of which you have adopted some or all of its values.

Now ask yourself again;

> *Do I share my fellow group members' views on our collective values and the means to realise them; the group being family, friends, work colleagues or fellow citizens of my country?*

You most certainly will answer no, not on everything; and that is because while the group collectively develops values on a shared basis, individuals within the group may or may not agree on all of the values, or the basis on which they are adopted. The group's unspoken rules for adopting and defending its values are what we call 'norms', an individual's attitude towards these values are the individual's 'beliefs'. The closer the beliefs of the individual members of a group are to their norms, the more cohesive the group is and vice versa.

By now it should be clear that culture is not exclusively a 'national' or an 'organisational' phenomenon. Any group will form its own culture over time. When a child changes school within the same city they face a period of adjustment to the new school culture, during which they are often isolated and their practices considered 'weird' or funny.

Culture therefore is born out of a group and thereafter held by its individual members as preferences towards a set of values.

Therefore, an individual does indeed adopt cultural 'values and norms' from their group(s) in the form of logical 'beliefs' or/and pure 'acceptance'; but because these adopted values and norms do not have to fully reflect those of the group(s), culture within the individual reside as 'cultural preferences'.

Culture and the Group

Having noted that culture is a group phenomenon, let's look at the psychology of culture, using national culture as a reference in most of our examples.

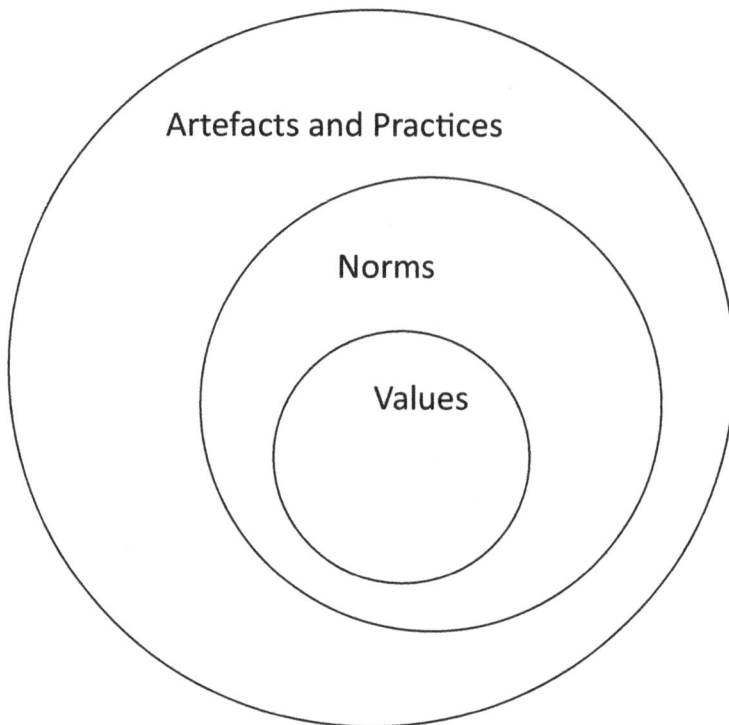

Figure 1.1   Values, norms and practices

Figure 1.1 below illustrates how culture manifests itself in a group:

VALUES

At the heart of every culture are the values which represent what the culture believes to be absolute, in terms of good or bad. A culture that has changed to respond to threats from invaders (as in our earlier example), will give rise to values that favour strength and bravery in men over older values of being in touch with the earth and its products. Likewise, a society that experiences poverty in the face of globalisation may give rise to values that favour achievement and wealth above general wellbeing.

These values are first established as an outcome of life experiences, and they are passed from one generation to the next through education in order to render the new generation fit for survival. As values are taught from an earlier age they become 'basic assumptions'. Although some later acquired values may change, many mainstream psychologists, including Sigmund Freud, believe that values acquired before the age of six years will remain with us forever. They will become an 'absolute truth' that is beyond question and is part of how we perceive our identity.

Most people today do not equate all their cultural values with the original purpose behind them. This is partly because that purpose may no longer exist, partly because values are seen as absolute truth with no need for justification, and partly because any questioning of how we perceive our values involves questioning of our identity, and with the exception of self-analytical and critical individuals, for most people this is not a comfortable experience.

However, it is important to note that not all 'values' have the same 'value'. The *Oxford English Dictionary* defines values as:

> *Principles or standards of behaviour; one's judgment of what is important in life.*

The term 'value' is typically used to refer to the most revered standards and absolute truth. In truth however, some values are far less important to their holders than others.

For certain groups or individuals, the value of 'patience' may weigh far less than the value of 'respect for authority'.

NORMS

As values reside within the individual members of the group, these members as a group will develop 'norms' to preserve their values. Social norms such as the favouring of local language and literature over those from other nations can arise from values that emphasise identity and the need to preserve it.

Likewise values favouring hard work, status and wealth will result in norms associating social status with a university degree.

With this last norm in mind, it is worth noting how a society can easily lose sight of the original trigger that gave rise to the value and often the persistence of this value along with the associated norms can become counterproductive over time. It is good to have a university degree if you wish to work in a field that requires it. Otherwise, school may suffice.

Higher education often entails sacrifice on the part of students or their parents. Unfortunately if an economy can no longer meet the subsequent aspiration of its university educated young workers, the norm and the value can become a social threat.

ARTEFACTS AND PRACTICES

Our arts, music, designs, fashion, buildings, shrines and monuments are all artefacts that represent our culture. So are our festivities and celebrations, how we treat children and the elderly, our approach to helping the poor, how many hours we work and what type of holidays we prefer. These are all practices directly influenced by our values and norms.

One of the most common sources of cultural stereotyping and cultural conflicts arises from assumptions others make about the values behind certain artefacts or practices.

Culture is deep and complex and not easily comprehensible especially to those 'outside' that culture. It takes time to know a culture. Experienced culture lovers will respectfully observe the artefacts and practices when travelling, making no assumption of what values lie behind them. As their interest in a culture deepens, so they start to enquire politely about the values. Some decide to live in a country for a year or more to better understand its culture. They now understand what 'values' members of the society share, which they may previously have misinterpreted.

We can summarise as follows:

- Values are what we accept as 'good' and form the core of our group identity.

- Not all values are equal. Some values are more 'valuable' than others.

- Norms are the rules that we use to preserve and protect our values.

- Practices are the way we behave as an outcome of the norms or directly from our values.

- Artefacts are representations that celebrate our values and norms.

What happens if the norms are at conflict with the core values in a society? Can such a case exist? It can, for example when it is forced on the society by a new regime after a revolution. The USSR imposed the communist norms on a society that had conflicting values. What happens is that with time, either the values or the imposed norm change.

Turkey is a society in which new norms where introduced by Kemal Atatürk which have so far prevailed over time with many of the values changing accordingly for many of the population; although there are increasingly dissenting voices and some resulting in social instability.

Within larger organisations that expand overseas and impose their values and norms on their subsidiaries and branches, the resulting dynamics are often exactly the same. Either the local subsidiary changes its values, or the HQ-imposed norms do. Worst-case scenario, if neither is possible the subsidiary either manages to buy itself out of the larger organisation, or is closed by that organisation.

A stable society or group is one whose norms and values are in tune.

Table 1.1 below lists a few examples of values, norms and practices that exist within the various spheres in our lives.

There is always a relationship between life spheres in that a family, a social or an organisational culture is strongly influenced by the other spheres and by the national culture in which they reside. However, what makes our life interesting is that each of these spheres may strive to break from the norms of the larger sphere it exists within. For example, an Italian family may adopt an American-style culture; loosening the traditional family grip on their young and encouraging them to work for their holiday money from an early age. Likewise, a family-owned or a large organisation in the Middle East may consciously and painstakingly adopt an organisational culture mirroring that of a typical German organisation; again, breaking away from the organisational norm in their country at large.

Table 1.1   Examples of values, norms and practices

Sphere / Group	Value	Norm	Practice
National	Cohesiveness and harmony	Shared responsibility and accountability	Group consultation. Competition is frowned upon
	Respect for authority	Obedience and non-questioning	Leaders in the government dictate policy
	Social achievement	One must work hard and strive continuously towards higher status	Workaholism and long working hours at the cost of family wellbeing
Family	Cohesiveness and harmony	Shared responsibility and accountability between siblings	Family decisions are made in consultation with all its members
	Respect for authority	Obedience of parents	Head of the family decides for the whole family
Workplace	Entrepreneurship	Individuals' initiatives are highly encouraged	Competitiveness between colleagues
	Stability	Detailed planning and validation prior to implementation	Resistance to change and facing uncertainty
Mountaineering Club	Exploration and discovery	Whenever possible, seek the unknown	High risk taking
	Safety	Avoid solo mountaineering. Use all possible safety measures	Rigorous training on safety and rejection of amateur or tourist mountaineers

Culture and the Organisation

It should now be clear that an organisation is just another group with its own culture. However, organisational culture merits books in its own right (and there are many), not only because of its significance to performance and productivity, but because this form of culture can be consciously and actively studied, changed and/or imposed according to specific aims and strategy of the organisation.

A small family owned company may start with an organisational culture that respects the family culture of its owners, which is likely to reflect the national culture in many aspects. As the company grows, the need to have an organisational culture that caters for faster decision making, higher innovation, efficiency and flexibility starts to become apparent; many such companies take active measures to change, often with the help of organisational culture consultants or through recruiting executive managers from larger organisations with the desired culture.

For large organisations, and especially multinationals, having the right organisational culture across its group becomes critical to success. If a multinational fails to implement a globally harmonious culture, it will face cultural crises on its cross-regional activities including both projects and processes. If on the other hand it imposes exactly the same culture across its group, it will isolate those whose 'national cultural values' are at conflict with the 'organisational cultural values'. Most international project managers have come across local branches of successful organisations that felt that the head office was unjustly imposing their culture on them without regards to their local needs.

However, observations and empirical data have shown that within multinationals that have actively developed and imposed an organisational culture, the organisational culture prevails over the national culture of the local branches.

A project manager, therefore, faces two main cultures when working on international projects within multinational organisations. The organisational culture and the national culture; both present within each branch of the organisation. The larger the organisation and the more international, the more likely that the organisational culture differs from, and somewhat overrides, the national culture of its branches.

That is not to say that the national culture becomes irrelevant. On the contrary it is just as relevant in multinationals as it is in smaller companies for the following reasons:

- Branches of successful multinational have an organisational culture that is harmonious across them. I stress 'harmonious' and not 'identical'. That is because the organisational culture has been consciously adapted by each branch to be in harmony with the national culture. At least, in terms of their more 'valued' values and norms. Local culture is always present.

- It is easier for an outsider to fit into a multinational as compared to smaller companies because the multinational's organisational culture is likely to be similar to the culture of other large organisations in their sector. This however can make it more likely for a project manager to lose sight of the presence and the significance of local national culture, and often to their own puzzlement, fail to get their team and stakeholders to perform and/or unheedingly commit a 'cultural' offence.

If an organisation manifests both the local and organisational culture characteristics, and given the difficulty for an outsider to both these cultures to determine what practices are influenced by which culture, how can an external project manager manage the cultural aspects within the project?

These questions will be addressed in detail in Part III, 'Culture and the Project Environment'. For now, let me assure the reader that the source of a practice, as either national or the organisational culture, is irrelevant to our purposes. The project manager needs simply to understand the values behind a practice, regardless of their origins.

We will now proceed in exploring how culture exists and is manifest within the individual.

Culture and the Individual

We have noted that culture is a group phenomenon and can only develop within a group. Thereafter, it will reside within the group 'collectively', while as cultural preferences within its individual members.

Thankfully, humans are blessed with the faculty of independent thinking, and this give us some role in determining how culture manifest in us.

Figure 1.2 shows how beliefs substitute the norms within the individual.

VALUES

A typical member of a culture will hold similar values to those of their group because these values have been taught to them and they have learned to use them as absolute truth and part of their own identity.

In every culture, there are individuals who 'question' the group's values and may refuse to adopt them. Challenging values takes courage, honesty and strength of character as the decision to adopt values that are different from those of your group often results in isolation. Depending on the group and the 'value' of the questioned values, some sceptics may risk being tagged as traitors or even becoming outcast or face the force of law. They are often perceived as a threat to the group's values and stability. More open and democratic societies are less severe in their reactions to such individuals; nevertheless, holding a different value system from the group often result in isolation and being perceived as 'strange' or 'eccentric'.

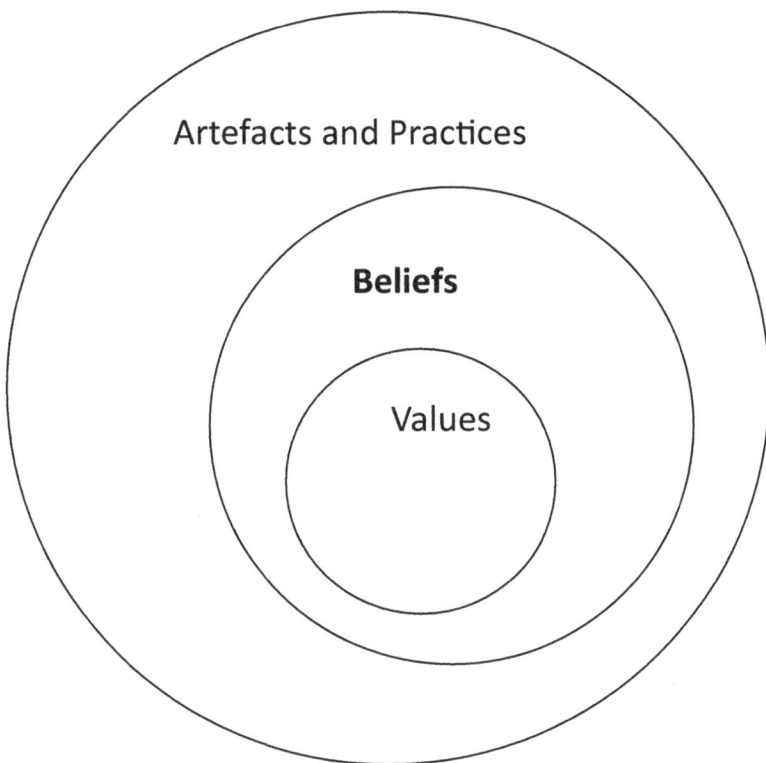

Figure 1.2   Values, beliefs and practices

BELIEFS

Norms are set by the group. An individual may believe that they can still respect the values by different means to those presented by the social norms, or they may decide to adhere to the norms regardless. The former is individualistic thinking; the latter, collective. In Saudi Arabia, many people are very proud of their traditional dress which includes a white rope with the red head cover worn by most men in the country. When they travel abroad however, they often change into Western clothes while on the airplane. Likewise, many Saudi women will do the same and change into Western clothes that are loose and colourful, simply adding a head scarf to cover their hair.

There is no hypocrisy in this; rather a sign of respect towards the culture of the country they are travelling to and an attempt at better integration. The values of their tradition and religion are not compromised as they are respected regardless, and the measure of breaking away from their norms is temporary.

There are also those who strongly disagree with group norms, even where they fully agree with the values behind them. They have the same aims as the group but disagree on how to realise them. Many political opposition groups are formed by such individuals who share the values of their fellow citizens but strongly disagree with the ruling party's approach to realising them.

PRACTICES

The practices of an individual may or may not reflect those of their group for reasons that can go beyond disagreement on values or norms.

The individual is a complex entity; far more complex than the group with more factors influencing their practices than just culture. A common mistake many make when they meet someone from another culture is to assume automatically that the practices exhibited by that person are a reflection of their culture. In doing so, they are unconsciously stereotyping.

Apart from culture, the individual's practices are influenced by their personal beliefs, personality traits and various acquired habits not related to culture.

The triangle in Figure 1.3 outlines the major elements present in each individual:

Human Nature is universal. We jump if we hear a sudden bang and laugh when we see something funny. Most people will rush to help if a pedestrian is hit by a car and offer assistance to an elderly person carrying a heavy load up the stairs. Human nature has its good and bad of course, but it is mainly universal and is inherited.

Culture as we have seen, is developed by the group and then adopted by both the group and its individual members. Culture is learnt through experiences and passing values down the generations.

Personality is the most individualistic part of our psyche. Part of our personality is our DNA; babies exhibit personality traits in the first weeks after birth. Part is learnt during childhood and adulthood. Some aspects of personality may change with time and some may change instantly following a significant emotional trauma or accident.

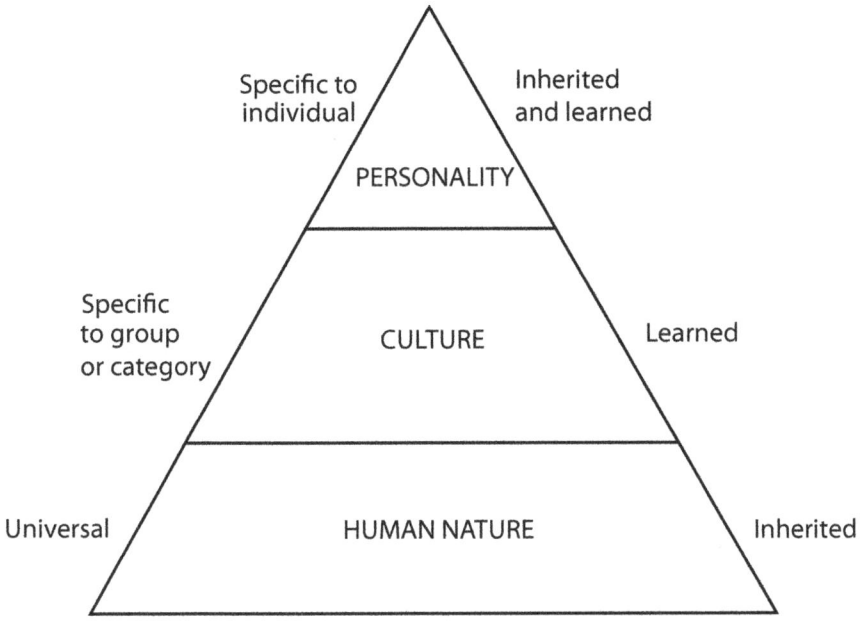

Figure 1.3   Three levels of uniqueness in mental programming
Source: Geert Hofstede, Gert Jan Hofstede, Michael Minkov, *Cultures and Organizations,*
Software of the Mind, 3rd Revised Edition, McGrawHill 2010, ISBN 0–07–166418–1.
© Geert Hofstede B.V. quoted with permission.

Personality is what makes you and me different, if we disregard the factor of culture. Being playful or contemplative, calm or slightly aggressive, emotionally strong or weak, logical or artistic, numerical or linguistic; the list is endless.

Let's now explore the complexities of the individual using as an example, an extremely culturally diverse personality: The Culture Soup!

The Culture Soup

Within large international communities such as those in Brussels or The Hague, the term 'Third Culture Kids' or TCK is frequently (and often incorrectly) used to make reference to those perennially relocating professionals that constitute a large number of these communities. The term TCK was first introduced by David Pollock and Ruth Van Reken in their book *Third Culture Kids* (2001):

TCKs being children (or adults who when children) never spent long enough in any culture to set roots. Moving home, changing schools and having to make new friends and go through the 'fitting-in' process every few years meant that these individuals had to adopt a culture that is neither that of their current or past geographical location, nor that of their parents' country of origin. A typical example is a child of a diplomat. TCKs grow to be culturally open minded and highly flexible with regards to moving and exploring; however, they do risk certain social and emotional issues during their development; which Pollock and Van Reken address.

You will note that the title of this section is 'The Culture Soup' and not 'Third Culture Kids'. This is because as project managers, the cultural aspects of the TCKs that are of concern to us are not exclusive to TCKs. For the multicultural project manager, what is important about the multicultural professional is the significance of the values, habits, traits and practices they have gained through their cultural exposure. Be that from their childhood (such as TCKs) or as adults who only experienced such exposure after having set cultural roots and gained a cultural identity. I call both these multicultural personalities, The Culture Soup; a soup, in which the original ingredients are so mixed together that it is hard to determine their origins with certainty. Every TCK is a Culture Soup but a Culture Soup is not necessarily a TCK.

For the multicultural project manager, working with a Culture Soup can be a despairing or an enlightening experience, depending on the project manager's own cultural awareness.

Let us now look at an example:

Consider Rabia Khan. Rabia is a third-generation Spanish citizen. She was born in Madrid where she studied and grew up. Her parents, calm and loving academics of Pakistani origin, retained a good part of their traditional culture inherited from their own immigrating parents. Throughout her childhood, Rabia would visit Pakistan with her parents for the summer holiday every third year.

On reaching university age, Rabia decided to study abroad in order to expand her international experience. She studied at the London School of Economics and graduated with top marks. Thereafter she got a good job at a large bank that sent her every second week to their branch in Lyon, France.

After three years, Rabia decided to continue into higher education. Her choice was an MBA in International Economics at Bocconi University in Milan, Italy.

By the time she completed her MBA she had a job offer awaiting her from the World Bank in New York to work within the department responsible for the Asia region. A few year later and following a few promotions, she was made a representative to part of the region. During the next five years she would spend between five to ten days a month in New York; the rest she spent mainly in Malaysia, the Philippines, Thailand, Vietnam or Indonesia. Her holidays were almost always spent in Spain or Pakistan.

We must not forget that Rabia's cultural exposure does not end here. During her studies in London and Milan her circles of friends resembled the United Nations and, as do the Asian and American people with whom she works today, they too have influenced her views and values.

Now imagine yourself having been assigned by the Vietnamese National Bank to work on a joint project with the World Bank. The details of this rural economy development project are irrelevant; what is relevant is that Rabia is the overall project executive and you are the local project manager reporting to her.

Before you have even met her, you were told by various colleagues that Rabia:

- is a tough manager;

- hardly ever stays overtime or arrives earlier than 9.30;

- often works from home (or her hotel);

- is very knowledgeable and up-to-date on world economics;

- is extremely organised, she records everything in writing and never forgets a thing;

- frequently reports to her boss (Asia region Vice President at the World Bank in New York);

- tends to excuse herself from meetings whenever there is strong conflict; returning once the conflict has blown over;

- has little patience with indiscipline and unexplained delays;

- tends to micro manage despite her senior position and frequently follows up and reviews her teams' work in detail (to their annoyance);

- lives alone.

Before you read on, take some time to reflect on this scenario with the limited knowledge you have of Rabia's history. Try to speculate what type of person she is. What are her values, personal traits, beliefs? Do you think she is an authentic person, honest with herself and others, at peace or at conflict with herself?

Let us now look at the layers of Rabia's psychology illustrated in Figure 1.4 below:

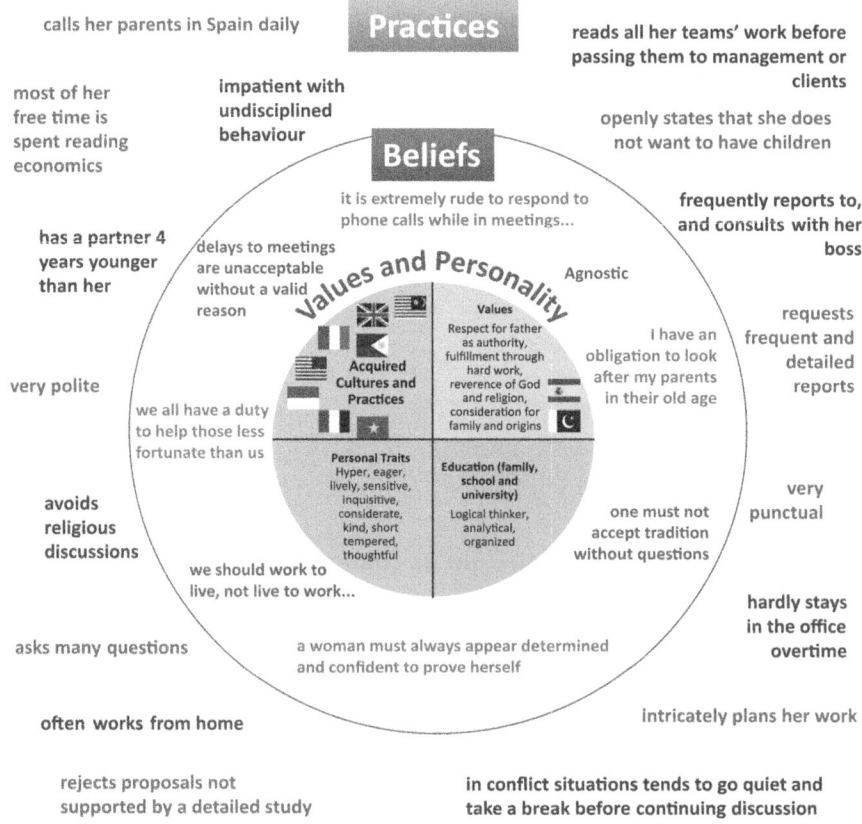

Figure 1.4   The psychology of Rabia – The Culture Soup

- The Inner Layer – Values and Personality – invisible.

- The Middle Layer – Beliefs – semi-visible.

- The Outer Layer – Practices – visible.

Values and Personality – The Core of the Mind

The inner layer of Rabia's psychology I have called 'values and personality' (Figure 1.5). The elements in this layer reflect the values and traits that influence Rabia's behaviour gained through her cultural exposure, education, family and personal traits and habits. This influence is often, but not always, subconscious, just as some elements of our own values and personality are subconscious. Rabia is aware of a number of facets of her attitude, for example some of her values and her beliefs. There are others of which she is partly or entirely unconscious of but are just as influential to her behaviour.

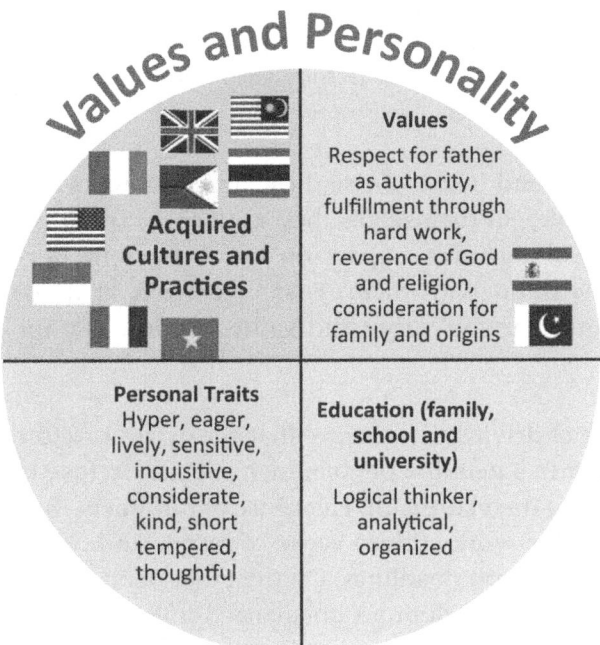

Figure 1.5   The psychology of Rabia – values and personality

VALUES

Table 1.2 lists some of Rabia's values and the influences that led to their development:

Table 1.2   Rabia's values and their source

Value	Source
Respect for her father as an authority figure and head of family	Pakistani authoritative culture
Fulfilment through hard work	Beliefs and values taught by her academic parents
Reverence of God and respect of religions	Muslim parents
Consideration for family and origin	Pakistani collective culture
Fear of driving	Being in a car accident when she was four years old resulting in an injury to her father's back (from which he recovered in a year)

I have chosen to add 'fear of driving' as a form of value to illustrate the nature of our 'values and personality'. The elements that make up who we are include cultural and environmental factors to which we have been exposed, but can also include, particularly in the case of fears or phobias, traumas from our childhood or later life.

Although we tend to categorise these deep elements as fears (negative) or values (positive), in themselves they are neither; each of them can have either positive or negative impact on our behaviour depending on the relationship we build with them. Fear of driving at its core is an over-emphasis of an otherwise very valid value within a certain context; *safety while driving*.

Rabia's fear of driving may ensure that she drives carefully. On the other hand, if it becomes a genuine phobia, then she may refuse to get into a car, which could make travel difficult. Her sense of fulfilment through hard work can instil a positive work ethic, a sense of responsibility and a willingness to respond to short-term deadlines. On the other hand, taken to extremes, it might encourage her to adopt an unbalanced lifestyle; spending extremely long hours working at the expense of her wellbeing. And, in the long term, her productivity.

PERSONAL TRAITS

Rabia is undoubtedly a clever individual. She is also somewhat hyper, lively, sensitive, considerate, kind but short tempered. This is her nature.

Self-awareness can play a big role in her personal development. If Rabia is aware that she is short tempered then she may also be able consciously to restrain herself when she feels she is losing her cool. Children are often taught to count slowly to ten before responding when upset. Rabia similarly, has learned to take a short break from conflict situations (often a short walk). This allows her to cool down and return to the situation with calmed emotions and better judgement.

EDUCATION

Education is not limited to school or university. It starts with our family and those around us. Rabia's family have taught her the importance of being well organised, which translates into the need to plan and validate her ideas carefully before proceeding with them. This has probably contributed to Rabia's preference for detailed management and control, as well as avoidance of uncertain situations.

As before, these characteristics could have positive or negative effects depending on the situation. Without doubt a complex project which has clearly defined outputs (establishing a partnership venture with a local bank in Vietnam) requires good deal of organisation and management. However, a project that is more developmental and emerging (establishing new services in Vietnam to aid growth in rural areas) may suffer from over planning and control; we don't exactly know what services we will need until we have done our research and trials and defined the appropriate financial requirement. This is likely to be a process involving a certain amount of trial and error.

ACQUIRED HABITS AND PRACTICES

We learn habits and practices from the various individuals and cultures we come across in our life. It is very unlikely for a person with high exposure to mixed cultures not to absorb any of their practices and even some values.

During an earlier project at the Italian base of an American automotive components manufacturer, I frequently had to manage the interface and coordination with the company's factories in Germany. At first I was shocked that the German partner would not make themselves available to talk outside the strict interpretation of working hours (apart from critical urgencies), but then I noted that out of all the various stakeholders in the project, the German partner delivered the best quality and punctuality. I made an effort to understand why this was and noted their excellent means of organising data and dividing work between them and diligently respecting the agreed process and medium for communication. They also appeared to resent meetings to address items that could be dealt with by email or phone, referring to such meetings as waste of time. During their working day, they produced far more than their colleagues in other countries who tended to work overtime, and consequently, were able to enjoy valuable extra time with their family. I have since consciously adopted the German partner's approach whenever possible. A Culture Soup's strategy would openly observe the practices of other cultures and decide to adopt those they agree with. This process can be conscious and deliberate as well as unconscious.

In another situation working in a less-organised environment, I found myself unconsciously adopting the work practices of those around me; needlessly multitasking; becoming lax about meeting times and sticking to agendas, resulting in wasted time and effort. Thankfully, a colleague pointed this out and I managed to reverse it.

More recently acquired habits and practices are the easiest to identify and manage. They all sit in the part of the subconscious that is easily recalled by contemplating the source and reasons behind them.

They are likewise possible to change with a little conscious efforts; assuming the act of changing them does not conflict with the norms and value of the group within which we operate.

Let's now look at the second of the three layers.

Beliefs – What is Right and What is Not

The second layer reflects what Rabia believes to be true or to be the right thing to do (Figure 1.6). Not everyone will share all their beliefs with others openly; sometimes it can be appropriate and at other times less so. Most of us consider some of our beliefs to be private and will not share them with others outside perhaps our family and very close friends.

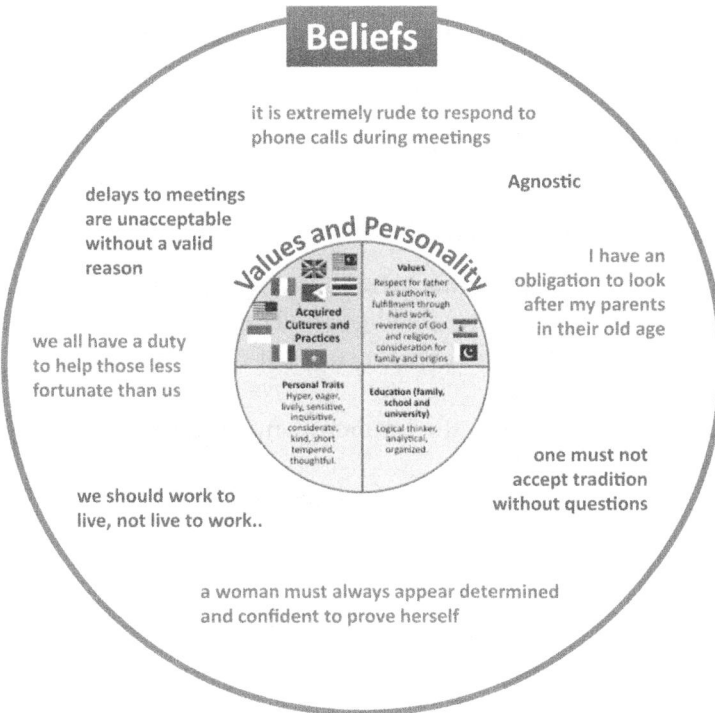

Figure 1.6   The psychology of Rabia – beliefs

Our beliefs are not necessarily in agreement or in harmony with our 'values and personality'. This is because the more mature a person, the more likely that they will question their own values and traits, overriding some personal traits and changing earlier beliefs.

Remember, we have identified that Rabia is intelligent and inquisitive so there is a reasonable chance that she will have a good degree of self-awareness, which will allow her to question some of her beliefs or reflect on her natural responses to certain situations, allowing her to adopt a more productive behaviour.

Clearly, Rabia is one of the small percentage of adults who are well aware of their 'values and personality'. Most of us will only have glimpses of our 'values and personality'; sometimes a particularly bad or unproductive experience may encourage self-reflection. However, there is a good chance that we may blame the experience on the behaviour of others and, even if we are aware of certain character flaws, for example a tendency to be overly critical of others, we may still find it very hard not to let our 'values and personality' rule our behaviour, particularly in situations of stress.

Let me be very clear about this, our psychological make-up is who we are and is neither intrinsically 'good' nor 'bad'. It is our behaviour on which we need to focus.

A final point on beliefs in this section: changing beliefs can sometimes be achieved through reasoning and intelligence. Thus, it is a human capacity that gives us a choice to break taboos and ensure self-determination.

Table 1.3 below illustrates the harmony and conflict between beliefs and value. In this case Rabia.

Table 1.3   Beliefs–value harmony

Belief	Related Value	Belief–Value Harmony
We have a moral obligation to look after our parents in their old age	Family collective culture	Full harmony
We should work to live, not live to work	Fulfilment through hard work	Managed harmony. Although Rabia works well, she makes a conscious effort not to allow it to compromise her quality of life. She ignores what she perceives as 'undue' guilty conscious. She also chose a career she truly enjoys making her work part of her quality of life
Agnostic	Reverence of God and religion	Managed conflict. Although still a believer, Rabia's views differ from her parents (and her own values)
It is safe to drive faster than I do, so long it is within the speed limits	Fear of moderate driving speeds	At conflict
One must not accept traditions without question	Strong Pakistani norms and traditions	Managed conflict. Rabia consciously questions her parents' traditions and may choose not to follow them. Yet, respect for the tradition and those who follow it is retained

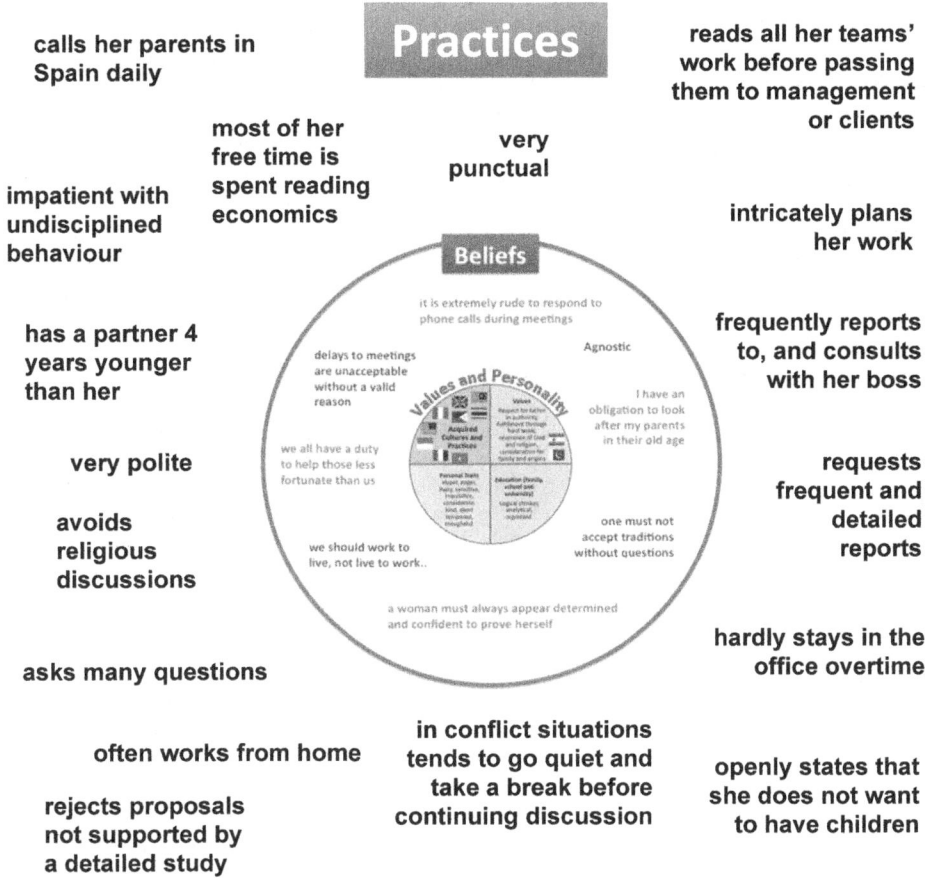

calls her parents in Spain daily

Practices

reads all her teams' work before passing them to management or clients

most of her free time is spent reading economics

very punctual

impatient with undisciplined behaviour

intricately plans her work

Beliefs

it is extremely rude to respond to phone calls during meetings

has a partner 4 years younger than her

delays to meetings are unacceptable without a valid reason

Agnostic

frequently reports to, and consults with her boss

I have an obligation to look after my parents in their old age

very polite

we all have a duty to help those less fortunate than us

requests frequent and detailed reports

avoids religious discussions

we should work to live, not live to work..

one must not accept traditions without questions

asks many questions

a woman must always appear determined and confident to prove herself

hardly stays in the office overtime

often works from home

in conflict situations tends to go quiet and take a break before continuing discussion

openly states that she does not want to have children

rejects proposals not supported by a detailed study

Figure 1.7   The psychology of Rabia – practices

Practices – The Way We Behave

The outer layer in Figure 1.7 illustrates Practices and these reflect the behaviour that we would observe in Rabia if we worked with her.

So now, back to your assumptions made earlier. Having understood some of Rabia's psychology, compare your notes with Table 1.4 which summarises the perceptions of Rabia's long-time colleagues who have come to know her better over the years.

Table 1.4   Perceptions of Rabia's long-time colleagues

Observation	Assumption
Never stays overtime or arrives earlier than 9.30 when in US	Enjoys her morning hours, coffee, bath and leisurely breakfast. Enjoys being at home or outdoors
Often works from home (or hotel)	Finds it helps concentration and prefers to do so if she does not have meetings that require office presence
Very knowledgeable and up-to date on world economics	She enjoys the subject of economics. She spends much of her personal time reading on economics
Extremely organised. Writes everything and never forgets a thing	Sometime too organised. She can tend to get drawn into details
Frequently reports to her boss (Asia, responsible at the World Bank in New York)	She respects both authority and knowledge. Her boss is very knowledgeable and she likes to share her plans with him and get his feedback. She sees him as a mentor
She lives alone. Has a partner four years younger than her	Rabia is enjoying life. Her job is exactly what she always wanted to do but she also realised that such a nomadic lifestyle will make it tough for a family. Not having a particular maternal urge or need to have a family, she decided against it
Walks out whenever there is strong conflict. Then returns in ten minutes	Rabia knows that she is short tempered and in strong conflict situations tends to either react in anger, or if she try to suppress her anger, she nevertheless is still unable to reason well under her emotions. She has realised that a ten-minute walk clears her emotions and mind. As such, she habitually calls for a coffee break in hot conflict situations to allow her to cool down before proceeding
Has little patience with indiscipline.	Both her home and academic educations taught her the merits of being disciplined and organised. She sees being otherwise not only as negative to the subject's performance but rightly so to others in their team. She therefore will not tolerate indiscipline and bad organisation
Is a micro manager despite her senior position and regularly follows up and reviews her teams' work in detail (to their annoyance). She also rejects all proposals not supported by detailed analysis and outline of the expected results	A practice arising directly from her value of not 'accepting' uncertainties until the related situation has been fully analysed and quantified. This renders Rabia a not-so-good delegator. She is aware that addressing this issue may improve both her and her team's performance and motivation. However, she has failed to do so to date
Rabia is a tough manager	During the 1960s growing up in Spain and being of Pakistani origin, Rabia learnt that women have to work harder than men to prove themselves professionally. We are moving towards sexual equality at the workplace but we are far from being fully there. As a result, Rabia retains a strong and determined stance, as well as a little distance from her staff to keep the relationships purely professional

IN THE EYES OF THE BEHOLDER

This example is based on a character I had the privilege to know and work with on a large international project not long ago, and aims to highlight the complexity of human personality and especially the Culture Soup, and the futility of attempting to psychoanalyse them.

I have gone into details in Rabia's psychology not to illustrate what the multicultural project manager should do. On the contrary, much of my own analysis of Rabia would most probably not fit her real inspirational character, and I never attempted, nor would I attempt to psychoanalyse any Culture Soup (or anyone for that matter). Apart from lacking the professional merits to do so, any attempt to psychoanalyse people with whom we have a personal or professional relationship is coloured by that very relationship and our own 'values and personality'. In other words, it is subjective and can never be correct.

Therefore, while the multicultural project manager must be aware of the complexities inherent in the Culture Soup, they need not (and cannot) be aware of an objective psychoanalysis. Our awareness of the complexities and conflicts present within any character serves to guard us from misguided assumptions and encourage us to open our minds to the possibilities.

The 'Working Culture'

Each individual will have an inherited culture from each group to which they were exposed for a significant length of time; including family, nation, university, social groups such as sport clubs and so on. Furthermore, any single group's culture will not be confined to its own developed values and norms, but will embed elements of the other cultures within which it resides. Would this not pose a level of complexity that would make it impossible for the project manager?

Fortunately not. I am deliberately repeating and stressing this point. Forgive me in doing so, but trust me, I have a purpose. The project manager need not be, nor should be a psychoanalyst; but should simply be aware of the possibilities.

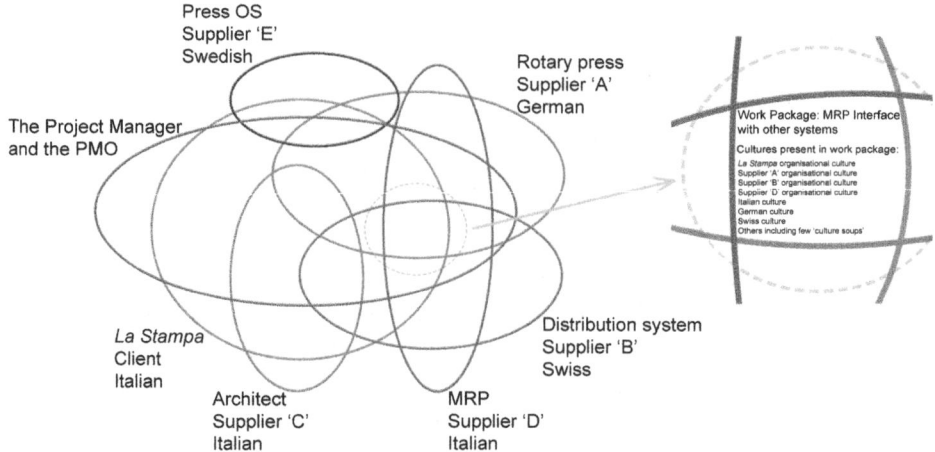

Figure 1.8   Cultural interfaces within *La Stampa* project

In the introduction, I described my experience at *La Stampa* newspaper in Italy, during a project that involved various suppliers and stakeholders from different countries and cultures.

Figure 1.8 illustrates how cultures can mix together in a project environment. Each circle represents the scope of work for each supplier within the project, some of which is performed in isolation from other suppliers (such as budgeting and delivery logistics) while other elements can only be performed in coordination and/or cooperation with other suppliers (such as installation of machinery, as well as training of users).

Thus in a project similar to that of *La Stampa's*, the project manager will not only face different cultures, but different mixes of cultures in different work packages (WP); with these cultures themselves representing a mix of national, organisational and other influences brought into play by the individuals involved in the project, such as but not exclusive to, the various Culture Soups.

We will use the term 'working culture' to refer to the professional working culture of a group or an individual regardless of its origins (national, organisational or a mixture of both) and so on.

It is the working culture of a group or an individual, and not the specific origins of that working culture, that the project manager must be aware of to manage the diversity efficiently.

PART II

Cultural Orientations and Project Management

In this part, we will review the key studies of 'culture and management', and explore in detail how cultures manifest in the norms, standards and behaviour of a society or group; be it within the context of social activities, family, politics and certainly, the workplace and project management.

Chapter 2

An Overview of Modern Culture and Management Studies

As anthropologists, social scientists and social psychologists explored the norms and behaviour of groups and nations, they came to identify certain commonalities in the way societies behave in a similar manner. These similarities of behaviour are driven by a set of values that the various societies have developed over generations.

To make sense of the information, researchers grouped related behaviours under logical categories know as 'cultural dimensions', 'cultural orientations' or 'value orientations'.

With such an approach, research can be conducted to empirically identify the position of a group on a certain cultural dimension. Take for example the dimension 'power distance' which measures how far a group is willing to accept the dominance of authority and respect the hierarchy. Generally, the Middle East tend to score higher on power distance, which means that at work, the hierarchical lines are meticulously respected and bosses are revered. Socially, there is a notable division between the classes and in the family, the father is a head figure who is highly respected and obeyed. Decision making is rarely democratic.

At the opposite pole of this dimension you have countries such as Sweden with a very low power distance and this is likewise reflected in various contexts within the society.

Through continued research and studies, social psychologists have identified the position of various groups and nations on various cultural dimensions' scales.

Let's review the background of key 'culture and management' theories that we will adopt for our multicultural project management approach:

Geert Hofstede and the 'Cultural Dimensions'

Geert Hofstede is a Dutch social psychologist that conducted the first, and one of the most comprehensive studies, of how values in the workplace are influenced by the national culture. Although not the first to identify 'cultural dimensions', he is the first to assign them the popular term.

In the early 1970s and 1980s, Hofstede and his colleagues carried out a major systematic study of work-related attitudes based on two questionnaire surveys, which produced a total of 116,000 responses from IBM employees in over 40 countries around the globe, making it the largest organisational-based study in history at that time.

A statistical analysis of the answers to the questions about the values of the IBM employees in different countries revealed common problems, but with solutions differing from country to country, reflected in the following orientations:

- *Power Distance Index (PDI)* – how far does the culture encourage superiors to exert power?

- *Individualism vs. Collectivism (IDV)* – do we think and behave as a group or do we encourage people to take personal responsibility for their lives?

- *Masculinity vs. Femininity (MAS)* – do we measure success in terms of 'power, riches and possessions' or 'quality of life, friends and relationships'?

- *Uncertainty Avoidance Index (UAI)* – how much anxiety do we experience and are willing to cope with in the face of ambiguity?

Michael Harris Bond and the Chinese Value Survey (CVS)

A Canadian living and working in the Far East since 1971, Michael Harris Bond is currently Visiting Chair Professor at the Department of Management and Marketing at the Hong Kong Polytechnic University. He had previously taught for 35 years at the Chinese University of Hong Kong and contributed to integrating the literature on Chinese psychology, editing *The Oxford Handbook of Chinese Psychology* (2010).

In the late 1980s and influenced by Geert Hofstede's culture study, Michael Harris Bond sought the help of Chinese colleagues to develop a list of basic values of Chinese people which became know as the Chinese Value Survey (CVS) questionnaire.

The results of the survey identified four Chinese cultural orientations, of which three were closely correlated to Hofstede's cultural dimensions. The missing dimension from Hofstede's study was Uncertainty Avoidance, while the newly discovered CVS dimension related to the social attitude towards 'time'.

Hofstede, who later adopted this dimension in his studies, calls it:

- *Long-term vs. short-term orientation (LTO)* – do our values place more emphasis on the significance of 'past and present' or the future?

To the researchers' surprise and delight, the orientation showed a strong correlation with economic growth, and came to show with time that it also predicted future economic growth. Indeed, the five Eastern economic dragons are amongst the top ten most long-term oriented cultures with China occupying the very highest position.

Trompenaars, Hampden-Turner and Value Orientations

Fons Trompenaars studied under Geert Hofstede's supervision at the Wharton School of Business marking the beginning of his career as a cultural researcher.

Fons Trompenaars, in collaboration with Charles Hampden-Turner, based his research on 30,000 people from various companies and over more than 40 countries. The sample size comprised 75 per cent of participants from management positions and the remaining 25 per cent from secretarial positions.

Trompenaars and Hampden-Turner divided their seven chosen cultural dimensions (or value orientations as they call them) into three different categories based on the sources of problems and dilemmas that a culture face. These are, relationship with people, attitude towards time and attitude towards the environment.

For the purpose of multicultural project management, we will be adding two of these seven orientations to our chosen dimensions:

- *Sequential Time vs. Synchronous Time (SST)* – do we view time as a series of sequentially passing events, or as interrelated events with the past, present and future?

- *Specific vs. Diffuse Index (SDI)* – do we allow our relationships to diffuse across our social and professional contexts, or do we keep them separate?

* * *

These research studies and their findings do not represent a comprehensive list of all research on the subject. However they provide an effective model when considering cross-cultural project management.

ONE: Cultural dimensions inter-influence and interact with each other. For example, there is a tendency for a 'collective' culture to be more hierarchical and respectful of authority; a mark of a 'high power distance' society. Often this is due to the same historical events bringing about both 'collectivism and 'high power distance' in the group. Furthermore, the same observable practice can arise from different dimensions or as a result of a mix of them. We therefore can only 'objectively' explore the influence of culture on project management by taking into account all the cultural dimensions collectively and not in isolation. This we will do in the following chapter. In this chapter, for the sake of clarity we will simplify our examples and make reference to one dimension at a time.

TWO: There is no escaping terminology and it helps to get the jargon clear from the onset. The following will be used extensively throughout this and the following chapters:

Cultural dimension: are a dimension of culture influencing certain norms, beliefs and practices in the group and its individuals.

Poles of a dimension: are the extreme high and low ends of the above dimensions. Few cultures sit at the poles, yet and for illustration purposes, we will be using pole examples wherever appropriate.

Cultural orientation: is the orientation of a culture with regards to one of the cultural dimensions. An orientation can lie anywhere between the extreme poles, including the poles themselves.

Life spheres: are the various spheres in which we live and operate. These I usually group into 'friends and society', 'the family', 'government and politics' and 'the workplace'.

There are two items to keep in mind before proceeding with this chapter:

Thus, Mr A.N. Other could be said to have a high orientation towards 'uncertainty avoidance' (relating to the UAI) within his family and workplace spheres, whereas he is neutrally oriented with regards to the MAS dimension in all his life spheres.

Throughout, we should keep in mind the fact that no specific cultural orientation is inherently good or bad, although there are some pole extremes. Whereas being at or near some poles may manifest negatively in certain spheres (which we will note later), in almost all other situations, an orientation towards a dimension is what works best for a given group; given their orientation in the other dimensions and how they interact together.

Table 2.1 below summarises our chosen cultural dimensions, their acronyms and the nature of their high and low orientations.

Table 2.1   Our chosen cultural dimensions

Dimension	Acronym	High Orientation (Pole)	Low Orientation (Pole)
Power Distance Index	PDI	High power distance	Low power distance
Uncertainty Avoidance Index	UAI	High uncertainty avoidance	Low uncertainty avoidance
Individualism vs. Collectivism	IDV	Individualism	Collectivism
Masculinity vs. Femininity	MAS	Masculine	Feminine
Long-term vs. Short-term Orientation	LTO	Long-term oriented	Short-term oriented
Specific vs. Diffuse Index	SDI	Specific	Diffuse
Sequential vs. Synchronous time	SST	Sequential	Synchronic

Chapter 3
Boss Knows Best!

If everyone is a prince, who will mind the mules?
Old Arabic proverb of unknown author

SUPARTS is a British multinational that designs and manufactures original and replacement automotive components; their clients include some of the largest automotive manufacturers in the US, Europe and Asia, as well as a number of global distributors and retailers of automotive replacement parts.

SUPARTS owns manufacturing plants in the UK, South America, Eastern Europe and South East Asia. They also hold long-term production contracts with manufacturing agencies in all continents.

A year ago, the board of directors accepted the global head of production's proposal to adopt new manufacturing standards and procedures, with the aim of increasing both efficiency and flexibility. Apart from the initiative's implications on the current internal processes and the various technologies used, it will also affect SUPARTS's interface with their clients; throughout design, making the prototypes and testing of components. This programme, which has a number of projects within it, is called 'Spring'.

Allen Young, a senior manager in the Welsh plant has been assigned as the global project manager of the industrial project within the programme, branded *Elastic*. Allen is a 44-year-old mechanical engineer who has been with the organisation for over 15 years, during which time he pitched and subsequently successfully managed local industrial modernisation projects. Apart from his proven experience in manufacturing, Allen is a seasoned project manager with excellent soft and hard skills.

* * *

Week 1 – First Stop, Slovakia

After kick-starting Elastic in Wales, and designing the project's blueprint to be rolled out across the other plants, Allen travelled to Slovakia, the second stop in the rollout process. His first action after agreeing the dates with the Slovak general manager was to send an invitation by email for a large meeting at the company's conference room to all the identified stakeholders. During the meeting Allen explained the project, its benefits and various areas it was designed to impact; and he advised those present that he would be approaching some of them individually for information and planning over the following couple of weeks. The overall reaction during the meeting was neutral; participants listened but didn't ask any questions, even when Allen invited them to do so. At the end of the meeting they left with a polite 'thank you'.

This somewhat disappointed Allen as he was accustomed to more inquisitive and enthusiastic reactions from stakeholders. The meeting felt more like a presentation. He wondered whether the Slovak culture was less pro-active and more reactive.

Next morning, Allen went to see Peter, one of the key design engineers of braking systems, with whom he had requested a meeting the day before. Allen asked Peter to explain the details of his design process and identify his designers and engineers involved at each step so he could talk to them in turn. Peter felt uneasy and explained that although he would be happy to do so, he would prefer that Bosac, the head of design, be present with them, but that Bosac was out for most of the week visiting two of their suppliers. This surprised Allen who responded by reminding Peter of the previous day's meeting at which he had made it clear that he would be making such requests; and that Bosac was present in the meeting and made no objection. Furthermore, that he expected the local managers to have already communicated to their staff some details of this project which was about to be rolled out in their own plant. 'Why waste Bosac's valuable time by asking him to be present in a meeting covering a process of which he was already well aware of? He would be informed of any relevant points afterwards'. Peter responded in the affirmative, adding, 'However, we really should have Bosac with us during this first meeting. He is the head of this department and we don't want him to feel we are bypassing him. He is away today and tomorrow, but I can arrange a meeting with the three of us first thing Friday morning.'

Allen accepted and thanked Peter; he did not want to be over persistent or cause unnecessary friction from the onset of the project. Nevertheless, he could not but help feeling somewhat frustrated. Here he was all the way from Wales, with his visit and its purpose well signalled in advance, and yet he faced such a scenario; why in the world would Peter, well known amongst the Welsh designers who worked with him for his professionalism and efficiency, request such a needless procedure?

Allen decided to turn his attention to production planning while awaiting the return of Bosac; this time, with a lesson learnt. He would go directly to the production planner and avoid risking a similar 'political' scenario by talking to the production manager who might react in a similar way to Peter and request the presence of the local head of operations.

It took little time for Allen to realise that his new approach was no better than the last. Novak, the 31-year-old production planner, looked nervous on meeting him. He greeted Allen politely and formally (not missing his title and insisting on calling him Engineer Allen) and asked what he could do for him. When Allen requested they go through the production planning process and any related interfaces, Novak offered to show him around the production floor. When Allen explained that he was familiar with their production floor through previous visits to their plant, and that what he was asking for was to be informed of the details of the official production planning process along with any established documentation and diagrams, as well as interfaces, just as if he himself was learning to do the job, Novak became more nervous and uneasy. He explained that with all due respect to Engineer Allen he would need to talk to his boss, the production manager, before sharing the requested information. Allen, who was about to protest as he had done with Peter, decided against doing so. He thanked Novak and assured him that he himself would talk to the production manager to get his authorisation.

Concerned, and starting to feel demotivated on this second day at the Slovakia plant, he went for a walk to mull over the day's events.

* * *

The power distance dimension looks at how far a culture encourages superiors to exert power. In a high power distance culture such as parts of Asia and the Middle East, being the boss means just that. Inequality is accepted. 'A place for everyone and everyone in their place.' Employees are frequently reluctant to express disagreement with their bosses, and prefer to work for managers who take the decisions (and responsibility) and then simply tell them what to do. This is often reflected in the country's social organisations and political structure, whereby a one-man autocracy, such as the head of the family, organisation or the state, is accepted and respected.

In a low power distance culture, superiors and subordinates consider each other to be equal, and both believe that social inequality in any society should be minimised. Employees have no trouble disagreeing with their bosses and expect to be consulted before any decisions that may impact their work are made. This however does not imply disrespect for the hierarchy or authority, both of which are present in low PDI cultures. A manager's higher rank at the workplace is offset by the subordinate's higher rank thanks to their technical expertise or in other areas such as sports, literary interests, being politically active, expertise in a particular hobby (for example, theatre acting) or voluntary social work. At the workplace therefore, the manager has higher rank, but boss and employees are equal as fellow members of the society.

As we shall see later, power distance reflects strongly on all social dynamics, starting from the family all the way to government and national institutions.

Hofstede defines power distance as:

> The extent to which the less powerful members of institutions and organisations within a country expect and accept that power is distributed unequally.

Back to our story. Where did Allen go wrong?

In failing to consider the difference between the UK's and Slovakia's PDI orientation.

The UK is a low power distance country. Therefore, Allen's approach to project management, which favours direct and open communication with the various ranks, bypassing the hierarchy once the project is approved, and approaching the desired stakeholders' directly and not through their bosses, works very well in Wales, just as it would do in the US, Sweden and other low PDI cultures.

Slovakia's orientation on PDI however, is very high. Allen's email invitation to the meeting, sent collectively to the various ranks of stakeholder, must have struck them as disrespectful of the local hierarchy; even though the senior managers did attend out of courtesy given Allen's position and seniority. Peter in turn, felt uneasy about bypassing his boss in this first meeting with Allen, and rightly, avoided allowing Allen to talk to his subordinates before he himself had spoken to his team to let them know what they may, and may not, share with Allen without referring back to him. Peter's motives with regards to discouraging Allen meeting his own team where three-fold:

1.   Peter wants Bosac to be informed and to provide approval.

2.   Peter's own authority with his team maybe compromised if they are approached by Allen, the senior manager from HQ without his having assured them that Allen has asked him for his say so.

3.   Peter's team would feel very uneasy about being approached by someone of high authority without their boss's support and reassurance.

Needless to say, Novak's reaction was exactly what Peter feared for his team.

The Origins of Power Distance Orientation

Whereas the origins of many dimensions are confidently traced in history (for example, uncertainty avoidance is directly related to a society's struggle in the face of wars, extreme weather conditions or other threats) power distance origins are more elusive.

Still, we do have some indication as to why societies should differ in their attitude towards power. Analysis of Hofstede's research data organised by country outlined a significant correlation to the following three factors:

•   The country's geographical latitude (the higher latitude, the lower the PDI).

- The country's population (the larger the population, the higher the PDI).

- The country's wealth (the richer the country, the lower the PDI).

Hofstede argues that the role latitude plays in determining a society's attitude towards power could be traced to the fact that societies living at lower latitude enjoyed a more fertile land which provided the society's basic needs of food and nourishment. Such a society's wealth is therefore its land.

It seems logical to assume that the biggest threat the society would face is that of invaders aiming to acquire their land. To protect against such threat, societies residing at lower latitude would organise themselves hierachically with a central authority that would efficiently oversee the groups' strategies of both defence and attack.

On the other hand, groups living at higher (and colder) latitudes did not enjoy such fertile land and their survival depended on adding industry to agriculture. Their major threat did not come from invaders but rather from nature itself. Societies that have learnt to fend for themselves without reliance or dependence on a higher 'other' stood a better chance of survival.

The role of wealth is even harder to determine. There are various factors associated with wealth that could be either the cause or the outcome of low PDI (or both). These include: lower dependence on agriculture, more modern industries, higher urban concentration and more social mobility, a better education system and a larger middle class.

The size of the population would logically influence the PDI; having a larger population would automatically reduce the approachability of higher authorities who would be far removed from the citizen. For example, the USA and its president. Similar authorities in smaller populations, such as Ireland, are far more approachable.

This reduction or extension of approachability has a direct emotional effect on how we perceive authority. To know somebody 'emotionally', is to empathise with that person and to judge them by the same standards, values and practices that we judge ourselves. Thus a step closer to equality and lower power distance.

Society, Family and the Government

Although I cannot recall the exact context, I still remember during my early adulthood, my father quoting a famous Arabic saying in response to a political discussion we were having: 'If everyone is a prince, who will mind the mules?'

Looking back today, the saying could mean one of two things:

- Accept inequality as a desired and appropriate trait of a functioning society.

- The mule's minder is just as relevant and deserving of respect as the prince.

Although I am certain of my own father's orientation leaning towards the lower power distance and that his quotation relates more to the second point than the first (yet, an element of the first was surely there as well), I am not sure what the orientation of the unknown author of the saying is.

Still, every nation or society must have their 'princes' and 'mule minders' to operate efficiently. What determines the difference between a high PDI and low PDI societies is:

Does the mule minder have equal rights to those of the prince?

Indeed, it is not about the society being divided into social ranks, but rather in the rights of each rank, and if they view each other as socially equal or not.

The family's attitude towards power distance manifests itself in how a baby is treated as early as a few months old. In higher PDI societies, there is a clear hierarchical status within the family that must be respected by all members from early childhood all the way through adulthood. In parallel and very much in correlation, responsibilities are clearly divided, with the highest being held by the head of the family. The head of the family is responsible for the whole family's wellbeing and family members are dependent on his or her guidance and leadership.

In lower PDI societies, as soon as children start to exert intellect or judgement, they are encouraged to reason and make up their own mind and decisions. The head of the family is the guiding 'teacher' rather than the authoritative 'leader'.

Governments and political leaders in high power distance societies tend to be more autocratic with authorities being more traditional and based on historical roots such as religion. Even within working democracies a difference between high and low PDI can be noted in 'presidential' vs. 'parliamentary' governments, whereby the parliamentary government dilutes the powers of the prime minister to that of the 'leader of the ruling party' rather than 'leader of the country'. It is the party and not its leader that leads the country. A high PDI society is more willing to accept inequality which is deemed necessary to satisfy people's need for dependence and guidance and to provide more security for both those up and down the power scale.

At the Workplace

Through my job as a consultant, which has permitted me to observe a very large number of organisations directly, it seems I have acquired the skill of understanding an organisation's power distance orientation merely by spending few minutes walking around their offices. Of course there is some exaggeration in this statement and I can never be certain of my immediate conclusions, nevertheless, I tend to get a good idea of PDI with a reasonable level of accuracy.

I cannot take the full credit for such a skill. The fact is, power distance is far more evident at the workplace than the other dimensions.

There are three easily observable factors that can tell us a lot about a company's PDI: office layout, dress code and the change to the employee's tranquillity when the bosses are present.

Table 3.1 outlines some of the PDI manifestations closer to the poles.

Table 3.1   Some power distance manifestations nearer the poles

Low Power Distance	High Power Distance
Use of open office space is preferred. Private offices for some bosses are meant to isolate their (regular) loud meetings and phone calls from their colleagues	Less open space. Sometimes never. Office size and the quality of its furnishing directly relates to the hierarchical position of its occupant
The general dress code is more casual. Staff and managers only dress formally for formal meetings with external stakeholders	The general dress code is formal, especially amongst the bosses
Staff attitude does not change in the presence of senior management	Staff tend to become uncomfortable or tense when a senior manager is present
Superiors and subordinates are equal. One day the subordinate will gain enough experience and knowledge and will themselves become a superior	Superiors and subordinates are unequal. It is the *exceptional* capabilities of the superiors that put them there
Manual workers have the same status as office workers. Lunch hours do not separate one workforce from the other	Manual workers have lesser status than office workers. Each workforce has its own lunch slot. Some companies have separate canteens for manual and office workers
A good manager will manage by delegating objectives and then assist their staff in meeting these objectives	A good manager tells their staff exactly what to do
Managers should consult their staff on major decisions	Managers hardly ever consult with their staff, nor are they expected to as this may reflect on the their lack of superior knowledge and confidence
Staff may openly disagree with their bosses	Staff rarely express disagreement with their bosses
Other PDI Social Manifestations	
Low Power Distance	High Power Distance
Access to education is equal for all classes	Higher classes have better access to education
Good students are those who show independent initiative in class	Teachers take all the initiative in class
Income distribution is less skewed	Income distribution is more skewed
Larger middle class	Larger lower and upper class
Inter-class social activities and friendships are normal. Often encouraged	Inter-class friendships and socialising are strongly discouraged
Children are left alone to play and to manage themselves wherever possible	Children are closely assisted and looked after by their parents and older siblings
Children are treated as equal, often consulted and the reasoning behind a decision is explained to them	Children are taught to respect their parents and follow their decisions. They are not expected to make up their own minds until adults
Politics and religion are separated	Politics and religion are not separated
Government officials and powerful public figures using status symbols such as expensive cars are suspect	The use of status symbols by government officials and powerful public figures is necessary to promote their authority
A small scandal can end a powerful politician's career	Even in the case of relevant scandals, it needs to be very substantial to end a politician's career
There is higher public participation in political discussion and processes	There is a general separation from, and mistrust towards politicians and official authority by the public

Chapter 4
You Are Not Alone!

No man is an island, entire of itself; every man is a piece of the continent.
John Donne, Devotions upon Emergent Occasions, 1624

* * *

A giant of a man with a large dark moustache, a kind expression and sympathetic brown eyes that invite trust and confidence; Bosac listened attentively to Allen as he shared his recent concerns with him.

A seasoned and well-travelled manager himself, he did not hesitate to inform Allen of how his email, the large meeting and direct approach to the stakeholders where perceived in the plant. He did reassure him though that it was 'no big deal' and no damage had been done, thanks to Allen's retreat and non-persistence. Bosac suggested that he accompany him to meet each of the senior managers informally one-to-one and ask their support; starting with the most senior.

Week 3 – Beijing, China

Content, motivated and full of enthusiasm following a pleasant and productive time in Slovakia, Allen flew to China to kick-start Elastic at the Beijing plant. He was now empowered with the experience of Slovakia and had made earlier phone contact with China's production manager to ask if he would kindly arrange his meetings with each of the relevant senior managers, starting with the general manager, as close to his arrival as possible.

Allen was greeted with courtesy and enthusiasm for the project and was particularly pleased to note the high interest the managers showed in his knowledge and technical capabilities. They were more than happy to introduce him to their respective teams so he might take the lead on starting Elastic immediately. With each manager, Allen agreed a weekly update on progress and use of resources, as well as immediate consultation should any exceptions requiring unplanned efforts arise.

On meeting each of the teams assigned by the impacted departments, Allen made sure to gather everyone's input in identifying the scope of the project from their perspective; he then asked that for each component on the scope, a team member be assigned as 'owner' with 'responsibility' for overseeing the efficient delivery of their component. On each occasion, there was a reluctance from the team to suggest someone for the assignment and a few made comments implying that, as the components were not delivered independently from each other, it was unrealistic to give each a different 'owner'. Allen assured them that he was fully aware of the interdependencies between the components, however, a responsible owner was necessary for each and the owner would have to manage their interfaces with other components. Each team, without exception, suggested their most senior member as the owner of all their components. When Allen tried to illustrate the downside of a single owner for all components the teams assured him that they would divide the work between them even if there was only one owner. Allen wisely consented.

A week later, and having been impressed by the teams' efficiency and professionalism, Allen felt that a show of appreciation was in order. He therefore invited the teams to a large dinner along with their functional senior managers. However, and to his surprise, all senior managers politely declined indicating current family and social commitments.

Not having the senior managers at dinner upset Allen somewhat; not so much for the loss of their company, but because he wanted to take advantage of the dinner to acknowledge the excellent performance of each team in the presence of their bosses. However, he knew that this acknowledgement could be made by other means and he resolved to writing an email congratulating everyone for a great job with a special thank you to (listing the names of the WP owners across the teams) for having most efficiently led and managed their part of Elastic kick-start, and noting that the dinner was meant to thank everyone for their performance. He made sure to copy all the senior managers including the general manager.

Over the next two days, Allen received polite emails from most invitees, including all the assigned 'owners', apologising for not being able to make it to dinner due to other commitments.

Allen didn't know what to think ... his immediate response was sadness!

* * *

Individualism vs. Collectivism (IDV) is probably the most powerful of the cultural dimensions, with the most deeply rooted values, and the strongest of influences.

At the extreme poles, societies operate in one of two ways. They either perceive their *overall progress and wellbeing as dependent on the sum of their individual members' initiative,* therefore shaping their values system to emphasise the importance of the individual's independence in order for each member of the group to reach his or her full potential; or they perceive their *overall progress and wellbeing as best achieved by working collectively as a group,* and in turn, shaping their norms and values to emphasise that the role of the individual is best realised by being an integral part of the group in all aspects.

One of the greatest cultural misconceptions of our time is associating collectivism with communist political systems that ignores the wellbeing of the individual; while associating individualism with egoism and/or a capitalist system that ignores the wellbeing of the group. Nothing can be further from the truth. *Both collectivism and individualism aim for the wellbeing of both the group and its individual members,* with neither being independent of the other. They differ however in their belief and approach.

There is no doubt that the West is more individualistic while the East more collective, and this is a matter for much concern to Western managers and project managers. Not so much because of its political and social manifestations (which are very significant in themselves), but mostly because almost all the key management theories have been developed in the West. That is, with individualistic rather than collective values, and have more notably than not, proven to fail in the East.

> *Individualism therefore is the degree to which a culture encourages people to act independently and take personal responsibility for their own lives. In a collective culture, such attitude is not acceptable as individuals are perceived as an integral component of the group, and expected to unquestionably behave for the wellbeing of the group, which in turn, will protect and support them throughout their membership to the group.*

Back to project *Elastic*. Did Allen 'put his foot in it'? Again?

If he did, we can't really blame him. After all, he did his best (successfully) to anticipate and avoid conflicts arising from difference in power distance between his own culture and the Chinese culture; and, whilst the implications of being at the opposite ends of the IDV dimension, can be very subtle, they have very significant consequences.

The UK, being a highly individualistic culture, emphasises the values of work delegation, named ownerships, responsibilities and accountabilities. A highly collective culture on the other hand, sees all these principles as shared by the group. The named representative of a group is exactly that: a representative.

It was for this reason that during the initial meetings with each team they all insisted on one person being assigned as owner to all their WPs. For them, they took the owner as representative and not as 'responsible' owner. Therefore, when Allen wrote his kind email of acknowledgement with particular thanks to the owners, copying all the senior managers, he did two things:

1.   Allen's email embarrassed the 'owners' who never saw themselves as above their colleagues in this work, and felt that the acknowledgement was uncalled for and could lead to disharmony between them and their team.

2.   The team members felt let down by Allen's email having clearly placed most of the merits not on the joint group efforts, but on their own assigned 'representative'.

Obviously, the teams and their representatives felt reluctant to participate in Allen's dinner.

The Origins of Individualism and Collectivism

There is no unanimous agreement on the origins of individualism and collectivism. However, empirical data shows two correlations:

- wealthier countries have higher IDV index;

- countries nearer the equator have lower IDV index.

Understanding cause and effect between IDV and the above correlation is a major challenge for anthropologists and social psychologists. A suggestion that higher IDV leads to a wealthier nation is met with the empirical contradiction that lower IDV leads to stronger economical growth. This was very apparent in previous decades with the Far East experiencing higher growth than the West.

We therefore can either conclude that higher IDV leads to wealth in poorer countries but then to negative growth in industrious countries, that wealth leads to higher IDV or that the relationship between wealth and high IDV is a coincidence. Either way, trying to analyse this dimension as uniform across the life spheres of a society, we can reach no realistic conclusion.

Is it collectivism at work, in politics, in organisation, in the family or in social dynamics that contributes to faster wealth? Which of these spheres contributes to social growth?

The relationship between geographical location and lower IDV is less evident and has similar reasoning to those of the origins of power distance. It is possible that in the harsher climates away from the equator, teaching independence to children was seen as means of survival despite the 'powerful others' who try to exert their influence on the lesser powerful for their own benefits. This could lead to a degree of higher IDV, however, as Hofstede notes, this factor only explains about 7 per cent of IDV differences and could easily be a coincidence or a research margin of error.

There is far more to collectivism and individualism than can be done justice in this brief chapter, particularly when considering that misunderstanding of this dimension has led to some of the greatest cultural conflicts of modern times. I therefore strongly invite the reader to refer to the Appendix for further elaboration of this most fascinating of cultural dimensions.

Society, Family and the Government

IDV manifests itself in a collective society mainly through the creation of tight groups. These groups are groups of friends, work colleagues, members of a religion (or sub-religion) or members of a social club that represents a common moral orientation.

The very same groups exist in individualistic cultures. The difference is that they are less tight and more open. If not only for new membership (which is often the case), at least in their relation to, and tolerance of, other similar groups.

Members of a social group in an individualistic society can come and go according to their needs, desires and availability. Members can even join multiple groups simultaneously, such as disconnected circles of friends (family friends from childhood, school friends, university friends, work friends, new friends through the tennis club). This independence and cross-membership is not approved of in a collective culture as it is perceived to threaten the solid values that a group has developed.

In a highly collective family, children are taught from a very early age to think in terms of 'we', with the family being the heart and core of 'we'.

Decisions are never made without consulting the family with the wellbeing of the family being the main consideration. These decisions will include the choice of husband or wife and field of study or career, or anything that would impact directly on the family's wellbeing. Individuals are expected to remain part of their family both organically and economically throughout their entire life and are expected to look after their parents in their old age. The family economics are represented by a common pot that is contributed to and shared by all its members. Marriage and the forming of a new family does not eliminate or reduce the membership to the original (parents) family, it adds members to it.

In an individualistic family the exact opposite is true. Children are taught and encouraged to make their own decisions, especially with regards to choice of study, career and marriage. They are also taught to fetch for themselves from as early as they can get a job (often starting with summer jobs during study years).

The structure of representative governments and their laws and regulations are strongly influenced by the national and regional IDV values. Within collective cultures the economy tends to be more centralised with higher import taxes; public services are rarely privatised as is often the case in individualistic culture.

Communism shares many values with collectivism and almost all communist nations are highly collective. However, the opposite is not true as the values of collectivism are not dependent on communism and many collective cultures are strongly opposed to communism. Suffice it to note that Portugal, Malaysia, Singapore, Greece and Turkey are highly collective cultures.

At the Workplace

In his book *Culture and Organisations*, Geert Hofstede beautifully sums up the psychological dynamic of collective and individualistic organisations as follows:

> *Employed persons in an individualistic culture are expected to act according to their own interests, and work, should be organised in such a way that this self-interest and the employer's interest coincide. Workers are supposed to act as 'economic persons', or as people with a combination of economic and psychological needs, but anyway as individuals with their own needs. In a collective culture, an employer never hires just an individual, but rather a person who belongs to an in-group. The employee will act according to the interest of this in-group, which may not always coincide with his or her individual interest.*

Indeed, most evidently individualistic and collective working practices are explained by this remark. In a collective organisation the organisation is the 'group' and its staff are members of that 'group'. Ideas and decisions are made in group consultation and likewise, attribution of success is given to the group. At some point the organisation (or department within the organisation) starts to resemble a social group with similar dynamics and emotions.

Individualistic organisations on the other hand expect its staff to take more individual initiative and to act as 'entrepreneurs' within the organisation. Competitiveness is encouraged and each member is rewarded based on their specific achievements and results.

It is important to note that both the organisation's industry sector and the functional role of each department play a major role in the IDV orientation. Whereas modern financial institutions tend to be more individualistic, manufacturing tends to be more collective, partly due to the nature of working conditions in manufacturing that lead to the forming of strong and cohesive unions. At the same time and within the very same organisation, the culture of the financial department is likely to be more collective than that of the sales and marketing department.

Table 4.1 below outlines some of the IDV manifestations closer to the poles.

Table 4.1   Some individualistic and collective manifestations nearer the poles

Highly Collective	Highly Individualistic
Harmony and consensus override immediate results	Immediate results override harmony and consensus
Confrontations and open discussions are considered harming to the organisational harmony	Confrontations and open discussions are considered healthy
Technical expertise in the subject matter is most important	Knowing how to source technical expertise of any subject matter is most important
Academic achievement is the highest reference a candidate can provide	Practical achievement is the highest reference a candidate can provide
Staff turnover is low	Staff turnover is high
Other IDV Social Manifestations	
Highly Collective	Highly Individualistic
Membership to social circles is tightly controlled and often exclusive	Social circles are open, cooperation between them and new memberships are encouraged
Close friends are perceived as an extended family and some family obligations are extended to friendship	Friendship has few obligations beyond honesty and integrity
Children are taught to think in terms of the 'family' in all major actions and decisions	Children are taught to think independently from an early age
The elderly expect to be looked after by their children during their old age	The elderly value their continued independence and invest towards it from their early age
Most people live with their parents until they marry. Some continue to live with parents after marriage	As soon as children grow and start to earn their independent income, they move out from their parents' home
Public services such as transport, healthcare and energy are public sectors	Public services are often private sectors. More recently, 'privatisation' of the public sector has been a recurring reality in individualistic countries
Centralised state-controlled economy	Open private-controlled economy
Equality prevails over individuals' freedom	Individuals' freedom prevails over equality

Chapter 5
Follow Your Desires!

Everyone has been made for a particular work, and the desire for that work has been put in every heart.

Jalal ad-Din Rumi,
Persian philosopher, theologian and poet (d. 1273)

* * *

Week 7 – Slovenia

'What a ride ...', thought Allen. China has been quite an experience and an eye opener. He had so far attributed the Chinese success during the recent decades to their flexibility to adapt, and somehow assumed that this implied that they have adopted modern Western-style work and management. How wrong he had been; Allen pleasantly felt an admiration for the Chinese culture.

Now in Slovenia, and following a week back in Wales after this most intense of his working travels, he felt happy and relaxed. He had been over anxious when he arrived fearing another 'cultural mishap'; after all, he managed to cause two in China. This time however, he was confident that finally he was doing things right.

The local plant director and production manager had met Allen for breakfast on his first morning in Slovenia, and had freed their entire day's schedule in anticipation to get him up to speed with the local status and introduce him to the key stakeholders. They had informed all concerned persons of project Elastic and had information and materials prepared for his arrival. Furthermore, they made it clear that they expected him to take the full lead.

Allen's meetings with the stakeholders only confirmed his first impressions. They were eager to work with him, discussed their effort requirements and arranged to be available a sufficient part of each week as purely 'project' resources. Allen took the lead and put together a high-level project schedule, assigning Work Package (WP) responsibilities and ownership to those he identified as both leaders and most proactive.

He then set up a meeting with the WP owners to communicate his plan and their responsibilities. To his surprise, almost all of them were in disagreement with their assignments. Lorenz, a senior engineer within maintenance, suggested that Allen's choice for the owner of maintenance WP should be Alfonz, the most experienced and horizontally skilled technician within the department, rather than himself, whose role was more about managing the overall maintenance activities and their related suppliers. All the other owners had similar arguments. When Allen outlined the reasons for his choice being their leadership skill and resourcefulness, they responded to the effect 'how is this significant in managing experts who know the context of their own work better than us?' Allen conceded and asked for their input in making a new choice of WP owners.

A few days later and having gained confidence from the team's openness, eagerness and overall progress, Allen suggested that they put in a few extra hours so as to complete the first stage of the project ahead of schedule and prior to his departure from the plant; this, he noted, would reflect excellently on their performance in the eyes of both local and corporate senior management. He suggested they work until 7.30pm (as opposed to 5.30pm) and Saturday mornings. He promised to pay daily for their dinner out of his own budget.

It was Miran, the head of IT who broke the brief silence that ensued:

'Why? We are on track, aren't we?'

'Yes, but we can achieve more if we put the extra hours.'

'Maybe I am missing something, if so please correct me. We don't have any urgencies which are not satisfied by our current plan. Right?'

'Oh no, we are doing great thanks to all of your and your teams' efforts. However, if we deliver the first stage ahead

*of schedule, it would be a significant achievement; and will
reflect well on the teams in the eyes of senior management.'*

*'Not in the eyes of our management. They expect delivery by the
planned date; earlier is not necessarily better, given that all is
proceeding well; why work late and weekends? I'd rather do my
own stuff in my own time.'*

Almost all the others, expressed their agreement with Miran.

* * *

Objective success, is realising your desires; nothing more, nothing less.

And that applies to masculine and feminine cultures alike. The difference
between a masculine and a feminine professional lies purely in what they *truly*
desire; with the masculine's desire being more oriented towards competitive
achievement and delivery, while the feminine, towards technical achievement
and overall benefits. While neither of these two poles need override the other,
where there is a choice to be made, that choice is clear for each.

Within social manifestations, this desire can be noted in the masculine's
orientation towards wealth and status, while the feminine, towards family and
social wellbeing.

The image of the highly successful yet miserable person is a subjective
illusion; such a person cannot be objectively successful. They are either of
masculine orientation and did not achieve masculine success, or of feminine
orientation and did not achieve feminine success. The saddest part of all is
that most such people themselves do not realise this. They define success by
their social or organisational norms when their personal values and desires
differ. More recently in the past half century, masculine success has become
a necessity for survival in many facets of the global economy.

The MAS dimension can be very subtle and confusing, not in the least
because a society's MAS orientation has a direct correlation with how their
gender roles are defined. Yet, the dimension has also the previously noted
effect on how success is defined and perceived; therefore bringing the non-
expert to believe that societies with distinctly different and separate gender
roles define success in terms of wealth and power (masculine); while those

that mix and overlap gender roles define it in terms of social wellbeing (feminine). A very understandable yet wrong assumption.

As we will see in this chapter:

- A masculine person strives on achievements, acknowledgement and status, making these their true 'desires' which are key to their happiness.

- Today's globally competitive economy is far more masculine than the average masculinity of its active participants, therefore forcing many individuals to act more masculine than they truly are if they are to progress at work.

- Gender equality does *not* imply overlapping of the gender roles.

- The distinction and separation of gender roles is *not* a mark of the masculine society.

It is due to the subtlety of this dimension that the multicultural project manager needs a deeper and more profound understanding of the MAS social orientation as compared to the other dimensions.

The role of men and women differ significantly from one society to another. Not only in terms of gender equality but more significantly in terms of what a modern society considers to be gender equality.

In pre-modern societies, the prime needs of providing food and sustenance (hunting), providing safety and protection (defending) and taking care of the newly born and youngsters (procreation and rearing), determined the roles of its male and female members. Today in modern societies, the development of industry and agriculture had rendered the role of hunting unnecessary, and the role of defence and protection as provided by the state with the aid of modern machinery and technology making it often as suitable for women to participate as it is for men.

A modern society in this specific context of 'gender role' is therefore a society whose development will allow male and female members to share largely the same roles *should they as a society wish to do so*, apart from the biological limitations of procreation and physical limitations of extreme labour and some defence roles; and have further given equal weight to male and female members' desire in determining what role they each want to play or share.

We can therefore deduce that many of the wealthy societies including Britain, the US, Italy, Sweden, Greece, Lebanon and Kuwait are reasonably modern societies.

These countries are meant to highlight that the differences in gender roles are not due to a lack of 'gender equality', but rather to what each society considers as gender equality and how they exercise their own ideal of male and female roles.

In Italy, women's roles are still mainly in the home while men are often the main breadwinner. This does not exclude women and men from crossing roles but it does, with the general agreement of both sexes, define them socially in the context of such roles. A career woman is likely to face specific difficulties at work due to her gender (and given the recent economical crises forcing women to take a more active role in the economy, these difficulties are becoming a major issue).

In Sweden, the roles of men and women are highly shared. Both work to provide provision. Both share and rotate the jobs of childcare and home maintenance.

Hofstede defines the MAS dimension as:

> *Masculinity stands for a society in which social gender roles are clearly distinct. Men are supposed to be assertive, tough, and focused on material success; women are supposed to be more modest, tender, and concerned with the quality of life. Femininity stands for a society in which social gender roles overlap: both men and women are supposed to be modest, tender, and concerned with the quality of life.*

By now, it should be clear why Allen did not find sympathy with his masculine desire to invest personal time to deliver ahead of schedule. While for him, early delivery represents a notable team achievement and a mark of its success, for the feminine Slovenians, it is an unnecessary achievement at the cost of their valuable personal time.

Nor were Lorenz and his colleagues happy about the work product ownerships being delegated on the basis of their management skills rather than their technical merits. In their feminine culture, it is the technical experts who take the lead; and most importantly, employees respect a technically proficient leader far more than a charismatic manager who lacks technical expertise.

The Origins of Masculine vs. Feminine Orientation

The origins of gender role are amongst the oldest and most elusive. Opinions vary as to the sources: religion, survival, physical attributes and even genetic psychological attributes.

Anthropologists and social psychologists have given many valid reasons and speculated widely. I will outline some of the most popular theories:

THE HUNTER AND THE BABY SITTER

Gender role was developed by the earliest societies on the basis of physical attributes. Thus the man assumed the role of protection and provision while the woman that of procreation, rearing and looking after the home and the young.

'OBEY THY HUSBAND'

There is little doubt that religion has played a major role in shaping the gender role. This role is not necessarily masculine despite popular perceptions. In many instances and contexts religion has played a major role in 'feminising' societies and liberating women from earlier oppressions. In other instances, the opposite also was true.

COLD OR WARM?

Societies living in colder climates tend to be more feminine than those in warmer climates. Some anthropologists suggest that in colder climates where survival is tougher, overlapping the gender roles increased resilience.

I'LL BE BACK IN A COUPLE OF MONTHS …

Trade and commerce flourished in certain societies thanks to their national products and geographical location. In these societies men often travelled to distant regions leaving all affairs at home for their wives to manage. This led to an extension of women's role and in turn, higher femininity.

Society, Family and the Government

Within many modern urban societies in the Middle East, such as in Jordan, Lebanon, Egypt and Syria (prior to the current conflict), there is a tradition of people socialising daily in cafes. This socialising is rarely gender mixed, yet the overall number of men and women in a average venue is generally balanced. When a couple marry, they continue to socialise daily with their respective friends, separately, just as they did pre-marriage; something they both deem necessary for their wellbeing. As the family grows, their social activities reduce; and as men get older, they become more tender and less masculine. At some point, social activities stop being gender segregated and preference for mixed socialising with other families becomes their new norm.

Another visible albeit less subtle aspect of the masculine society is the display of status symbols, which is often essential for successful persons to be accepted as such. This acceptance does not end in social integration and is key to networking and business relations.

Paradoxically, within the masculine family, the young boys rather than the girls have a tougher time growing up. In wanting to ensure their future success, they are often treated in a 'toughening' manner by their father, while their mother who does not disapprove of her husband's treatment, plays a more tender and comforting role. The young girls who will grow to play a lesser role in the economy but higher in the family and home management, do not need such toughening. Indeed, a masculine society highly values femininity and tenderness in women and young girls are treated tenderly by both father and mother. Quite often, more tenderly by the father.

Within the feminine state, there is a higher emphasis and budget on health, educational and social service to guarantee a minimum standard of living for all its citizens.

Full democracies occupy the two poles of this dimension with their system, law and regulations representing the general desires and values of their citizens. Consider the defence expenditure against that of education and health in the USA (masculine), and the Netherlands (feminine). They could not be more different, with the former being the strongest nation on earth while still struggling to put together an efficient national health service, and the latter being relatively militarily weak but with impressive national health service that is equally available to all its citizens, rich and poor. Ironically, those who argue that they are at a disadvantage in the Netherlands are its wealthier citizens who can afford private health care but the state would not allow it, for fear that private health services may compromise the quality of the national health system, and in turn the wellbeing of its less wealthy citizens.

At the Workplace

Most visibly, masculinity and femininity is noted in organisations through their recruitment process; from how a candidate's CV is perceived, all the way to selection.

Any candidate from one pole of this dimension who applied for position within an organisation of the other pole must have experienced some puzzlement or shock at the process.

Within a masculine organisation, managers need to demonstrate strong assertiveness, determination and competitiveness and they are rewarded for these qualities as well as their results. In a typical American investment bank, 'masculinity at work' can be noted at its very peak. In one international bank I worked with, the title 'Vice President' was held by over 10,000 employees; 'Managing Director' by over 500. What is more significant than the titles themselves is that their holders are meant to act in a way that reflects them. There is a strong feeling of personal ownership by senior managers and the use of terms such as 'My World' and 'Your World' are common when referring to their departments or areas of influence. Every good team player exerts all their effort and energy to achieve more and there is always some sense of urgency. Working hours are usually long even when no truly crucial deadlines are approaching (I say truly as masculine organisations tend to treat all deadlines as crucial).

On the other pole, feminine organisations tend to be more relaxed. Managers may feel the same sense of ownership as their masculine counterparts but its significance for them is more technical and less exclusive and statuary. No big titles and loud terms are used. Most employees have higher technical interest in what they do and are less concerned with competitiveness and acknowledgements. They do what they believe is right regardless. The hours are normally shorter than those of a masculine organisation; however, in the case of a truly urgent deadline, members of a feminine organisation do not fall short of their masculine counterparts in staying as late as it takes to get the job done.

There is no evidence that masculine organisations are more productive than feminine organisations. Nor the reverse. Industry sectors tend to lean towards one pole or another even within the same larger culture (city or nation). The differences between a masculine sector in a masculine society and a feminine sector in a feminine society becomes very evident. A good example to contemplate is the American bank JP Morgan (highly masculine) and the Swedish furniture group IKEA (highly feminine).

No one can claim that one orientation is better than the other. Most likely, switching the poles between the two organisations will end in the demise of both, as each orientation is best suited to its own sector.

Back to our recruitment process, CVs in masculine cultures loudly note and praise their candidate's achievements and capabilities. During job interviews, candidates are expected to confidently outline their outstanding capabilities and what makes them perfect for the job. In a feminine culture, such CVs and interviewee behaviour is considered arrogant, bragging and somewhat embarrassing. A good professional is a humble professional who does not need to over-outline their achievement. The interviewer will make sure to ask the right questions to determine the candidate's suitability for the job. The entire recruitment process is more relaxed with a give and take of a two-ways discussion.

Table 5.1 below outlines some of the MAS manifestations that are close to the poles.

Table 5.1   Some masculine and feminine manifestations nearer the poles

Highly Feminine	Highly Masculine
Management salaries are lower	Management salaries are higher
Working hours are shorter (often restricted by the organisation itself). Working evenings and weekends are rare	Working hours are longer. Working evenings and weekends are common
Deadlines and urgencies need to be justified	There is a constant sense of urgency and approaching deadlines.
There is higher emphasis on technocracy	There is higher emphasis on management
Technical expertise are important	Knowing how to source technical expertise is more important that being an expert
Public or frequent acknowledgements can be embarrassing	Employees and managers expect to be publicly acknowledged for their achievement
Organisations provide social services to their employees such as sport clubs and recreational activities	There are fewer social services provided by the employer. Often none
Other MAS Social Manifestations	
Highly Feminine	Highly Masculine
Success is defined in terms of the quality of family life and social relationship	Success is defined in terms of wealth, power and status
Modesty is a virtue	It is important to show one's success
Gender equality means that men and women share and overlap their roles	Gender equality means that men and women agree to retain distinct and more traditional roles
Sport is pleasant and leisurely	Sport is highly competitive
Moderate to low expenditure on cars, clothes and mobile phones	High expenditure on luxury cars, designer clothes and latest mobile phones
Career path is chosen on the basis of interest	Career path is chosen on the basis of opportunities
Both parents are tough and tender towards their children, depending on the objective	Towards the boys, fathers are tough while mothers are tender
Both parents deal with facts and emotions	Fathers deal with facts, mothers with emotions
Lower defence expenditure. Higher expenditure on health, education and social services	Higher defence expenditure. Lower expenditure on health, education and social services
Higher taxes escalating with increased income	Lower taxes often reaching a roof at moderate levels of income
Environment is high on the political agenda	Environment is a lower priority on the political agenda
Higher aids to poor countries	Lower aids to poor countries
Preference for negotiation in resolving international conflicts	Preference for show of strength to resolve international conflicts

Chapter 6

Are You Sure?

Better the devil you know than the devil you don't.

Irish proverb

* * *

Week 9 – Slovenia

'I never thought I would come to dread Fridays ...' thought Allen during the early morning walk from his hotel to the plant.

It seemed to him that Slovenians had a love affair with details. Not that he had anything against detailed diligence; he himself did his good share of regular planning and reporting, but this level of detail seemed more befitting a bureaucratic government office rather than their dynamic company.

Earlier during the previous week when the various WP owners had presented their meticulously detailed plans for him to integrate in the local master plan, he had explained that he did not require all these details, and would only be making use of the summary activities. He asked if they could resend him the plans with only the summary, keeping the details out for clarity purposes, which they did. Little did he know he would have to go back and request the details a couple of days later.

He had assumed that the WP owners in their enthusiasm for project Elastic and their good knowledge of project management methodology, had wanted to use this project to establish their teams' standards for subsequent projects and for this reason had gone beyond reasonable levels of detail in their own planning. When on Friday's project board meeting he was asked for a report to include a breakdown of daily activities, hourly resource usage by name, technical specification and quality of products, all identified risks and issues that have an impact beyond a single day's work, he was taken by surprise. He had never expected senior managers to request such detail. Back home in the UK, presenting data of this kind to senior managers would not have gone down so well.

'And is there any value to such detailed planning into the future, given that the most minor of unforeseen events and deviations will certainly force the plans to be modified, well before the currently planned activities are due?' Allen kept thinking as he approached the plant to prepare for the project board's weekly Friday afternoon meeting.

* * *

Uncertainty Avoidance Index (UAI) can be defined as the degree to which members of a group experience discomfort or anxiety towards ambiguity.

A common mistake is to confuse uncertainty avoidance with risk avoidance.

A risk is the possibility of an event resulting in negative consequences. A risk is an object of concern.

Therefore on the basis of this traditional definition, there is little ambiguity in a risk. We know what the risk is, we can estimate its probability and impact should it happen and we can plan certain measures to guard us against it.

The ambiguity of uncertainty comes from not knowing what to expect. And by not knowing we cannot devise a response strategy. In other words, *ambiguity has no object*. If there were an object we could identify, it would no longer be ambiguous. We would know exactly what we have to 'fear'.

A project faces a risk if a number of its suppliers are in a region that is experiencing political and civil turmoil. Clearly the risk to the project is falling short of supplies and not being able to deliver some of its outputs on time.

The project manager may devise a strategy whereby they will complete their orders from the affected countries as soon as possible; at the cost of early payments and local storage until the supplies are needed.

On the other hand, a long-term and large project (or programme) may face uncertainties if a new political party is elected to government. How will this government address taxes and regulations relating to the project's sector? Are we to expect higher taxes on imported supplies or more rigid working regulations? Which parts or processes of the project are going to be effected, and to what extent? We can only wait anxiously to find out.

Once the new laws and regulations are published, uncertainty will cease and the project will now face known risks, if it does not undertake measures to comply.

You may wonder why any organisation with common sense would place itself willingly in an ambiguous situation? Perhaps it wants to be innovative. At the very heart of innovation (and invention) is experimentation. Progressing through trial and error. Before we try something, we can only guess what the results may be.

Of course, not every trial faces ambiguity. Many face a handful of eventualities in which case the experiment is designed to determine which it will be. However, the most innovative of inventions come from trying something completely new. We have no idea how the investors may react, how the market may react and how any third parties crucial to the product may react. The risk is not the uncertainty. The risk is deciding to face the uncertainty. The risk is that we will fail in the face of uncertainty. The uncertainty is unknown.

Apple's iPhone and iPad are great examples of facing uncertainty. Many uncertain factors were at play that could have 'made or broken' these products entirely.

Paradoxically, some uncertainty avoidant cultures tend to rate higher on risk facing than lower uncertainty avoidant cultures. However, we can now understand the motive. High uncertainty avoidant cultures experience higher anxiety in the face of ambiguity. Sometimes the only way to break this anxiety is to force the ambiguity to be revealed and manifest itself as an object (in our case risk).

Imagine for example that you are the project manager of a 'mission critical' project within your organisation and that on each meeting with the senior sponsor you get the impression that something is not right but you can never understand his evaluation of your performance. This sponsor can influence your managers' own opinions. You have tried in various conversations to get some feedback from the sponsor but he repeatedly has given very little information and remained neutral and factual in all that is said. You are now getting the impression that he is being particularly cold in his communications with you. You are aware of this sponsor's reputation as emotionally neutral and generally inexpressive, still, you cannot help but feel increasing anxiety that this coldness has gone beyond his usual character and is possibly due to some misperception about you.

At some point, you start to feel so anxious that you decide to face this ambiguity and ask him some direct questions. You want to bring any possible dislike or mistrust on his part into the open so you may rectify them; or if you are lucky, discover that in fact he has nothing against you and approves of your work.

You are consciously aware that this course of action may result in the risk of your removal from the project, and even demotion. Yet, there are many who would take such a fearful risk rather than face a long unnerving ambiguity and would prefer to take action to turn the ambiguities into risks.

Slovenians, belonging as they do to a high uncertainty avoidant society, aim to provide as much clarity around expectations as they believe is possible. This can easily become counterproductive as we will note in the later chapters, especially in light of modern planning software that makes it possible to plan product delivery, time, resources, risks and various other elements far into the future and in very meticulous detail.

Uncertainty Avoidance and Innovation

The influence of culture on innovation has been explored by Shane (1993; 1995). His research suggests that rates of innovation are predominately influenced by weak uncertainty avoidance. He also suggested that weak power distance and strong individualism are also linked to higher innovation, although to a lesser extent.

Yet, and as logical as Shane's findings seem, they were strongly contradicted by a significant observation that the French researcher and author, Philippe d'Iribarne made:

During the 1990s the French automotive manufacture Renault and the Swedish Volvo created a joint venture. France scores high on UAI, while Sweden, very low.

A mixed team was established to work on the design of the new car. In 1998 Philippe d'Iribarne wrote:

> In the joint team, the French rather than the Swedes produced the more innovative designs. French team members did not hesitate to tryout new ideas and to defend these aggressively. The Swedes, on the other hand, were constantly seeking consensus. The need for

consensus limited what ideas they could present, even what ideas they could conceive of. To the Swedes the expression of ideas was subject to the need for agreement between people; to the French, it was only subject to the search for technical truth. The French were primarily concerned with the quality of decisions; the Swedes with the legitimacy of the decision process. In the negotiations within the team, the French usually won. They had the support of their superiors who were involved all along, while the Swedish superiors had delegated the responsibility to the team members and were nowhere to be seen. The danger of this asymmetric structure was discovered too late. A mutual distrust had developed at top management level that led to the termination of the venture.

I find d'Iribarne and Shane's contradicting observations both fascinating and enlightening. Geert Hofstede responded to this contradiction by stressing the fact that the observer can never be free from his or her bias. In this case, the French high UAI (d'Iribarne) and the American low UAI (Shane).

However, there are some absolute truths beyond the bias in *both* Shane's and d'Iribarne's observations:

- Creativity and innovation require a moderately lower uncertainty avoidance. However, this relationship is non-linear and, beyond a certain point, lower UAI can be counter-productive to creativity.

- A structure that allows free flow of ideas requires fewer processes and procedures, as is often the case in lower uncertainty avoiding cultures.

- Implementation of creative and innovative ideas requires better-developed and structured processes and procedures as in a higher uncertainty avoiding culture.

- Because of a multitude of other significant factors to UAI, the constraining effect of high UAI on creativity and innovation is only observable at the extreme poles of this dimension.

We therefore must face the UAI with caution and keep in mind in the later chapters that unless we are dealing with the extreme poles of the dimension, there will be very little we can observe or influence with respect to innovation and structure. This should make our job as multicultural project managers somewhat easier.

The Origins of Uncertainty Avoidance Orientation

Anthropologists and social psychologists have searched for a link between historical instability and uncertainty avoidance. It would seem logical that cultures which repeatedly faced uncertainties to their way of life, such as wars, famine or extreme weather conditions, would develop a higher orientation towards uncertainty avoidance. Empirical data, however, does not support this assumption.

Geert Hofstede, having searched for a correlation between uncertainty avoidance and power distance, has noted that the heirs to the Roman Empire scored high on both dimensions. However, the heirs of the Chinese Empire scored high on power distance and low on uncertainty avoidance.

Finally, Hofstede notes in his book *Cultures' Consequences* that:

> All in all, the statistical analysis does not allow us to identify any general sources of weak or strong uncertainty avoidance, other than history.

Society, Family and the Government

An uncertainty avoidant culture feels discomfort in the face of what is different. This can generate some forms of racism or xenophobia *at the extreme higher UAI pole*. In a moderately high UAI culture, group members have a preference for the company of their own; be it school group, university group, work group or social status group. This is easily observed in large social events and parties where those present 'mix and mingle' far less than they would in a lower UAI culture.

An expatriate in a moderately high UAI culture may be offered all the appropriate courtesies with the very best of intention. But their social relations with members of the hosting culture will unlikely progress beyond such courtesies.

Families within higher UAI cultures emphasise cleanliness and safety, which to them comes from better hygiene (often exaggerated), responsible behaviour, avoiding strangers and keeping to one's own social circle.

In lower uncertainty avoidant cultures curiosity overcomes natural anxiety. The attitude is that 'different' is just as good, if not sometimes better. Children are encouraged to explore and mix socially. Both horizontally (varying cultures) and vertically (social class), even hygiene is given less importance than in higher UAI families, with the view that a reasonable exposure to dirt is harmless and will better develop a child's immunity system.

Just as families in higher UAI cultures build stricter norms to guard against uncertainties, so do the government laws and regulations. These laws and regulations highlight the extent of anxiety or discomfort that the nation feels towards ambiguity. Hofstede noted that whereas Germany (high UAI) has laws for the event that all other laws become unenforceable (Notstandsgesetze), Britain (low UAI) does not even have a written constitution.

At the Workplace

My approach to planning training and consultancy services is relatively unstructured. In any training for which the participants are of a similar profile, I prefer to keep a loose schedule with only high-level agenda items for the main areas I intend to cover. The details I then elaborate, change and adapt as I proceed with the training, on the basis of immediate participation and feedback. This approach allows me the flexibility of providing the right information in the right way to the right audience; and I take a similar approach to delivering consultancy services. The alternative (a detailed pre-set agenda) would never be flexible enough to cater to the exact needs of most clients, since these only become clear during execution.

This approach is much appreciated in the UK and the US where it tends to be the norm for most consultants.

In 2007, I was asked to pitch a training course for a group of project and programme managers within Fiat Auto in Turin, Italy. I sent my proposal with the course content based on the participants' profiles provided by the client. I was surprised when Fiat HR called to say that the schedule was at too high a level and that they required a breakdown right down to most detailed topic in order to authorise the training. I tried to explain that this would almost certainly reduce the value to the participants, as I would have to abandon the flexibility to adapt my training to their needs during the very course. Sadly, HR insisted that although they might agree with me, the rules of the company dictated that details be set prior to any training approval.

I can now rationalise this experience on the basis that Italy rates much higher on uncertainty avoidance than the UK, hence the discomfort at an ambiguous agenda. This manifested itself in Fiat's requirement for an extraordinary detailed training schedule prior to approval. In all fairness to Fiat and the participants in my course, once we had started, I did ask the participants how they would feel letting go of the agenda and addressing immediate needs and concerns within the larger context of the session. The response was enthusiastic and by the end of the event all the participants gave positive feedback to HR. Fiat remains a major client of our training organisation.

Table 6.1 below outlines some of the UAI manifestations closer to the poles.

Table 6.1   Some uncertainty avoidance manifestations nearer the poles

Low Uncertainty Avoidance	High Uncertainty Avoidance
Managers are younger	Managers are older
Academic qualifications are less relevant than experience	Academic qualifications are more relevant than experience
Less governance and control overall	Higher governance and control
Few written processes	Processes are elaborated in detail and formally documented
Less structured execution	More structured execution
Higher innovation	Lower innovation
Other UAI Social Manifestations	
Low Uncertainty Avoidance	High Uncertainty Avoidance
Social groups are more open	Social groups are more closed
Higher racial integration	Lower racial integration
Loose social norms	Rigid social norms
Comfortable with ambiguous situations	Ambiguous situations are highly stressful
Children are left alone to play	Children are meticulously looked after and never let out of sight
Children are encouraged to mix with others of different culture and social class	Children are taught to mix with those of their own culture and social class
Lower bureaucracy	Higher bureaucracy
Younger politicians	Politicians are older, often beyond retirement age
It is very unlikely that a political career will run in the family	Political careers often run in the family and politicians have a higher chance of being elected where this is the case
Less rules and regulations	More rules and regulations

Chapter 7
Safeguard Your Status

I wear many different hats; one at work, one at home and one at my social club.
'Wearing many hats' is an English idiom

* * *

Thinking back on the team dinner in China, Allen felt a surge of embarrassment return and wondered if on his next trip to the plant, his 'dinner performance' would have been forgotten.

Having finally convinced enough people to accept his dinner invitation, which proved less difficult once he extended his invitation in person, the party of 14 team members and two senior managers went to a traditional local restaurant after work.

One of the senior managers was Chong who knew Allen well from his three years acting as the global quality director based in Wales. It was Chong who had earlier suggested that Allen avoid naming any particular persons when acknowledging a team's performance, and that he approach the teams in person to extend his dinner invitation rather than by email. Now Allen wished he had better noted Chong's hints during the dinner itself.

Allen had felt completely relaxed after the third beer and, prior to the meal being served, he chatted and joked openly with the group in a most amicable and informal manner. Following the British fashion, he had dropped all formalities and restraints for the evening. He also took it on himself to encourage the seemingly shy and conservative participants to drink more, 'loosen-up' and join in an unrestrained conversation. He believed that the team would appreciate a relaxed attitude given their otherwise formal environment at work.

*The next day, Allen asked Chong if they might lunch together. He
wanted to talk to him about the previous evening's dinner. That
morning he couldn't help but feel that the team was talking about and
possible even laughing at him. Not so bluntly as to be impolite, but
to an extent that was clearly noticeable. Allen couldn't recall doing
anything particularly wrong the previous night! It's not that he got
blind drunk or made a fool of himself … right?*

* * *

One of my favourite business travel destinations is the US; especially if I
anticipate a busy agenda that will leave me with little time in the evening for
culture or recreational activities.

After work and before dinner, I would go to a nearby bar. I never had to
make an effort to chat to people. Just by sitting at the bar and ordering my
drink, sooner or later someone will start chatting to me and by dinner time I
often end up with a dinner companion.

When I first experienced the Americans' openness to strangers and their
desire to talk about issues varying from politics, weather, sport, family and
work; including personal topics which often made me blush, I was surprised
yet pleased to have made friends so quickly and easily. Just as amazed as I was
dismayed when by the end of that evening hardly any of my new friends cared
to exchange contact details or stay in touch, but simply left me with their best
wishes for my trip. I later on got used to these brief and pleasant friendships
that an evening may bring. I never heard again from the vast majority of my
temporary American 'friends'.

Those travelling to the Far East, the Middle East or Mediterranean Europe
will tell a very different story; in these countries it is particularly hard to make
acquaintances or friends without being introduced. You may sit in a popular
bar every evening for a month, yet apart from the barman and tourists, no one
will chat to you. If you take the initiative to chat to the locals you are likely
to get a polite, formal and courteous response enquiring about your origins
and impressions of their country, after which they will excuse themselves to
return to their own company. However, should you be so lucky as to strike
up a friendship during the evening, then it is highly likely that they will want
to exchange contact details and will keep in touch. Should you ever return
to that country, these friends are likely to meet you again and invite you to
lunch or dinner, and may get offended if you decline their offer.

These apparently opposite social attitudes have puzzled members of the other cultural group. Eastern societies tend to see the Americans' openness as excessively intrusive, and the idea of confining a seemingly close relationship to one particular event as insincere. The Americans on their part find Eastern societies and some Europeans to be distant and lacking in openness.

Both opinions are clearly coloured by the cultural expectations of the given travellers.

Talcott Parsons described two opposing types of societies: Specific and Diffuse. A specific society tends to separate their life into specific areas with distinct relations and behavioural codes for each. Thus, if we make friends at the bar this by no means implies any correlated relationship to these friends at work or at the tennis club. On the other hand, a diffuse society does not distinguish between relations and behavioural codes for each area but rather 'diffuses' them across all or most life spheres.

As a result, a specific culture finds it easier to build fast and close relationships in one area (the bar or the club, for example) as this does not imply any formal or informal commitment in another. Naturally, this is not the case for a diffuse culture whereby friendships in the bar will diffuse to the club, social circles, family and other areas; implying the need for prudence in making a careful selection of who one befriends, and to behave and be perceived consistently across the different life spheres.

A manager in a diffuse culture is therefore a manager who will behave as a manager with their team at work, during out-of-work activities and even in the event of a coincidental meeting in the supermarket or any 'out of context' situation. This is in stark contrast to the 'specific' British or American manager who drops all formalities with their team the moment they step outside the office.

> *A specific culture is a culture that separates life into specific and distinct areas across which relationships and behavioural codes do not cross; whereas a diffuse culture is a culture that expects relationship and behavioural codes to be uniform throughout.*

Kurt Lewin's Circles

In a study on social-psychological difference between Americans and Germans, Kurt Lewin, the late American–German physiologist identified two personality types as concentric circles representing life areas with the centre being the most private. These two personality types are referred to as U-type and G-type and are illustrated in Figure 7.1.

The U-type personality is typical of a 'specific' culture such as the US with the private space being confined to a small circle in the centre. Much of what is considered private in a 'diffuse' culture such as one's car, the kitchen at home, personal clothes and many other belongings are considered public in a highly specific culture with solid lines separating them.

The G-type personality is typical of a 'diffuse' culture such as Germany in Lewin's study with private space occupying a much larger circle leaving a very small public space. The same areas that are publicly separated by solid lines in the U-type are not so distinct in a diffuse culture. Relationship in one diffuses into the other.

The cultural aspects Lewin's circles are meant to illustrate can be split into two categories; Privacy and Status.

PRIVACY

The American U-type inner 'private' circle is far smaller than the German's. Indeed, visit an American's home and ask for a drink, or to use their washroom, and they are likely to point you in the direction of the fridge and/or washroom and ask you to help yourself; this applies even if getting to the kitchen and washroom requires walking through various rooms of the house. In the U-type circle, apart from bedrooms and the 'home office', almost the entire home is considered public and sharable with visiting friends.

The opposite is the G-type larger 'private' circle, which is more evidently manifested in the Far East and Middle East. Most homes have a 'guest' room; that is, a guest reception room where visitors and friends are received. Furthermore, they also have a guest washroom, therefore retaining all family living quarters in the home as 'private'. Ask for a drink from your closest Middle Eastern friend and they will bring it to you. This is not formality; this is merely because the drink is in the kitchen which is a 'private' space.

Interestingly, private and public spaces represented in the circles are not confined to physical items but also to personal information on wealth, health, work, family and relationships. Therefore, the American is far more comfortable speaking openly about their intimate relationship than a German, Middle Eastern or a Chinese would be.

STATUS

Beyond the inner private circle we have the public space. Here what is distinct between the two types is not only the scope of the space considered public, but whether it is a public space or public spaces. That is, do we have one public space encompassing the various life spheres and demanding a uniformity of behaviour, image and status; or do we have multiple public spaces that do not mix and where one's behaviour, image and status may differ?

The first is the German (or Far Eastern, or Middle Eastern) diffuse G-type; the second is the American (or British or Australian) U-type.

WHEN G AND U MEET!

Conflict or 'discomfort' arise when the private area of a 'diffuse' individual overlaps the public area of a 'specific' colleague or friend.

An American visiting the Middle East could easily embarrass and make a local colleague uncomfortable by asking them about their marriage and other family matters; or, whether they may borrow the colleague's car for an errand. On the other hand, a Middle Eastern visitor to the US could make their American colleagues uncomfortable by repeatedly refusing to join them in out-of-office social activities because the visitor prefers not to mix professional and social relationships.

The Origins of Specific vs. Diffuse Orientation

Observations of social trends have shed some light on the cause and effect of SDI orientation:

Mobility – Mobile cultures such as in many parts of the US and New Zealand, where people frequently relocate across vast distances in their lifetime and emotional attachments to personal belonging become loose. This in turn will reduce what a mobile culture considers as being 'private' or 'personal'. As a result, it is quite common to borrow friends' cars and use their homes during their absence, which is unconceivable in many parts of the lesser mobile Europe and most of the Middle and Far East. The more mobile the culture is, the more specific it tends to be.

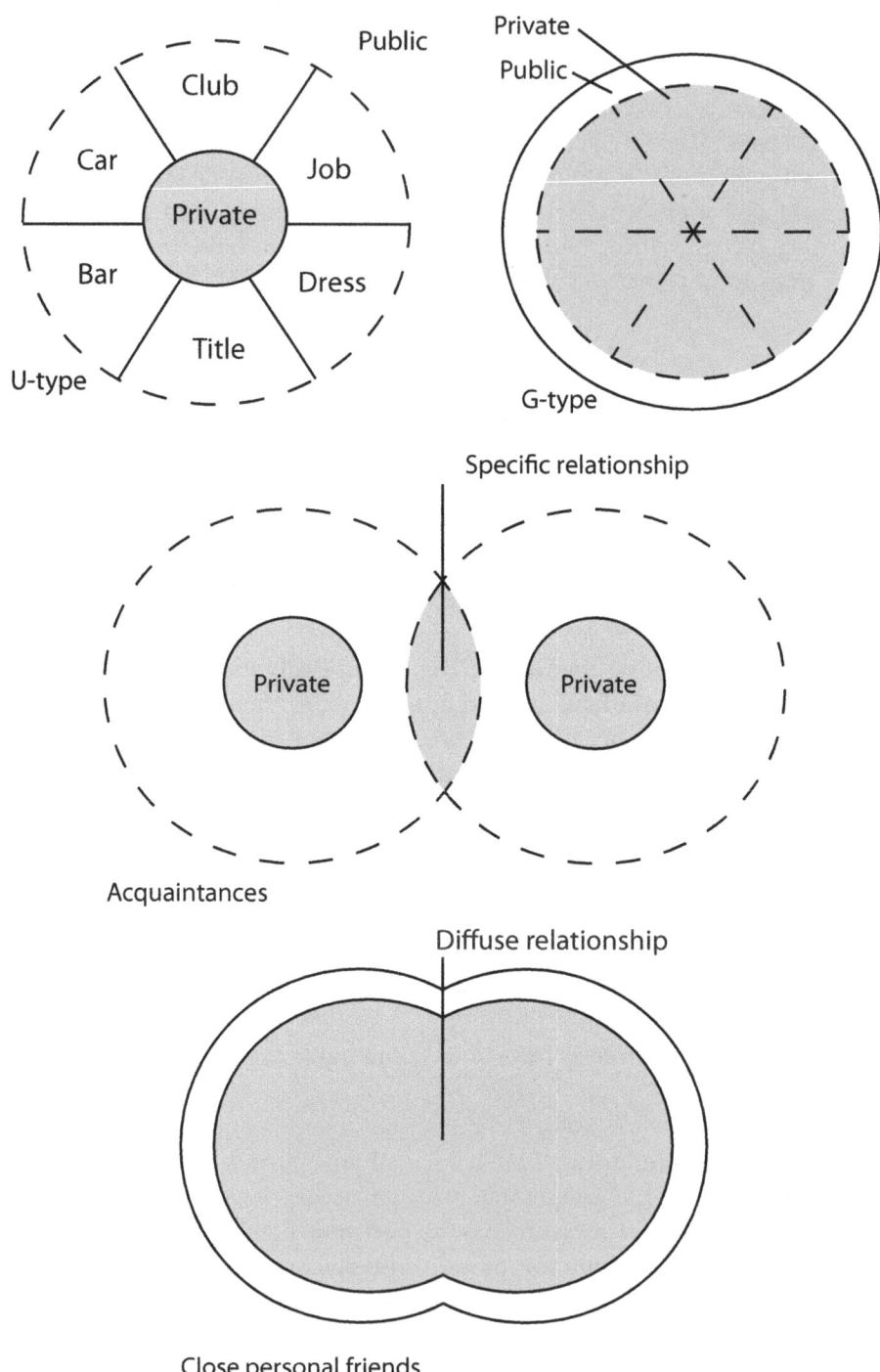

Figure 7.1 (*Inspired by*) **Kurt Lewin Circles**

Collectivism – Both logic and empirical data from Hofstede's and Trompenaars's research suggests that collective cultures are more diffuse than individualistic ones. Naturally, within a collective culture, where most of our actions, decisions, reward and punishment are not a matter for the individual but for the group, it is harder to split a collective philosophy into separate distinct life spheres. Once a solid group has formed, which may include family members, close friends or long-time working colleagues, this group will naturally diffuse its dynamics from work to home to leisure.

Society, Family and the Government

In highly specific cultures such as the US, friendships are specific to the context of their formation; for example, at a bowling club. These new friends may remain friends for a lifetime without ever diffusing their friendship outside the context of the club. Should they happen to meet by coincidence at a restaurant or a store, they will greet each other, have a brief chit-chat about certain club news and the impressive score made by one of the teams the previous week, and then depart with a 'see you Saturday at the club'.

In a specific culture, it is quite usual for an individual to have 'cycling friends', 'bowling friends', 'family friends' and 'book club friends' who remain distinct and never mix.

In a highly diffuse culture, when people meet for the first time (usually through an introduction from a common friend or acquaintance), their conversation tends to be conservative and polite with questions such as 'what line of work are you in?', 'which district do you live in?', 'what are your political views?' and so on. These questions are aimed at establishing 'who' the person is and considering whether they are fit to be trusted as a friend. Only once some trust is established will the conversation become more relaxed and move to true areas of interest. This friendship formed in one context will diffuse into others. Friends will invite each other to join them at dinner parties, social outings or family events (the last stage of a solidly established friendship). If they do not play tennis together it is not due to separating the specific life spheres, but rather because one of them does not play tennis.

Diffuse cultures tend to perceive friendships in specific cultures as shallow and superficial as they isolate their friends into one part of their life. This perception is incorrect. The separation of life spheres into distinct areas does not imply any lesser loyalty or obligation than in a diffuse culture.

I came to understand this through direct experience during my university studies in London. I had always integrated well with various cultures and made friends from different nationalities. However, given my own background, most of my friends were British or Middle Eastern. With my British friends I spent social time in the university bar and playing snooker. With my Middle Eastern friends I spent the rest of my leisure time including evenings and weekends. As such, I always held the impression that if I ever needed a favour, it was my 'diffuse' Middle Eastern friends who would rush to help.

As end of year exams approached, I faced particular difficulties with 'thermodynamics'. I had missed many sessions during the year and was struggling with some of the theory. I turned to my classroom friends for help.

To my surprise, it was my seemingly 'less close' British friends who made every reasonable effort to help me, including one of them committing to a full day each weekend to help me with the subject. I was very moved, just as I was very surprised when, after all this was done, my British friends remained friends within the original context of the university bar and snooker only. I understood then how easy it is for cultures to misjudge each other. My British friends were just as close to me as my Middle Eastern friends. I had simply judged them by my own subjective standards.

Within the dynamics of family members, there is little difference between diffuse and specific cultures. The parents, with their role of providing a safe and pleasant home for their children as well as guiding them in what they perceive as the best academic and social education, are naturally diffuse. Even in a specific culture.

The differences are noted not in the family's internal dynamics, but in how they share their external friends and acquaintances between them. In specific cultures, friends are unlikely to share in the family's activities. They would be known to the family in the capacity of 'George's tennis partner', or 'Simona's friend from the book club'. Even when invited home for lunch after a tennis match, the conversations with the inviting friend's family is unlikely to extend beyond pleasantries and questions on tennis. Should a youngster's parent venture into asking his or her friends about their studies or their family, the youngster would feel uneasy and may get cross with his parent's intrusion.

Likewise, adult friends of a youngster's parents are unlikely to have any authority over them.

In a diffuse culture, the interaction between friends and family is much closer. Parents want to know all about their children's life outside the home, and would therefore ask them to invite their friends over so they may learn more about them. As friendships in a diffuse culture are not constrained to a specific sphere, good parents want to make sure that their children are not befriending bad company that can negatively influence them socially and academically. In diffuse cultures adult friends of a youngster's parents are seen as 'aunts' and 'uncles' and given authority and respect.

Fons Trompenaars's research on this dimension has identified cultures, including those of China, Indonesia, Nigeria and Kuwait, as more diffuse whereas Russia, US, Canada and much of central Europe as more specific.

Although government systems of ruling monarchies, democratic presidencies, parliamentary elections and autocracies and dictatorships can exist today at both poles of these dimensions, looking back historically, you can note an evident relationship between the political systems and the two poles of this dimension. Namely, specific cultures are more democratic and scrutinising of their governments than diffuse cultures.

Specific cultures assess members of their government on the basis of meritocracy within the specific context they occupy. Therefore, there is little concern about a minister of education's understanding of agriculture and vice versa, or about the head-of-state's social and recreational interests.

A diffuse culture on the other hand does not make or accept such solid distinctions of contexts. This does not mean that the minister of education should be an agricultural guru, but he or she are expected to have some expertise in the various government duties, and the more senior the member of the government is, the more they are expected to be general experts. The head of state is therefore a guru in the various spheres of life extending all the way to their hairstyle and dress preferences in some extremely diffuse cultures, becoming the fashion of choice for the general public.

It is important to note that the above scenarios tend to manifest only at the very extremes of the specific and diffuse poles. Germany and France, which are markedly diffuse in comparison to the USA, do not manifest any of the above.

The process with which our laws and regulations are developed show a strong correlation with the SDI dimension. In highly specific cultures, laws are established for a specific context as to regulate a specific sphere. Later on, these laws are expanded and 'diffused' to larger contexts. Lobbies in the USA are perfect examples of groups pushing for laws and regulation for a very specific area.

Within a diffuse culture, the process of developing laws tends to follow the opposite direction, with generic laws being established to cover a much wider context; these are later refined, tuned and positively fragmented to cater for specific contexts.

Interestingly, the end result of these laws and regulations may not differ as an outcome of this dimension, with the only difference being the historical process of their development.

At the Workplace

During my higher education, I wrote a thesis titled 'British Operations in Saudi Arabia – A Cultural Managerial Conflict'. The thesis outlined my research to identify Saudi Arabia's orientation on Geert Hofstede's original four cultural dimensions, and how such orientations affected British working practices in the country.

At the time, my father, a civil engineer working in Saudi Arabia during the country's most lucrative construction years, had many connections with senior members of large Saudi and British multinationals. I sent him my questionnaire, which he distributed in equal numbers to British and Saudi managers in different organisations.

Here is one of the comments a senior British manager made about doing business with Saudis:

> It is very difficult to get to the point when establishing a new agreement. The Saudis seem to be interested in discussing everything and anything apart from business. Whenever I tried to move the discussion towards our intended venture they would beat about the bush and move back to discussing social topics. In the end, rather than settling an agreement in a couple of meetings, it would take a

couple of month between the office, restaurants and even day trips to the dessert before signing anything. I cannot deny the pleasant nature of the Saudi's and their sincere hospitality, but it is frustrating when you want to get on with the work and feel that much time is being lost.

And here is one that a Saudi businessman made about doing business with the British:

The British are respectful and polite, yet, they seem to be in a rush to sign a considerable and binding agreement as if they were merely selling a car or a house. They want us to enter into a long-term business relation without getting to know each other. This makes me feel very uneasy and often I had to reject promising opportunities because I don't want to partner someone I don't know. The British would not marry someone they don't know, yet would enter into a binding partnership after a couple of meetings! I find this to be puzzling and contradictory.

These British and Saudi comments highlight some of the tensions that may arise in negotiations and business development. The internal work dynamics are also significantly different, with managers and bosses in diffuse cultures enjoying a wider influence than managers in specific cultures.

Another significant and seemingly contradictory aspect is that employees in specific cultures are more flexible and willing to extend their role to areas outside their defined job description. Often they are expected to do so if the project or process requires it. In diffuse cultures the exact opposite is true with employees being uncomfortable about being asked to perform a job outside their formally defined responsibilities.

The reason for this is quite simple. Within a specific need or context such as a project, for an employee or manager to actively participate in another's areas of responsibility would not be seen as intrusive since such participation is *temporary and specific* to the current project needs. In a diffuse culture, participating across others' areas of responsibilities is perceived as interference that would diffuse 'beyond' the current project context, and naturally bring about power conflict.

Table 7.1 outlines some of the SDI manifestations closer to the poles.

Table 7.1   Some specific and diffuse manifestations nearer the poles

Highly Specific	Highly Diffuse
Logic is the main factor behind new agreements	Relationship is the main factor behind new agreements
Communication is very direct and to the point	Communications are seemingly indirect and diplomatic
Behavioural codes at work do not diffuse to outside work and vice-versa	Behavioural codes are homogenous at work and outside work
Employees are more flexible to perform jobs outside their formal role	Employees are uncomfortable and often unwilling to perform jobs outside their formal role
Other SDI Social Manifestations	
Highly Specific	Highly Diffuse
It is easy to chat to people and make fast acquaintances	Without being introduced, it is difficult to make friends or acquaintances
When meeting someone for the first time, it is not unusual for the discussion to include intimate topics such as emotional relationships and private family matters	When meeting someone for the first time, the discussion tends to be polite and formal with questions aimed at knowing the character and integrity of each other
Friendships made in one life sphere, such as the tennis club, do not diffuse to other spheres	Friendships made at the tennis club easily diffuse into other life spheres
Friends of a youngster's parents have no special relationship or authority over them	Friends of a youngster's parents are considered 'uncles and aunts' and given respect and authority as such
Politicians are public servants whose job is to perform a political task and are scrutinised on their political performance with little interest in how they conduct their own affairs so long as they remain within the law	Politicians are figure heads and the more senior they are, the closer to a national role model they should be. Their conduct outside politics is just as important as their conduct within politics
Politicians enjoy little privacy and protection from the media	Politicians enjoy higher privacy and protection from the media.
Laws are developed for specific contexts where they apply and later extended to cover the wider context and other needs	Law start as generic laws (moral conduct, ethics, and so on) which are later refined to closely fit the more specific contexts the law may apply

Chapter 8

Gantt! What Gantt?

Plan the work and work the plan.

Popular best-practice quote

* * *

Week 11 – Italy

'I knew this was going to be difficult' thought Allen as he tried hard to enjoy his first dinner in Veneto, in the company of Mr Orlandi, SUPART's Italian partners and owner of a high-quality production agency.

He did not expect to find everything ready for his arrival as was the case in Slovenia; he knew better than that. But he definitely did not expect to find a shortage of power supply, missing essential auxiliaries, displaced and disconnected machinery and lack of labour resources!

Apparently, and as Mr Orlandi explained, only a month ago the agency won a competitive parts' production contract for a large trailer axles manufacturer, resulting in the need for rapid expansion of their industrial and labour resources. Of course, they still planned to kick-off Elastic during Allen's visit and any delays would be kept to the very minimum, Mr Orlandi assured Allen as he filled his glass with the most excellent local Amarone wine.

To accommodate their new production contract, the agency needed to increase their factory space and redesign the layout, acquire new machinery, increase their power supply and hire new resources. They had already rented two neighbouring hangars; however, these were not equipped and required a complete set of facilities including water, gas, air and electricity. Allen had no doubts that kick-off of the Italian project Elastic would have to be postponed a few months as he could see no way in which the agency could be ready anytime soon. However, he was not going to return to Wales now that he was here; at least he should take advantage of his presence to get some initial planning completed and responsibilities allocated. The rest would have to wait for another trip.

Week 12 – Italy

To Allen's great surprise, the last week since his arrival saw more done in preparation of the new production capacity than he could ever have imagined. On very short notice from the agency, professional contractors were there laying the facilities lines in the new hangers, and temporary workers had been contracted to start the work until the new permanent labour was hired; all within a timescale which would have been inconceivable in the UK. The following Monday the electricity supplier was due to complete the final installations and connect the increased power supply to the main boards. It was starting to look as if he would be able to kick-off the project before his departure. Until …

Until that is, the Italian electricity supplier announced a few weeks delay due to a recent change in government regulation. As far as Allen could see, that was it for his new hopes.

What followed was a show of artistry and creativity. The very next day there were electrical engineers sourced independently by Mr Orlandi's friends and contacts in the industry, working on the electrical installation in the new hangars. A large portable power generator was ordered to be on site by mid-week 13, and a lawyer's letter was sent to the original electrical suppliers noting the incurred costs and all intention to legally pursue reimbursement if they did not provide the electricity before the generator arrived. Sure enough, the electricity made it in time. Other obstacles that materialised due to issues with other auxiliaries were likewise resolved.

Now Allen and his team in Wales were on a high, with one objective in sight; to kick-off Elastic before the end of week 14.

In the rushed setup, significant safety compromises were noted that needed immediate changes and in response, detailed and comprehensive instructions and guidelines where immediately sent to the Italians from the Welsh HQ, along with two experts to help implement them.

None of the instructions were considered by Mr Orlandi since they were too costly. Instead, he and his managers identified the crucial safety issue and the legal obligations and internally devised cheaper and faster internal ways to comply with manual temporary measures, postponing the full permanent rectification of the problems until after start of production, when they would have a better understanding of the needs and more free resources to implement an effective and stable solution.

It was music to Allen's ears when a month later, over a working dinner in Wales, senior managers (including the global head of production) expressed how impressed they were with the Italians and that had a similar situation arisen in their own plant, they did not believe they could have met the deadline so efficiently and effectively.

* * *

Prior to the development of modern project management techniques and software, the choice to plan, and how to plan, was greatly influenced by the culture, with members of synchronic cultures preferring to address multiple tasks simultaneously without pre-planning the details, and members of sequential cultures choosing to pre-plan and finish one task before starting the next. This cultural influence is still present in project management today, although to a lesser extent. Given software-aided planning which allows us to plan multitasking resources with a reduced risk of overloading available capacity, the option of high-level synchronic vs. detailed sequential planning is often a matter of logical preference rather than cultural tendency.

It is worth noting that just as synchronic cultures have learned to sequentially plan so sequential cultures have learned to synchronically plan, and this owes its thanks to the recent developments in the disciplines of project and programme management.

Fons Trompenaars wrote in his book *Riding the Waves of Culture*:

There is accumulating evidence that sequential planning processes work less well in turbulent environments. They are too brittle, too easily upset by unforeseen events. The fact that they tend to concentrate on the near future testifies to the vulnerability of long sequences. Synchronic plans tend to converge or 'home in' on predetermined targets, taking into consideration fusions and lateral connections between trends that sequential planning often overlooks.

Trompenaars is not incorrect in his observation; however, there is another significant point that is clearer to us project managers. As we shall see later, synchronic cultures are at heart chaotic cultures while sequential cultures are 'ordered and systemised'; and although synchronism is not without its advantages, the lack of order does make it very hard to manage larger initiatives involving multiple parties and complex interdependencies.

A major breakthrough in making the best out of synchronism while retaining key controls and order has been addressed formally with the continued development of programme management and agile project management methodologies in the past decade. All of which recognise the need to retain flexibility by continually synchronising and managing synchronic activities; while avoiding detailed planning when the environment is too turbulent and end customers' needs are rapidly changing. Something that is true of many of our modern industries today, especially technology.

For synchronism to achieve its full positive potential it should be a 'managed synchronism', and this is exactly what sequential cultures are learning today. Otherwise, synchronism risks becoming a chaotic task juggling.

Sequential vs. Synchronic Time (SST) and Other Time Orientations

Although 'Sequential vs. Synchronic' orientation is our prime focus for multicultural project management, we should be aware that it is only one of three elements within the cultural time orientation. Fons Trompenaars divided time orientation into three subcomponents:

- sequential or synchronic;

- time horizon – long-term vs. short-term orientation;

- clock or event time – quality vs. punctuality.

Long-Term vs. Short-Term Orientation (LTO vs. STO)

The second subcomponent of time, 'the magnitude of time horizon' corresponds to Hofstede's long-term vs. short-term orientation (LTO vs. STO), which was identified by Michael Harris Bond through the Chinese Value Survey.

Most companies in the US think and plan on the basis of two to five-year strategy while in China, plans are made on a minimum basis of 15 to 20 years, if not longer. In LTO cultures there is an emphasis on long-term lasting results even at the cost of temporary short-term results. In the US, compromising the next five years for the sake of stable growth 15 years ahead is unthinkable. A CEO responsible for such a strategy would be long removed from their post having 'failed' to provide shorter-term results.

What is most significant about this orientation is that it has been shown to clearly and significantly correlate with the culture's national economic growth. China, Japan, Hong Kong, India, Taiwan, Korea and Brazil are all closer to the LTO pole.

From a business perspective, little can be said to be more significant than this orientation. Most notably in forming strategies and long-term plans, but also in the form of performance evaluation and employees reward, which is based on a much longer term compared to a short-term oriented culture. This affects all working dynamics and the orientation diffuses to all business functions and personnel.

From a project management perspective, although the effect of this dimension is felt directly through the businesses decisions on which projects to undertake and to prioritise (in the form of Portfolio Management), once a project has been decided and a project manager allocated, the impact going forward is lesser, and mostly limited to the following three areas:

1. SUPPLIER SELECTION AND MANAGEMENT

Long-lasting supplier relationships are more valued in LTO cultures than in their STO counterparts. Suppliers are selected on the basis of a long track record of quality and reliability. This is the case even when it is possible for a project to obtain similar supplies from a cheaper alternative.

A project manager in an LTO culture may find that they have less choice as to suppliers' selection and need to adhere to a list of the organisation's 'preferred' suppliers if not 'one' specific supplier for the type of product or service.

However, and although this restriction may push the budget of the project somewhat higher, it does make for more efficient and reliable procurements reducing a significant part of the project risks.

2. TEAM'S ENTHUSIASM AND MOTIVATION

In an LTO culture, performance evaluation, bonuses and promotions are based on a longer-term performance than in an STO culture; making project performance less influential to its team's overall evaluation. This does not imply that project teams in an LTO culture care any less about the project performance. However, in an STO culture where the project performance has a higher impact on their performance evaluation and reward, the project manager could expect greater zeal and enthusiasm from the team.

3. STRATEGIC ALIGNMENT

Alignment between the project output (products), outcome (results), and the organisational strategy is a key discipline within 'Portfolio Management'; organisations implementing the discipline receive a better overall value for their projects' investment. As such, be it an LTO or STO culture, if strategic alignment is properly implemented, there will be no impact in this context due to this time orientation. However (and despite the increasing global maturity of project management), the majority of organisations still fail to implement project portfolio management, and it is in these organisations that a long-term or short-term perspective plays the most significant role.

LTO cultures naturally look further ahead into the long-term, making them more 'strategically aligned' overall. Indeed, working within an LTO culture, a project manager will find that members of the project team, especially senior members, are more focused on the overall benefits and value of the project outcome than the direct project deliverables. Without a formal strategic alignment process, this would not be the case in an STO culture.

Most of the organisations I worked with were mainly of an STO culture. Although the value of strategic alignment was well understood by top management, when implementing the process itself, it took some effort to get project managers and senior team members to grasp the value of the concept. Not long ago, I was hired by a Brazilian organisation (Brazil is an LTO culture) to design and set up a Portfolio, Programme and Project Management Office for their worldwide operations' projects. I was amazed by how much easier it was to get everyone to understand and adhere to the newly implemented 'strategic alignment' processes within the portfolio management component. It made immediate sense to members of the organisations as, for them, the process was nothing more than structuring and formalising something they had always valued and performed (although less efficiently due to a lack of structured process).

Quality vs. Punctuality

Note that 'quality' in this context refers to the overall quality criteria of a product or service. That is, as well as durability and reliability, it includes the scope of functionality through the agreed set of specifications.

Making a choice between quality and punctuality (time) is a regular project management trade off. Classical project management illustrated the relationship between time, scope and cost as the triangle in Figure 8.1, whereby only one side can be fixed at a time. For example, should we have limited resources and it also seems that we will fall short on the quality by the agreed deadline, we face two options:

- compromise quality by reducing the scope;

- postpone the deadline to give the available resources more time to comply with the original quality.

Yet, such a decision is not dictated by business logic alone and culture plays a good part in making it. In the case of a project aiming to release a product quickly into a fiercely competitive market, the decision on what to compromise is probably less influenced by the culture; however, in the case of a less critical 'time-to-market' project, or projects aiming to deliver internal products to the organisation such as a new material resource planning (MRP) or document archive software, the decision of what to compromise is often influenced by the culture.

Some cultures, such as in Britain and the US, tend to emphasise punctuality and meeting deadlines above quality, often to the detriment of results and ending with a failed product, on the basis of the overall value it delivers to its users. I have repeatedly witnessed American executives pushing to meet unrealistic deadlines as long as the very essential features of a product are met. The release date and being able to say 'we finished on time' rating being far higher than usability. I have witnessed multi-million euro projects managed in this way, resulting in products that were abandoned within a few months of their release for this very reason.

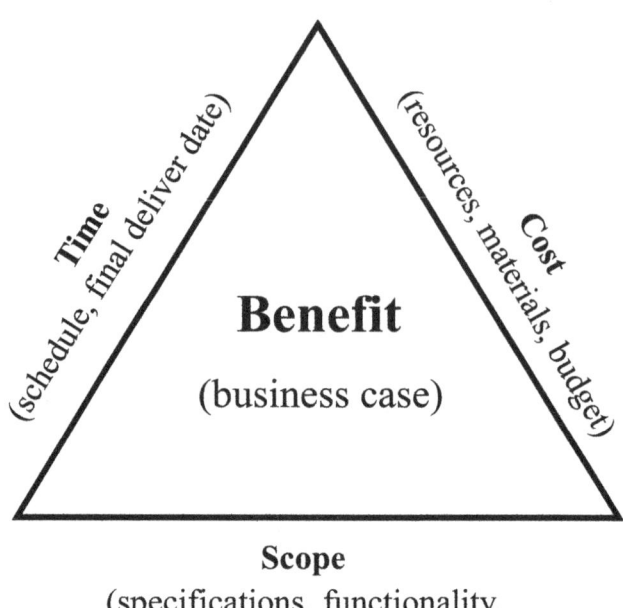

Figure 8.1   Classic project management triangle

On the other pole, I have also witnessed the opposite, with quality rating much higher than deadlines – often to an exaggerated extent. In these cases timelines are stretched so far that when the product is released, most stakeholders have lost interest. Furthermore, gaining support and buy-in for new projects is much harder as those who pay for it or have to provide the resources, have little confidence in the planned delivery dates.

It is important to note that cultural orientation towards quality vs. punctuality applies not only to large initiatives or significant projects, it also applies to the smallest tasks. An American manager requesting a progress report from an employee by the end of a working day is unlikely to be disappointed in terms punctuality, although the report may be short of some of the relevant information without adequate time to gather it. Most likely this lack of information will be noted in the report as a follow-up update to be communicated subsequently. An Italian manager making a similar request under similar circumstances is unlikely to get any report in time, complete or reduced. Towards the end of the working day, they are more likely to receive an email from the employee noting the delay and the reasons; and they will rarely object to it.

A conflict may arise, however, if the manager is American and the employee is Italian or vice versa (archetypically speaking).

There is no absolute right or wrong in this respect. Balance and the ability to decide on priorities for each specific situation on the basis of value is key. The two questions to ask ourselves should be:

- What will happen if we delay delivery?

- What will happen if we compromise the quality?

  Time Orientation can be defined as the way in which a culture perceives time in terms of overlapping of events and actions, longevity of present vision, and compromise for the sake of punctuality.

The Origins of Sequential vs. Synchronic Orientation

Going back as far as the early humans and prior to stable settlements, the early man and woman behaved synchronically as it is the natural thing to do and, at the same time, represents a lack of order which would need to be developed by a society prior to its being present. The early human therefore lived in very small unordered groups that decided what they should do (hunt, move to safer ground, eat, and so on) on a day-to-day basis.

As the early human started to form larger groups, stable settlements and societies developed, formal leaderships arose, rules for the protection and preservation of the group and means of organising and sharing essential tasks such as hunting, gathering wood, building huts, and preparing food were developed. In short, order was being introduced for the wellbeing of the larger society.

Naturally, as small settlements grew into what became today's towns, cities and countries, so did the essential systems needed to organise these increasingly complex societies.

For one reason or another (including those which will be noted in the next section), not all cultures introduced rules and systems to the same extent. On one extreme, some only introduced the very essentials resulting in overall chaotic societies, while on the other extreme, some cultures went so far as to regulate and manage each and every conceivable situation, this meant that they became much too rigid and that their system risked disintegration from within. Speaking to my Dutch brother in law and other Dutch friends they all agreed that the Dutch social system, in its attempt to order everything conceivable, has become overly bureaucratic, rigid and inflexible with increasing overall inefficiency. And indeed, there are strong calls to reverse the system where this is most evident.

The origins for 'long-term vs. short-term', and 'quality vs. punctuality' orientations are elaborated in the Appendix.

Society, Family and the Government

Although no civilised culture can exist without social norms, laws or regulations, many cultures impose the minimum requisite norms and regulations to avoid total chaos, leaving much of their social dynamics synchronic.

It should be noted that this is not necessarily because of a failure to adopt a formal and structured social system (although in some cases it can be), but more often a choice. Indeed, if you are British, Dutch or of any other highly ordered and sequential culture, think of what social aspects you loved most when you last visited Italy or other highly synchronic culture. Most such visitors make reference to the slower social rhythm and a sense of carefree relaxed social dynamics.

Queuing to pay at a supermarket counter in the UK, you may observe a certain anxiousness amongst the fellow queue members to get through the line and continue with their daily errands. Everyone waits in polite silence, looking at their watches and scrutinising the counter employee's efficiency in serving the customers. Should it happen that someone knows the counter employee and starts a conversation, those waiting will give each other the appropriate looks and may make polite remarks to make it clear that they do not appreciate the extra wait.

In Italy, the experience is somewhat different. Those queuing are more relaxed and do not seem in a rush. While waiting they will chat amongst themselves or check the news on their mobile phones. Should the counter employee start to chat to an acquaintance in the line, which often happens in chat-loving Italy, not only will the chatting be loud and merry (about a new born baby, Sunday's family lunch or whatever is the subject) but the people in the queue will listen and join in. Of course, there are many who would rightly point that this lax attitude is very inefficient. For their part, the Italians will argue: What do you need efficiency for in a supermarket queue? And even if you do and you are in a hurry, why didn't you postpone your shopping till you had more time rather than turning what would had been a joyful shopping trip into a stressful job?

There is no right and wrong, it is the context that determines what works best. For example, given a similar Italian queue during working hours at the post office, with people needing to send their mail and return to their jobs, the above synchronic orientation does result in highly unjustified delays.

Trompenaars made a note of how, in Italy, when serving salami at a delicatessen counter, the butcher will ask all others waiting clients if anyone else wants salami while he has it out and unpacked. If you were there, are a sequential person and do not want salami, this may irritate you. However, it is far more efficient overall than the Netherlands or UK whereby, regardless of how many other customers want salami, the salami will be repacked after each serving only to be unpacked again a couple of customers later.

Within the family, which represents the group held most dear by all nations, all essential duties are organised, be it a sequential or a synchronic culture. We therefore find that in synchronic Italy and the Middle East, no lesser emphasis is placed in planning well for the family health and wellness, provisions, doctor's visit, choice of schools, study time and bed time for the young, as compared to a sequential culture. Of course some families are chaotic and find it hard to manage and organise their duties efficiently, but this is not due to the national culture but rather to the culture of the family itself and the personal traits of its members.

Laws, regulations, government offices and formal procedures are proof that most synchronic cultures are capable of developing and imposing an ordered system where they see fit. So much so, that they are likely to overly exaggerate and end up with highly bureaucratic government agencies.

Italian bureaucracy is a testimony to this. A few years ago my then UK-based company established an Italian legal entity. Setting up the Italian SRL (limited liability company), took approximately ten times the time and effort, and about 20 times the cost, of that of setting up a limited liability company in the UK (Ltd). Likewise, hiring an employee in Italy involves far lengthier and more costly procedures as compared to the UK.

When I noted this to my Italian lawyer, she acknowledged the point, noting that the British processes for setting up a company or that of hiring an employee are too lax and leave many loopholes and open possibilities for fraud and corruption. Possibly true, but the fact is there is far less fraud and corruption in the UK than in Italy, due in no small part to the society being sequential and playing by the rules. As such, the Brits prefer to risk a relatively small amount of fraud and corruption rather than penalise the vast majority of its law-abiding citizens with rigid controls and bureaucracies.

Another reason why laws and regulations are more flexible and efficient in a sequential culture is that sequential cultures have much more experience in generating efficiency out of a regulated environment. They are better at optimising processes.

Just as a synchronic culture may fare better where order is not critical, so do they fare worse where it is.

At the Workplace

Creativity and managing the unexpected are the most noted practical outcomes of a synchronic culture.

The very fact that people in a synchronic culture do not have ordered systems that guarantee their turn in a queue, and often find themselves having to face lengthy and tiresome bureaucracies, forces them to devise 'creative ways' and means to get what they want despite the obstacles.

Again, necessity is the mother of all invention and, in a synchronic culture, the need to find 'other means' has often resulted in creativity. This is not speculation, it is visible in synchronic cultures.

Consider the arts. Which nations have fared best and which worst? You may agree that art at its highest expression tends to flourish in highly synchronic cultures; yet, production and realisation of artistic concepts (design) flourish in sequential societies. There is a very significant lesson to learn:

- synchronism breeds creativity;

- turning a creative concept into a creation (product), requires a system (sequential).

Interestingly, this mirrors the effect of uncertainty avoidance on innovation and the implementation of innovative ideas.

Italians are renowned for their creative designs. Beyond design, however, Italian products fare lower on quality and performance in comparison to the less eye-pleasing products of some 'sequential' cultures. Compare the Italian Alfa Romeo to the Japanese Toyota and you will get the picture.

Creativity does not end with art and design. Being creative manifests in how we overcome difficulties and unforeseen obstacles and events. A creative person is better equipped to handle a turbulent situation.

In a highly sequential culture, work is planned in detail with exact resources allocated to activities. All is studied so as to avoid conflicts of resources and ensure best use of time and money. This approach works very well as long as no unexpected event throws a spanner in the works.

The unexpected event is not a risk that has been identified, monitored and assigned a contingency. The unexpected event is just that; unexpected and taking the stakeholders by surprise. In such an event, a sequential culture will find their plans thrown off track and will struggle to devise a recovery. A synchronic culture, on the other hand, would be more at ease. In part, because their initial plans were not so detailed into the future. But more importantly, because they are accustomed to chaotic situations and have developed an ability to creatively recover from such an event.

The Italian story of Allen and Project *Elastic* is no fantasy. It is based accurately on a situation I found myself in a few years back as a programme manager tasked with moving the production of truck trailer's axles from my American client's plant in Wales to a partner production agency in Veneto, Italy; and the government regulation that seemed to cause a delay in electricity supply was an increase of value added tax (VAT or IVA) from 20 per cent to 21 per cent in Italy. This unreasonable reason behind the delay in electricity supply was what led the Italian owner to believe it a false excuse and take his successful action against them.

The moral at the heart of my story is that the seed of this programme's successes was contributed by the American client, Welsh plant and Italian agent in equal measure. Much of what was achieved could never have been completed efficiently if not for being intricately planned and tracked by the sequential partners. Yet, with so many unforeseen obstacles, many less-resilient organisations would have thrown the plans out of the window with resulting delays and overruns, had the synchronic Italians not creatively resolved them with a sustained focus on end value.

Table 8.1 below outlines some of the SST manifestations closer to the poles.

Table 8.1   **Some sequential and synchronic manifestations nearer the poles**

Highly Sequential	Highly Synchronic
There is a preference to finishing an activity before moving to the next, even if no logical dependency requires it	There is preference to toggle between activities and multitask
Initiatives are well planned and responsibilities allocated prior to execution	There is less emphasis on planning. Projects are often divided into high-level components that are executed as seen fit by those responsible for them
Higher use of project risk management and contingency planning	Formal project risk management is rare
In a smooth, stable and low-risk environment, execution is efficient	In a smooth, stable and low-risk environment, execution is less efficient with tendency to go off track on time and budget
Should a negative unforeseen event materialise, it will disrupt the plans and resolving it would result in much delay and extra costs	Should a negative unforeseen event materialise, a synchronic culture is more likely to come up with faster and more efficient solutions
Creativity is lower, but turning a creative idea into a product or service, is more efficient	Creativity is higher, but turning a creative idea into a product or service is less efficient
Other SST Social Manifestations	
Highly Sequential	Highly Synchronic
People plan their activities well in advance assigning defined timeslots for each	People make note of their activities and perform them when free time allows
Daily or weekly activities are perceived as another 'job'	Daily or weekly activities are easily perceived as, or mixed with, leisure
The rules of the road are respected	The rules of the road are mere guidelines
Everyone arrives on time for social and leisure events	People rarely arrive on time. Delays of an hour for social events are normal and expected
The logistics of a leisure activity such as a picnic are well planned and organised	As far as possible, the logistics of a leisure activity are decided on the spur of the moment
Rules, regulations and processes are clearly defined and well adhered to	Rules, regulations and processes are less clear and only adhered to when they cannot be avoided
Public services and government processes are fast and efficient	Public services and government processes are slow and bureaucratic
There is little allowance for 'exceptions' and 'preferential treatments'	There are many 'exceptions' and 'preferential treatments'

Chapter 9

Correlations amongst the Cultural Dimensions

There are correlations between the dimensions. These vary on the basis of their social and historical origins, and the deeper values that lie at the core of cultural dimensions.

Some of these correlations are immediately apparent, other less so, and more importantly, some apparent connections can be misleading.

Let's look at some of the correlations and the reasons behind them. However, before we do I must stress a word of warning. *Correlations are tendencies and far from certainties*. In many instances when we brainstormed logical correlations amongst my research groups, we found that our conclusions were contradicted by the empirical data.

For example, we speculated that masculine societies would score higher on the power distance dimension. The basis for our speculation was that high power distance societies would breed a desire amongst members to reach the top of the hierarchy implying a striving for status, wealth and/or power; resulting in higher masculinity. Likewise, members of a masculine society striving for status, wealth and power would result in a higher power distance society. When we analysed the actual empirical data, not only did we find that no such correlation exists but that there is a slight inclination to the opposite.

Collectivism/Individualism vs. Power Distance

Perhaps the strongest and most easily apparent correlation between the various dimensions is that of collectivism and power distance. Researchers have identified similar origins for both dimensions; geographical location and wealth.

We noted earlier how societies located near the equator historically enjoyed more fertile lands but that this put them at risk from envious invaders. Consequently, they developed a hierarchical structure that was efficient for attack and defence; this, in turn, led to higher power distance.

Why should this dimension lead to a more collective society? There is no certain answer to this beyond some empirical evidence. However, it is not an unrealistic speculation that the need for better defence against aggression not only required an efficient hierarchy, but also a cohesive and well-coordinated society which resulted in higher collectivism, particularly in historical societies in which defence required the involvement of all its able-bodied members, as apposed to today's professional and specialist armed forces.

Wealth also played a role in shaping IDV and PDI; wealthier countries are more individualistic and have lower power distance. Although the reasons for the influence of wealth are not fully understood, there is direct evidence that growth in poorer countries and developing economies is positively related to individualism.

What is the cause and what is the effect is not clear, especially when you consider that although individualism and economical growth are related, in the longer-term and in industrialised nations, the opposite effect has been shown to be true with the countries experiencing the highest growth being more collective.

Beyond noting the similar origins of individualism and power distance, you may observe and deduce logically that collective societies operating in larger groups would naturally need a stronger hierarchy to be managed efficiently. The opposite is just as true.

Uncertainty Avoidance vs. Power Distance and Individualism

Research data has shown that there is a correlation between uncertainty avoidance and 'power distance and individualism'.

In high uncertainty avoidance cultures there is a higher level of anxiety when facing the 'unknown'. As we have seen, this unknown is not limited to work and politics, but extends to the society at large, with its members being more at ease amongst their closer friends and relations rather than in the company of strangers or new acquaintances. This results in the formation of tightly closed groups, which are naturally collective.

As uncertainty cannot be avoided completely, regardless of how high a society's UAI orientation, its members will feel comforted in being able to share the resulting anxiety with others; therefore preferring group decisions and dynamics to individual initiative.

Another correlation with uncertainty avoidance is power distance. Given that power distance is correlated positively with collectivism, this would imply that high uncertainty avoidance societies are also high power distance societies. True, but there is more to this correlation than just the collectivism and power distance correlation.

Employees in a high uncertainty avoidance culture favour a manager who tells them exactly what activities they need to do over a manager who delegates objectives and allows them the freedom of deciding the means and activities to achieve them. This preference towards instruction arises from the anxiety of not wanting to make a wrong or 'uncertain' decision for which you may be held accountable. This implies a higher power distance since decisions and their accountability are confined to the managers.

It is important to note that 'cause and effect' flows only in one way in this case. While high uncertainty avoidant societies are likely to be more collective and oriented to higher power distance, the reverse is not true. Being collective or of higher power distance does not necessarily result in higher uncertainty avoidance.

Specific/Diffuse vs. Individualism/Collectivism

A collective society is a society that shares their ideas; making decisions and allocating activities and resources collectively. This makes it harder to separate their various life spheres completely and, as a result, most of the dynamics of many of these kinds of societies become diffuse.

Likewise, an individualistic society will see no particular benefit in extending social and professional relations beyond their specific context. On the contrary, diffusing relationships will result in larger groups that require greater involvement in decision making and coordinating activities; something that is often perceived as a hindrance in a non-collective society.

Dimensions Present a Tendency, Not an Absolute

Dimensions present a tendency and not an absolute. At both the group and the individual levels, we may willingly adapt our cultural inclination in order to be flexible and obtain the best value from a specific environment or situation.

Just as important, don't forget that at the extreme poles of each dimension some practices can becomes truly 'negative' to the wellbeing of those involved. In most of my earlier discussions I have attempted to steer away from elaborating negativities and rather focused on the items that present a positive argument for each pole.

For example, I used an American Investment Bank to represent a highly masculine organisation and a Swedish manufacturer to represent a highly feminine organisation. In both examples, any physical, verbal or psychological abuse of employees is unacceptable and the organisation in which these take place will fall foul of both internal and external regulations.

The fact is, within developing countries that do not have actively implemented regulations to protect working standards and employees' rights, near pole masculinity and very high power distance often result in abuse and unfair treatment at work.

PART III
Culture and the Project Environment

In this part, we will review the influence that culture has on some of the key project management practices. We will consider the overall environment rather than the individual members of the project team (which we will address in the following part). The environment in this context implies the country, the region and/or the involved groups and organisations.

Please note that what follows is not a comprehensive list of cultural influences within our context. Culture does influence most aspects of project management practices down to minute detail; however, most of these influences do not need managing as a culture. For example, senior managers in feminine cultures have a higher preference for technical details as compared to masculine cultures. As a proficient project manager, part of your initial job is to discuss and establish management reporting needs prior to project start, which will result in the correct reporting content and format regardless of culture.

We therefore will only concern ourselves with those influences that either need to be actively managed, or of which the project manager should be aware in order to avoid shock or disappointment when they face an unfamiliar culture.

Chapter 10

Organisational Structure and Project Management

The structure of organisations, that is the overall organisation and not how projects are organised, is arguably the most influential element (outside the influence of the project manager) on the efficiency and success of project management.

In the past two decades, the increasing number of projects and the emphasis on the need to efficiently manage their implementation has seen various theories and studies offered to identify the 'optimal' organisational structure that caters for projects' efficiency and success.

Today, we have three main types of organisational structures within which projects are performed:

The Functional Organisation

No mystery to anyone. The vast majority of organisations worldwide have a functional structure, divided purely by 'functions'. Figure 10.1 below is a simple illustration of a functional organisation.

The functional organisation is an organisational structure that caters primarily for process and production. A traditional factory producing agricultural fertilisers or kitchenware will require this structure to keep efficient control over its various functions: financial accounting and control, design and engineering, manufacturing, HR, marketing, sales, customer service and so on. The top level in the structure reflects these functions, with each having a director responsible for its overall efficiency.

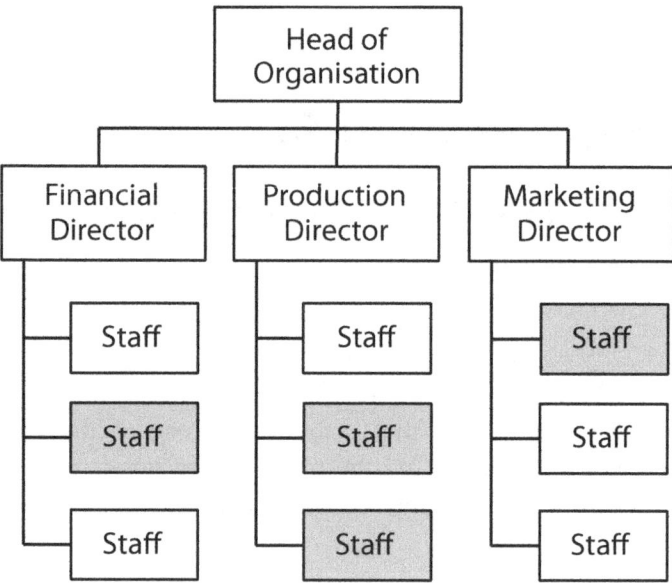

Figure 10.1   The functional organisation

Traditionally, projects in functional organisations have either been rare or small and have not warranted the need for a change in the structure. Small projects could be implemented efficiently without having to resort to project management practices, while larger less-frequent projects such as establishing a new production line would have been outsourced to external suppliers.

Today, and apart from very small companies, few organisations can claim to be sufficiently immune to significant projects warranting an organisation structure that caters for them. The past few decades have brought rapid technological developments and globalisation, resulting in higher uncertainties, competition and a more sophisticated customer with frequently changing requirements. Henry Ford is quoted to have said of his cars that, 'If I had asked people what they wanted, they would have said faster horses' and after the Ford T-Model was launched in 1908, he also famously said, 'Any customer can have a car painted any colour that he wants so long as it is black.'

Despite the apparent absurdity of Ford's remarks, he was not wrong, not for an era when the optimum benefit for the customer and therefore value and growth for the organisation came though standardisation. The T-Model production lasted 19 years from 1908 to 1927.

In other words, upon the launching of the T-Model along with its sales, marketing and other related functions, Ford could sit back for over ten years and concentrate on business development and higher efficiency and productivity with little attention or concern towards the slowly changing sector's demands and technology. As such, project management maturity and efficiency was a far lower priority. Indeed, at the time, project management was a discipline associated mainly with construction and some military interventions (and it was rarely called project management).

Today, were the Ford Motor Company to follow the strategy of its founder, it would not last a decade. Perhaps not even a couple of years.

Twelve years ago I assisted an auto component manufacturer and supplier to Fiat in Italy in setting up a Project Management Office (PMO). The PMO role was to plan, coordinate and track the design and delivery of breaking systems for Fiat autos. Given that on average Fiat had about 10 new car models in the pipeline at any one time, and given that some of these models were cancelled before completion, at least one new car was released every second year. The product development programme of a new car had hundreds of projects under it. Consider the wider programme, including technology, manufacturing and global marketing, and you can see why car manufacturers today are no longer simply process and production-based companies.

So what happens when we implement such a large programme in Ford or Fiat? Thankfully, almost all larger organisations have now modified their organisational structure to better cater for project management. However, and most importantly, in much of the lesser-developed parts of the world, there are many medium and large organisations that have retained a purely functional organisation despite their need to frequently implement projects. Even in the developed world, many small and some medium companies still retain a purely functional organisation.

Making reference to Figure 10.1, let's consider a company with a functional organisation in which the marketing director wishes to explore the feasibility of launching one of the company's product lines in another country. Initial research shows that for the product to fit the local needs of the target market, it must be modified from its current specifications. The marketing director in cooperation with the financial and production directors allocate resources (in grey boxes) to the task. They take it upon themselves to each coordinate their own resources as the organisational structure dictates strictly functional authority. One of the team members is often allocated as a project 'leader' or project 'coordinator' with conscious effort to avoid the title project 'manager' since the only manager that has authority over the entire project team across the various functions is the CEO; and often within functional organisations the term 'manager' implies direct 'authority' over the managed resources.

A project in a purely functional organisation faces the following major difficulties:

- the project manager (leader or coordinator) lacks authority in the project;

- the project manager often faces political conflicts with functional managers resisting or refusing to allocate pre-agreed resources;

- whenever a conflict arises due to resource shortages, even with regards to pre-agreed allocations with their functional manager, their functional role will almost certainly take priority over their project role regardless of the motive of the shortage being their project or process roles, and regardless of true urgencies;

- management support is very scarce as it comes only from the functional managers who lack the time to dedicate to the project.

The Project Organisation

As the name implies, a project organisation is an organisational structure that has been modelled to cater for projects and not processes. This type of organisation, although very fit for the purpose, is not at all fit for process-based organisations even if they undertake many projects. The project organisation is illustrated in Figure 10.2 below.

Typical examples of project organisations are construction companies, event management agencies and software development houses. These organisations work purely on the basis of projects for external clients. Permanent members of a typical construction company may include the board of directors alongside financial and support staff. They will also employ a number of professional construction engineers from their market sectors (housing, hotels, commercial).

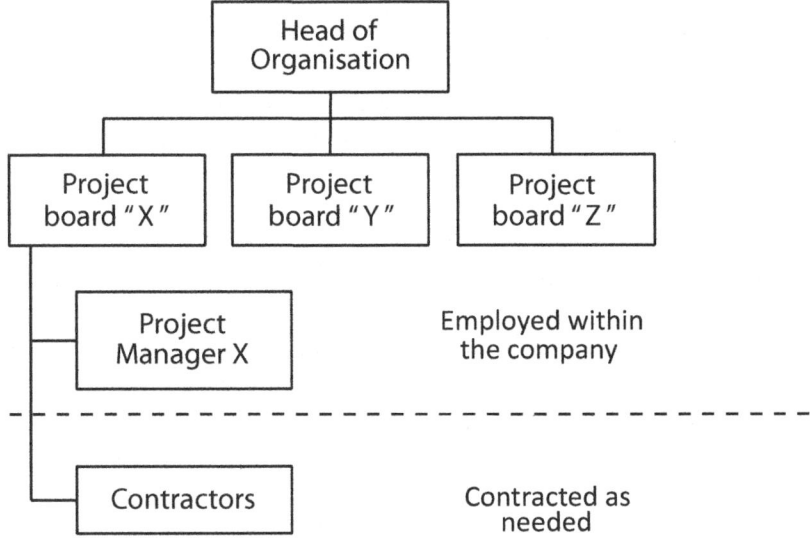

Figure 10.2   The project organisation

These construction engineers will represent their sectors as business units within project board x, project board y, and so on. For each project within each of these units, there is an engineer acting as the project manager (project x manager, project y manager and so on). Sometimes, when only one project is present within a business unit (say commercial construction), the head of the unit will act as the project manager.

Almost all other members of the organisation are brought in on a contract basis for specific projects. HR, financial control, administration and other functions are centralised in a small unit that sits near the board of directors.

In terms of scale, a company that constructs a handful of mid-sized hotels a year may easily not exceed 20 permanent staff members.

Software development houses and event management agencies have very similar structures.

The role of the project manager within a project organisation is both technical and hands-off, as projects do not cross functional lines to merit the role of a purely hands-off project manager. The support roles of planning, tracking and coordinating resources is the management norm of such companies.

The drawback here can be the lesser functional controls due to the lack of formally established departments and the higher use of suppliers and contractors, but that is compensated by the overall efficiency the projects would gain from the organisational structure. It is a structure fit for its purpose.

The Matrix Organisation

The 'project' matrix organisation is a compromise between the functional and the project organisation, in being a mix of both. There are weak matrix, moderate matrix and strong matrix organisations catering for different extents of project management needs. An electronic company, such as a mobile phone manufacturer releasing various models each year (projects), will require a strong matrix to be efficient. Indeed, within the 'Archibald–Prado organisational project management maturity model', they identify that from a scale of 1 (lowest maturity) to 5 (highest maturity), an organisation must be at least a strong matrix organisation to achieve a maturity level of 4.

Note that the above is not a formal requirement and the organisational maturity is determined through self-evaluation. To my knowledge there is no formal certification for organisational project management maturity. It is well accepted, however, that any organisational structure that is less than a strong matrix will render the implementation of complex and large projects difficult.

The strong matrix organisation illustrated in Figure 10.3 resembles a functional organisation at first look. However, there is an additional role that is added at the top level of the organisation, the director of project management. The title varies from one organisation to another. Throughout my career I have come across the titles 'organisational programme manager', 'manager of project managers', 'head of projects and programmes' and 'projects and programmes director'. They all meant the same thing.

The director of project management is a formally appointed role by the CEO to the board of directors and has equal weight and authority as other members of the board. Depending on the size of the organisation, the director of project management may have permanent staff that act as project executives and project managers within the organisation. When a project team is proposed, their roles and time allocation (for example two days a week of the maintenance engineer) is coordinated and formally agreed between the director of project management and their functional managers.

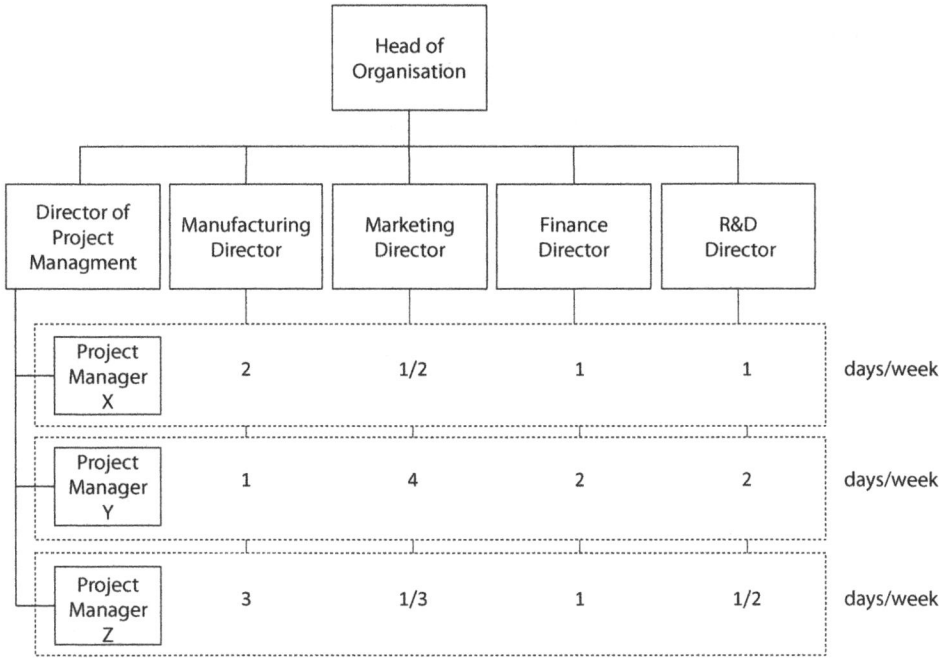

	Manufacturing Director	Marketing Director	Finance Director	R&D Director	
Project Manager X	2	1/2	1	1	days/week
Project Manager Y	1	4	2	2	days/week
Project Manager Z	3	1/3	1	1/2	days/week

Figure 10.3   The strong matrix organisation

Although a similar agreed resource allocation is performed in functional organisations, the difference is that when conflict arises, the project managers find themselves at the mercy of the functional managers without a manager of their own to support their cause.

Not so in the matrix organisation where an unresolved conflict is escalated all the way to the director of project management if necessary until resolved on the basis of true organisational priorities without operations taking precedence as standard practice. Furthermore, in a strong matrix organisation, the project dynamics are well communicated and understood by all functional managers and senior staff. If this is not the case, then the director of project management has fallen short on performing their duties.

A strong matrix organisation aims to provide both processes and projects with the priority and support they deserve on the basis of their overall value contribution to the organisational strategy.

Without an understanding of the organisational structure and its significance to efficient project management, managing the cultural diversity in projects will be challenging. This will become clearer in the following sections.

Before We Proceed

At the risk of being repetitive, I will re-highlight the main items to keep in mind when considering what follows within the project environment, for I cannot over-emphasise their significance to effective multicultural project management:

- Does our international project involve only our organisation or a number of organisations? In the first case, the organisational culture is likely to dominate over the national and regional subsidiaries' culture and we have clearer guidelines of what to expect.

- Has the project manager performed projects with this international team before? If so and they know each other well, then hopefully there will be fewer conflicts due to culture; nevertheless, this book will help improve the multicultural management. If the project manager has never worked with the international team before and the project involves a number of organisations, then they are about to enter the stage for which this book is mainly written.

- If an international team is composed of members of various organisations coming together for the first time, a question to ask yourself is: is there a dominant culture or cultures? That is, is it a French and a German organisation building an airport in Dubai? In such a scenario, and although we still should never stereotype, we can expect significant archetypical behaviour. That is, the French to act as French, the Germans to act as Germans and the locals in Dubai to act as Arabs. This is merely an expectation and the project manager will find that many perceived archetypes, are instead part of a 'Culture Soup'.

- What is the professional and educational background of the multicultural team? Are they 'Culture Soups' like Rabia? In many international programmes, such as those of the European Commission or the United Nations, as well as many projects in cultural melting pots such as Brussels, you may find that archetypes are a minority and the standard member of your team is a Culture Soup.

- What are the organisational structures of the organisations taking part in the project? Functional, Matrix or Project Organisation?

- Are the project resources fully dedicated or part time? Do they report to the project manager and the client only or do they have a functional manager to report to as well?

The Culture Soups are the hardest to predict due to their rich mix of values, habits and practices arising from so many different cultures. Yet, they are truly the most interesting to work with and more importantly, likely to be mature and not easily offended. By virtue of their rich experience they are organically 'culturally aware' and are flexible to adapt to what is perceived as better practice for the overall project objectives.

Chapter 11
Roles and Responsibilities

For project management to be effective, key roles and their related responsibilities must be clearly established and communicated. These include:

- *The Sponsor*: The person or group that authorises the project and its budget on the basis of the expected values and benefits such as net increased profitability, higher savings, reduced staff turnover, higher competitiveness or legal compliance.

- *The Client (or customer)*: The person or group for whom the project is being undertaken. The client has the overall responsibility of foreseeing that the project output (product or service) achieves the expected results and benefits.

- *The Users (represented by the Senior User(s))*: The person(s) or group(s) that will make use of the project output. The users have the responsibility of contributing to the user specifications, and validating and testing the project output. Note that the user is not the end user of the final product but the user of the project's product. For example, if our project output is a new production line for a new car model, the user is not the end customer who will buy and drive the car but the production engineers, technicians and operators who will operate and maintain the production line.

- *The Suppliers (represented by the Senior Supplier(s))*: The person(s) or group(s) supplying services and/or materials to the project.

- *The Project Manager*: Managing and coordinating the project activities and resources in order to achieve the expected results on time and budget.

• *Project Support*: The person(s) or group providing planning, coordination, tracking and logistical support to the project manager and stakeholders. Also called the 'project team'.

These key stakeholders are often referred to as the project organisation when outlined hierarchically. However, given that the terminology is also used to describe an overall organisational structure that caters exclusively for projects as noted earlier, we will only refer to these stakeholders as the 'key stakeholders'.

On the other hand, the term 'technical stakeholders' will make reference to the stakeholders directly involved in performing the project tasks and activities.

Finally, the wider term 'stakeholders' makes the classical reference to all persons who are involved in the project, impacted by it and/or themselves have an impact on the project; be it positive or negative and be they internal or external to the involved organisations. Stakeholders could either be 'internal stakeholders' (internal to the organisation using the term), or 'external stakeholders' (outside the organisation using the term).

'Stakeholders' includes both 'technical' and 'key' stakeholders as well as all persons performing activities on the project, all the users and suppliers, any personnel whose working processes are to be changed due to the project or its output, and any impacted (or impacting) external stakeholder (such as residents and commuters in the area where a major construction is to take place).

Stakeholder roles are not necessarily exclusive. Most small projects and even some larger projects will have the same person acting in more than one role, such as the department manager acting as both sponsor and client. Likewise, the project manager may undertake the additional role of project support if the size or complexity of their project does not warrant a separate project support entity.

Although key stakeholders must be clearly identified regardless of the culture, in some cultures there is a higher need to strongly emphasise the roles and responsibilities and formally communicate them to all stakeholders. Needless to say, lack of role definition and of appropriate participation, especially in terms of the sponsor and client, will result in compromising the project manager's authority and efficiency, particularly within a functional organisation.

Higher power distance has both its advantages and disadvantages in this context. Higher PDI departmental and functional managers feel a stronger ownership and are more protective of their staff and department, therefore resisting 'outsiders' interference especially if such 'interference' intends to make use of their resources. Likewise, if their people are approached directly by the project manager they will feel uneasy and insist that the project manager speaks to the boss and not to them directly. This often results in lesser harmony and longer timescales as the project manager is required to await the department managers' availability; as well as loss of accuracy in increasing the chain of communication.

On the positive side, a high PDI culture is more likely to have the organisational roles and responsibilities well defined, and for their members to respect authority and comply with management decisions even when they disagree; which can be preferable to democratic decisions when interests are at conflict and efficiency is of the essence. The project manager, having gained formal and visible support from the sponsors, and having made known and clear the key stakeholders' roles and responsibilities, will enjoy a formal authority which will counteract the negative aspects of higher PDI and result in higher response and cooperation overall. This formalised authority is of particular importance in organisations that lack a matrix or project organisational structure; more likely to be the case in higher PDI cultures, as the culture is less at ease with horizontally crossing authority lines, and the norm is more often than not a vertical functional organisation.

In lower PDI cultures the opposite is just as true and the project manager is less likely to face 'political' and 'power' struggles when managing and coordinating resources across functions, with bosses and employees being less resistant to outsiders' intervention so long as it does not impact the efficiency of their work. However, in the event of conflicts arising from resource availability, the project manager has less influence in establishing their project as a priority over the functional processes, even when this is the case. This can be counteracted by the same formal sponsor support as in a higher PDI culture (which should always be present for project management to be efficient), albeit to a lesser extent. What is more important is to clearly communicate to the relevant stakeholders the priorities in terms of the *overall benefit to the organisation*, and, should conflict arise between the project and functional priorities, the project manager should re-evaluate the priorities with the concerned functional manager(s).

This approach is not merely accepted but appreciated in lower PDI cultures as it improves communication and harmony and outlines that both functional and project roles have the same aim: organisational benefit. The result should be (and is expected to be) that whenever a project–function conflict arises, priorities are allocated on the basis of maximum organisational benefit and minimum damage; with neither the project's nor the functional needs taking priority over any other basis.

In a collective culture there is a higher emphasis on the manager's technical knowledge than in an individualistic one. An individualistic culture is more likely to place higher emphasis on managerial competence and the ability to 'source' technical know-how rather than the manager having the know-how themselves. The project manager will therefore find that the key stakeholders in a collective culture are more technically proficient, with their roles clearly defined based on their technical context. By technical proficiency I am not merely referring to technology but to the technical aspect of a functional role. Therefore, a marketing director in a collective culture will be a marketing expert with related academic and/or professional achievements. In an individualistic culture this is not necessarily the case and 'general' knowledge of the competence area is often sufficient; senior managers are only expected to know enough to manage their technically proficient resources. Indeed, while in an individualistic culture it is not uncommon to perform a shuffle of top management roles that results in the head of personnel becoming the head of business development (as in the reshuffles of some cabinet-based governments), in a collective culture such a practice is almost unheard of.

As a result, in a collective culture the project manager can expect higher technical support from key stakeholders. Likewise, the stakeholders will expect the project manager to be technically proficient in the context of the project's deliverables. Indeed, whereas in an individualistic culture, project management consultants with methodology expertise tend to work in various sectors (myself in automotive, finance, IT and editorial); in a collective culture, management skills and transversal methodology expertise are not seen as sufficient by themselves. The project manager is expected to be a technical expert in the specific context of their work and, as a result, the chance of their frequently crossing sectors is less likely.

In an individualistic culture the key stakeholders (often including the client) lack technical expertise of the project deliverables as they have been assigned to the project roles on the basis of their management rather than technical proficiency, and the project manager will need to work more directly with the technical resources to plan and coordinate the specifications and quality aspects of the deliverable(s).

A word of advice if you are part of a collective culture and about to manage a project in an individualistic culture: *Do not assume that your client understands exactly what they want.* This presents a significantly high risk that the end product may not meet the client's expectation. Make sure you clearly outline the technical specifications and their expected benefits right from the beginning, and obtain the client sign-off prior to proceeding. This strategy is also valid for a collective culture but you will find that they are more likely to expect you to do so. An individualistic culture risks losing track of the business case and its benefits if not formally managed.

* * *

As we had seen earlier, while collectivism (low IDV) is positively correlated with higher power distance (PDI), masculinity and femininity (MAS) holds no correlation to either. Still, the MAS dimension has an influence on the key stakeholders although to lesser extent. This influence is not dissimilar to that of individualism.

A masculine culture favours good management and leadership over technical know-how, while the opposite is true of a feminine culture. The same advice above given for projects in an individualistic culture applies to a masculine culture. If the culture is both masculine and individualistic, this advice cannot be overstated.

Both uncertainty avoidance (UAI) and specific vs. diffuse (SDI) influence the formality of relationship with management. In higher UAI cultures the relationship with management is more formal, as it is in diffuse cultures. This is mainly due to the emphasis higher UAI cultures place on clearer definition of roles, with authority and formality reinforcing the hierarchy.

In a diffuse culture, formality is also preferred but for different reasons. A diffuse culture does not distinguish behaviour codes across the various life spheres. Therefore (particularly with regards to senior management such as the sponsor and client), do not expect company social events and dinners to take a lax turn and do not indulge in out-of-work informalities. If you are of a 'specific' culture working in a 'diffuse' one, please do not be tempted to, and retain some formality in such events; observed behaviour outside work will directly influence how you are perceived at work.

Chapter 12
Planning and Tracking

'Planning and tracking' is arguably the most significant of all project management skills. Not only due to its ubiquity in all types of projects and programmes but also due to how it differs from its counterpart in processes. Project planning and tracking is a skill that was developed specifically for project management. I have never come across a planned project that did not have a Gantt chart.

Yet, and despite the term planning being obvious, it is worth a brief elaboration to explain the different meanings the term has in different countries.

An American project plan is a document that includes all the project information required to obtain authorisation prior to project start. This includes the business case, the scope, the key stakeholders, the project schedule (Gantt), risk and issue management approach, the proposed project controls, communication and the budget. The American project plan is the equivalent of the Project Initiation Document (PID) in the UK.

The term 'project plan' in the UK traditionally refers to the 'project schedule', which includes the project timeline and the planned resources.

On the basis of British terminology, we will use the term 'project planning' to refer to activities such as identifying the main deliverables in the project proposal, identifying the project work breakdown structure (WBS), assigning work packages (WPs) to owners, identifying activities and their resource requirements, identifying constraints and dependencies and developing the project schedule, as well as planning the delivery of desired results through the identification and realisation of related performance indicators. We will also include specification planning where applicable.

Tracking refers to the follow up on the project activities and resources to identify progress against the project plan. We will include specification tracking where appropriate.

Let us now review how culture may influence project planning.

Product vs. Value

The term 'value' is often used interchangeably with the terms 'outcome', 'benefits' and 'strategic results'. Although these terms do differ to some extent in their meaning (a difference that will not be addressed in this book), they do make a similar reference when used to describe a project planning and tracking approach. Value, outcome, benefit or strategic-oriented project planning are all driven by the final results that organisations wish to achieve; and these results are aligned to the organisational strategy and clearly noted in the project business case outlined in the initial project proposal (also referred to as the Project Charter or the Project Brief).

Therefore in value-oriented planning, project planning starts by determining what indicators we can monitor in order to track the realisation of the business case. Thereafter, the WBS and the activities within each of its components (WP or work component), are evolved and planned on the basis of their realisation of these indicators; which are referred to as Key Performance Indicators (KPIs).

This approach to planning is more common to programme management than to project management. However, with the evolving methodologies emphasising value realisation alongside product delivery, the approach is increasingly being used in project management as well.

An example of value-oriented planning would be planning for a project or programme that aims to improve the overall quality of a manufactured product. The quality manager(s) alongside others in the organisation determines a set of desirable and measurable outcomes that point towards the improved quality; these are the KPIs. Typical KPIs might include: 'percentage scrap rate', 'percentage rework rate', 'percentage customer rejects' and so on. Thereafter, the entire planning process is completed with the KPIs as the objectives, which are represented by a set of intermediate, related milestones to be tracked periodically.

Compared to product-oriented planning, value-oriented planning is more flexible to changes in the product specifications, resources used and timeline, so long as the end results remain valid or are improved. It does however suffer from a higher risk of 'losing track', arising from the fact that benefits (and therefore value) are only realised after the project has delivered some of its products; sometimes, value is not realised until a significant time after the project is closed. It is therefore unrealistic to track progress towards benefits and value during the initial and execution stages of the project. The validity of the business case may be tracked from day one, but our progress towards realising it may not be, at least, not until some outcomes are achieved; and in the interim, the project risks higher delays and cost overruns.

Product-oriented planning takes a different approach in that once the initial project proposal is approved on the basis of the business case and outlined product(s) to be delivered, the planning proceeds by identifying the product(s) delivery milestones and the activities required to achieve them.

The advantage of this approach is that both planning and tracking are based on clearly defined product deliverables, making it less likely for managers to lose track of these deliverables at any point in the project lifecycle. The disadvantage is in the loss of flexibility should the need for change arise, as well as a higher risk of losing sight of the original business case and delivering a product that is no longer relevant.

In both these approaches, specifications need to be planned once the products are identified, and subsequently, tracked; a good project plan is an appropriate mix of both the approaches. Yet, culture has its preferences which may often override an 'appropriate' mix, forcing the project plan to be biased towards either value or product planning.

* * *

Within higher power distance (PDI) cultures, organisational politics is strongly present and senior managers are expected to demonstrate well-defined results on a regular basis. As such, there is higher emphasis from senior management towards product-oriented planning with specific well-defined deliverables. While this can be seen in the positive light of clear management accountability, it does have a tendency to overlook the final value. In the less political lower PDI cultures, there is a more open and fluid vertical communication with the organisational strategy being shared beyond the top management levels. Therefore, there is higher emphasis on end results and less on the product itself; favouring value-oriented planning.

Individualistic (high IDV), higher uncertainty avoidant (high UAI) and masculine (high MAS) cultures also favour product-oriented planning. Managers within an individualistic culture share less between them than in a collective culture. Not because members of an individualistic culture wish to withhold information from their colleagues, but rather as a direct outcome of their higher tendency to take individual initiatives as opposed to making group consultations and decisions prior to taking the initiatives; as would be the case in collective cultures (low IDV).

What happens if the culture is extremely high on both power distance and individualism? Would this result in a complete disregard of 'value' during planning and tracking? My guess is as good as yours; however, we are unlikely to face this extreme combination as PDI and IDV are directly and inversely correlated, and although some nations do not follow this noted correlation and combine both individualism with high PDI or the reverse, they are never at both extreme poles of this combination. Geert Hofstede's research data shows no country that exhibits either very high individualism with very high power distance, or very high collectivism with very low power distance. Therefore within a typical organisation, a preference towards product-oriented planning arising from higher power distance is likely to be somewhat offset by a preference towards value-oriented planning arising from higher collectivism; and vice versa.

Higher UAI, which can cause anxiety in the face of ambiguity and manifests in the need for higher clarity, will result in a preference for more detailed planning and thus, in turn, a preference towards product-oriented planning.

While the MAS orientation does not influence strategic thinking, a highly masculine culture, with its members striving for competition and visible achievements, can lose track of the projects' strategic alignment and the end value that it is meant to deliver; instead placing a disproportionate emphasis on planning and delivering short-term product-oriented milestones.

I have repeatedly witnessed masculine organisations delivering products doomed to be hastily abandoned, because when the product was delivered within the project's constraints, it still failed to provide the expected value. This was either due to losing track of the business case during planning and execution, or to being overly ambitious with new innovative technologies despite users' warnings as to their usability.

On the other hand, a feminine culture with its greater focus towards value and final results is more likely to prefer value-oriented planning; and while this is perfectly valid, it can lead to inversely disproportionate emphasis on value and therefore to losing track of intermediate deliveries, resulting in higher costs and delays.

Typically, a sequential culture (high SST) will place lower emphasis on planning and tracking the overall value as compared to a synchronic culture (low SST). However, it should be emphasised that this is not due to the sequential culture being any less aware of the strategy and the need to deliver value, but rather to the fact of their nature being more ordered and organised, which means they have a tendency to over-emphasise product-oriented steps at the cost of the final arrival point. A sequential culture risks losing track of purpose while a synchronic culture risks arriving at their purpose too late or at too high a price.

In a single sentence, the effect SST on planning and tracking can be summed up as follows:

> *Classical project management methodologies are sequential while agile project management and programme management methodologies are synchronic.*

Yet, I would repeat myself and remind my reader that the development of these methodologies has allowed many organisations with either natural preference to learn an alternative approach and use it when most of value.

Top-Down vs. Bottom-up

Another highly significant project planning approach is made through the choice of either top-down or bottom-up planning as illustrated in Figure 12.1 below.

As the term signifies, top-down planning starts at the highest level of the project's stakeholders. At first, the top of level of the WBS is established and owners are assigned to each of its components (WP), thereafter each owner needs to breakdown their component into further components and assign further owners. Finally, the major steps (often referred to as summary tasks) within each component are identified alongside their owners, and these in turn are broken down into tasks and activities. The process needs to be guided by the project manager or project planner throughout, who will also help establish the various dependencies and resource requirements for the activities.

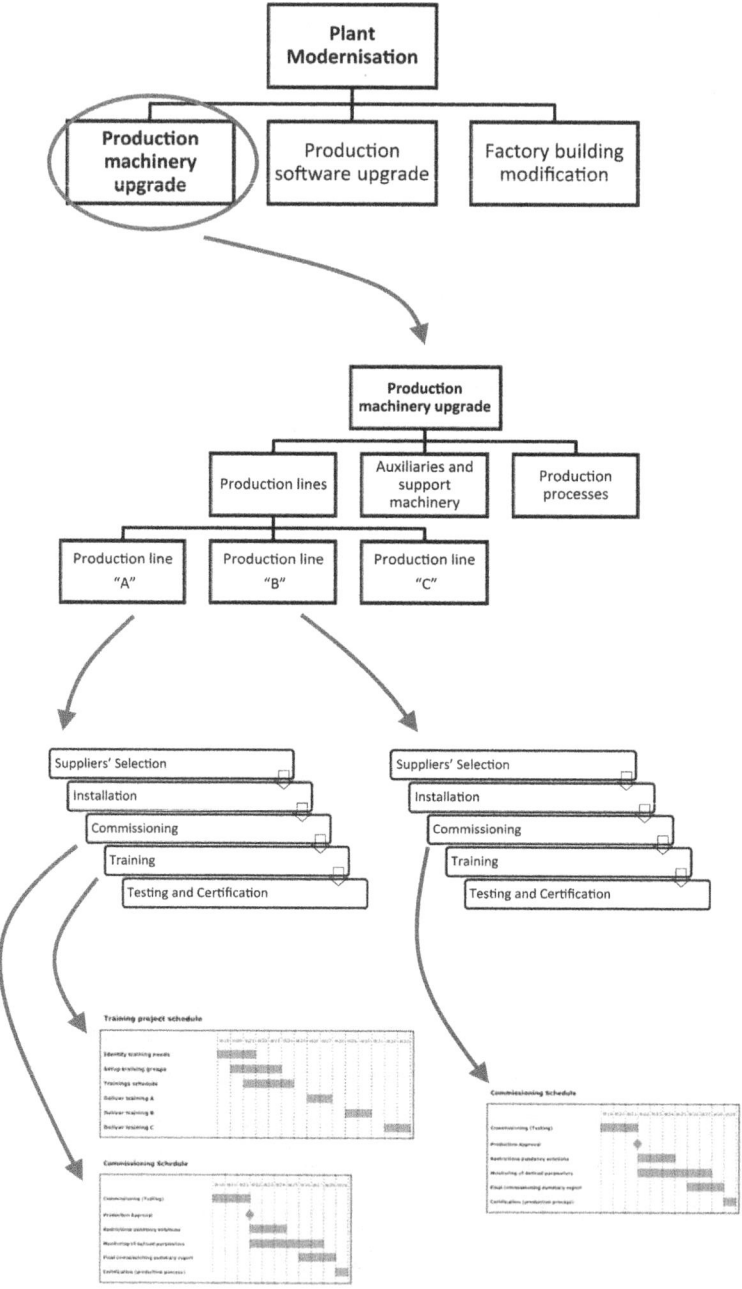

Top-Down Project Planning

Figure 12.1   Top-down vs. bottom-up project planning

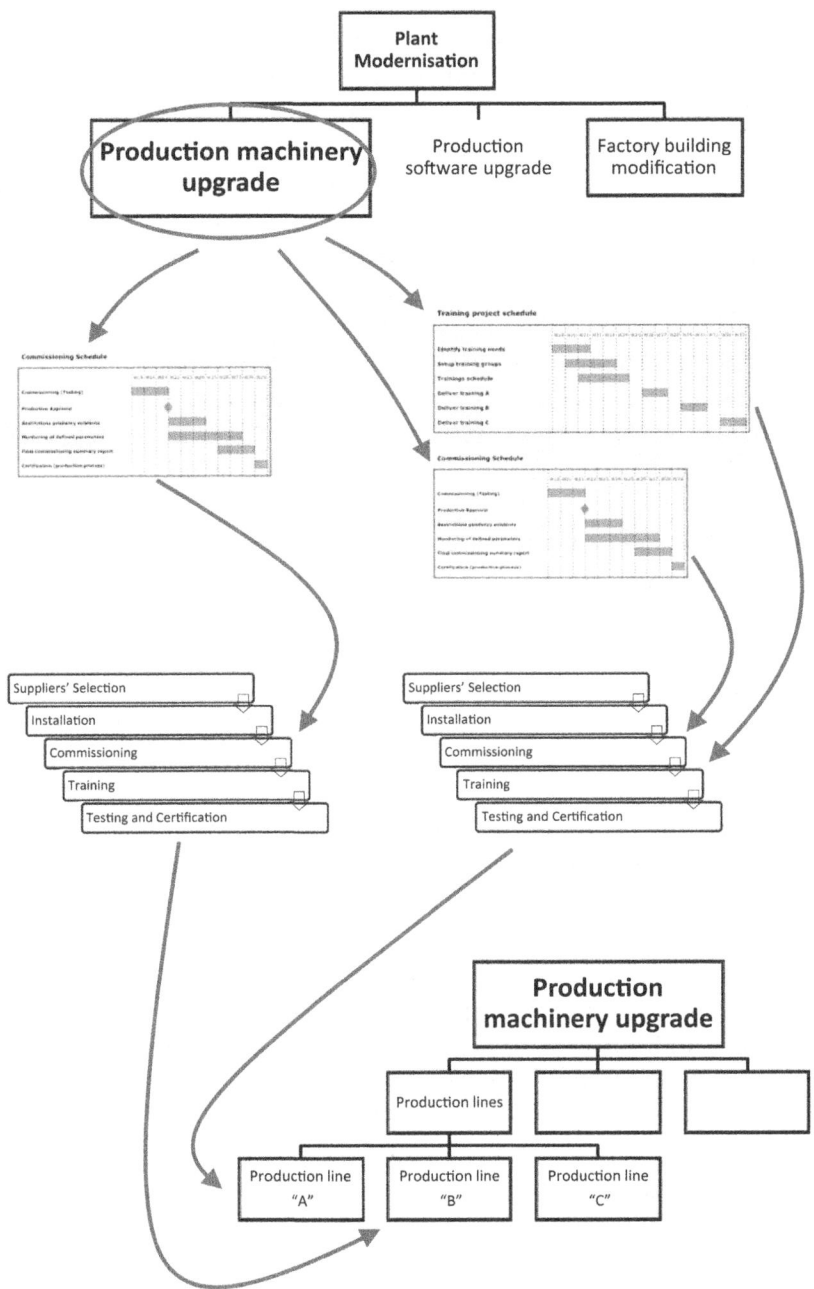

Bottom-Up Project Planning

Figure 12.1   Top-down vs. bottom-up project planning (*concluded*)

Bottom-up planning follows the opposite direction. The first step remains the same, in that the senior stakeholders first establish the component at the top level of the WBS alongside their identified owners. Thereafter, planning takes a jump to the operational levels. For example, if the project involves a plant modernisation and one of the first level components is to upgrade the production machinery, the next step will be for the project manager to start talking to the various production and maintenance staff to understand their input and needs, thereafter, he or she will talk to their supervisors, then their managers, then the heads of production, maintenance, and so on. Once sufficient information has been gathered and requirements understood, the project manager needs to structure the activities using logical summaries that can be incorporated into the WBS components, they also need to establish the various dependencies, resource requirements, and so on.

Despite the immediate appeal top-down planning has over the seemingly chaotic bottom-up process, the latter does have highly significant advantages. For example, in projects involving the use of highly innovative technologies whereby top management are not in a position to determine the component beyond the top WBS level and attempts to do so (which are not uncommon), end up with an impractical plan that only frustrates the technical resources assigned to execute it.

On the other hand, beyond its appeal of clarity and logical flow, top-down planning has an advantage in being far more strategically aligned. Indeed, many bottom-up planned projects risk losing sight of strategy and failing to deliver value.

Bottom-up vs. top-down planning was, and still is, a key area of discussion with various perceived pros and cons for each, along with evolving methodologies and software to enable you to incorporate the best of both.

* * *

Higher power distance, collectivism and higher uncertainty avoidance all influence a preference for top-down planning.

In a high PDI culture, managers are expected to know what needs to be done and tell their staff exactly what and when to do it. In his book *Interpersonal Behaviour*, Harry Triandis reports the story of a Greek employee being asked by his American expatriate manager how long it would take him to complete a certain report. The employee later said to one of his colleagues, 'He is the boss! Why doesn't HE tell me?'.

However, it is only fair to note that the better-defined roles and structured hierarchy in higher PDI cultures do cater for more efficient top-down planning than in low PDI cultures.

Likewise, within a high UAI culture the boss is expected to dictate what is to be done as they are less willing to risk their employees' taking the wrong decision with regards to performing the assigned activities; nor are the employees willing to risk the responsibility of such a decision.

Why does a collective culture prefer top-down planning?

A collective culture works in groups, be it at the senior, middle-management, operational or technical levels. Project planning as such reflects this collaborative effort and consequently top-down planning comes more naturally to them. Furthermore, and as noted earlier, senior managers in a collective organisation are more technically proficient than their individualistic counterpart. Add to that their higher cross-functional exposure through frequent collaborations, and that empowers them with the knowledge that makes their project planning technically feasible, with a low risk of being impractical. Often the end result (something that I have witnessed in collective, moderate PDI and low UAI organisations) is a practical and realistic top-down project plan that is strategically aligned and incorporates the details of its products' deliverables.

High Level vs. Details

Almost all project professionals have come across project plans that are either planned at too high a level to be accurate, overly detailed to be realistic, or anything in between. Most well-planned projects, however, often have both a high level and a detailed plan, with the first being the main tool for management reporting and decision making, while the second for planning, tracking and reporting on the activities and their progress. Needless to say, the high-level plan should be a summary of the detailed plan. The detailed plan is the working plan.

How detailed should the project plan be?

There are many factors that influence this decision. These include the stability or instability of the sector, our lack of familiarity or familiarity with the type of project, its complexity or simplicity, whether the stakeholders are spread-out or reside within a single department, whether the project activities are dependent on external events or only on internal events, and so on. In each of the noted examples, the first factor would lean our decision towards more detail while the second, towards higher-level planning.

Using the first pair of factors (stability or instability of the sector), lets look at an example. A residential construction project is far more predictable with stable overall resource availability, materials costs, suppliers' consistency and clearly set client requirements as compared to an innovative software development project with its frequently changing customer requirements, changing available technologies, fluctuating suppliers' pricing and so on. As such, detailed planning against established construction designs would make sense and should provide us with reasonable estimates of both durations and costs. Not so in the second case, where apart from mapping the immediate near future, planning should stay at high level.

* * *

Here again cultural orientations can manifest in a preference for one or other option; but none are as influential as uncertainty avoidance.

The higher the UAI orientation of a culture, the more anxiety they experience when facing any unknown and this manifests directly in their project planning and tracking; our tools for mitigating ambiguity and nasty surprises. There is a need to know exactly what to expect, what is to be done, by exactly whom and when; by both the managers and the subordinates. However, more often that not this sinks into far too much detail to be realistic. The result is merely an illusion of clarity.

One of my earlier clients for whom I helped establish a PMO with methodology, tools and procedures was a multinational organisation with a 20,000 plus employees and a particularly high uncertainly avoidance orientation. They went beyond my recommendations and started using the planning software to determine the exact project timelines and correlated resource needs for the entire fiscal year; down to single activity and man-days. Considering they had a vast number of annual projects varying in duration from days to months, with hundreds of 'part-time' allocated resources, their plans were simply meaningless and I made this very clear to the senior management. Nevertheless, my comments were not well received until, with the passing of time, they noted first-hand that the most minor of changes or unexpected events required the plans to be continually modified.

At any point of time, they noted that their earlier expectations of what is to be done, who will do it and when (beyond about one month ahead) bore almost zero resemblance to the current reality.

An overly frequent tracking cycle is another symptom of high uncertainty avoidant organisations, with the downturn that if the tracking cycle is more frequent than necessary, few activities will be accomplished from one cycle to another. Some of the technical stakeholders may also justly find it disruptive and demotivating to have to report so often on so little progress.

Planning details are also influenced by the PDI and SST orientations, although to a lesser extent than above. High power distance often results in more detailed planning as an outcome of the managers' needing to identify the exact tasks and activities for the subordinates to perform, as opposed to delegating objectives or WPs as in lower PDI cultures, and therefore reducing the necessity for details.

Sequential cultures, as compared to synchronic cultures, are likely to plan in more detail. However, this is not due to a preference for details but rather because synchronic cultures find it both hard and unfavourable to plan in detail, preferring a high-level plan that can more flexibly be implemented as seen fit closer to the implementation time; not an invalid approach and definitely has its advantages as we noted earlier. However, where detailed planning is necessary, a synchronic culture may struggle to do so.

Vertical vs. Horizontal Allocation

Unless a project is strictly confined to one functional area and can be satisfied by the use of resources belonging to only that functional area (vertical), the project will have to make use of resources from a number of functional areas (horizontal).

Apart from very small ones, the vast majority of projects have to make use of cross-functional resources; that is, horizontal resource allocation.

In diffuse cultures, where there is higher tendency for the organisational structure to be functional, resistance to the project manager wishing to accesses non-dedicated resources for planning and tracking of activities is not uncommon. However, unlike in the case of high power distance where such resistance is based on respect for vertical authority, in the case of a diffuse culture it is due to the functional managers and their resources perceiving cross-functional use of resources as disruptive to their functional efficiency.

Making clear the temporary nature of this horizontal resource usage and its value to the overall organisation is key to unblocking such resistance. Given the importance of relationships in diffuse cultures, such communication must be diplomatic and calling for higher management intervention to unblock resistance should only be used as a very last resort.

The same reasons behind the need for clearly defined roles and responsibilities in diffuse cultures have a significant influence on how project responsibilities are later assigned to WPs and activities. Diffuse cultures (in a not dissimilar way to collective cultures) emphasise higher value on technical know-how and less on resourcefulness and managerial competence; the reverse is true of specific cultures. Therefore being assigned a responsibility outside one's technical proficiency is neither the common nor a comfortable proposition. An employee from a specific culture which emphasises resourcefulness and managerial skills is more comfortable with crossing roles and may even appreciate it as an opportunity for learning and growth.

Each of these two poles has its advantages and disadvantages. While you can expect greater flexibility from resources in a specific culture, something which is highly valued in projects with less clear outcomes or higher uncertainty, there is a risk of losing track of quality as a result of the lower technical proficiency of the managers. On the other hand, diffuse cultures pose a lesser risk to quality but at the price of less flexible resources and therefore delays.

Technical vs. Political vs. Strategic

Given that the vast majority of organisations do not enjoy limitless resources, that more often than not our projects need to adjust to unforeseen events at various points in their lifecycle, and that the market requirements and our client needs may also change during the project implementation, it would be wise to account for such unforeseen changes from the very start.

As such, efficient specification planning would require that each major attribute within the specification is given a priority on the basis of its contribution to the expected benefits and overall value; which should then be outlined in the project's business case.

This will prove particularly useful should a need arise to cut the project budget or its timeline, forcing the project manager to compromise the specifications in order to meet the new constraints.

In such an event, the project manager and senior stakeholders will find their decision on what attributes to focus on, what to freeze and what to cut out altogether, made considerably easier in light of their logical prioritisation.

However, and despite the fact that logical prioritisation should always be made on strategic basis – that is, in considering the net contribution an attribute or functionality will provide towards realising the project business case – this is not always the case.

I have witnessed three main types of prioritisations:

1. *Strategic* – as explained above and as a prerequisite for efficient project management and positive final project results.

2. *Political* – when a product attribute takes a higher priority than its strategic due on the basis of the power or seniority of the person who suggested or sponsored the attribute.

3. *Technical* – when a product attribute takes a higher priority than its strategic due on the basis of its innovative or challenging nature.

You may argue that technical prioritisation has a validity to it and should not be dismissed lightly; I agree. However, where this is the case, the weight of a technical attribute automatically becomes a strategic weight. Consider, for example, projects that deliver automobile production lines, with the project scope covering aspects from the first finished concept design all the way to the first market ready car. The simplified car attributes include:

1. engine power (high vs. low);

2. fuel efficiency (high vs. low);

3. interior size (large vs. small);

4. interior furnishing (luxury vs. basic);

5. noise insulation (high vs. low).

Let's look at three distinct car markets; family cars, luxury (executive) cars and sport cars. Clearly, when we prioritise these five attributes, the prioritisation will significantly differ depending on the target market. The fuel efficiency takes priority over engine power for a family car; the opposite is true of a sports car. Table 12.1 below illustrates an example of 'strategic' prioritisation for these markets.

Table 12.1   'Strategic' prioritisation of a new car features based on three different markets

	Priority		
	Family Car	Luxury Car	Sports Car
Engine Power	Low	Medium	High
Fuel Efficiency	High	Medium	Low
Interior Size	High	Medium	Low
Interior Furnishing	Medium	High	Low
Noise Insulation	Medium	High	Medium

It should therefore be clear that when a technical attribute makes a significant contribution to the business case, it takes a strategically higher priority. An environmentally friendly car powered by renewable energy will place 'fuel efficiency' alongside the innovative technologies that enable its sustainable performance at the top of the priority list.

* * *

In a high power distance culture, the more senior a manager the less their decisions are questioned and the higher weight the decisions are given. Therefore, there is a 'natural' and I dare say 'strong' tendency for prioritisation to be overridden by politics. Thankfully this is often compensated by the fact that many high PDI cultures are also collective cultures; and collectivism here again has the opposite effect.

As in the case of value-oriented project planning noted earlier, collective organisations, in sharing their strategy and decisions, are more likely to prioritise on a strategic basis and thus to an extent override the influence of the higher power distance. However, a significant risk of strong political prioritisation does manifest in a high PDI individualistic culture, as for example is the case in parts of Switzerland, France and Belgium.

Low uncertainty avoidance cultures tend to favour trials and experimentations with less-experienced anxiety towards the unknown outcome; and this is what makes low UAI an essential orientation for creative and innovative work such as research and development. Consequently, in particularly low UAI cultures, there is a tendency to be too 'lax' towards the strategic outcomes and overly focused on the newer and more innovative attributes, resulting in technical prioritisation.

In a similar way, members of a highly feminine culture with higher interest in the technical context of their work can lose sight of the strategic values of the product attributes and overly focus on their technical perfection, once again, resulting in technical prioritisation.

Would a highly masculine culture be the opposite? Ironically no. Highly masculine cultures thrive on challenges and the more challenging a product attribute proves itself to be, the more it earns undue attention at the cost of its strategic value. The driving forces of a highly masculine culture are notably different from a highly feminine one, but the results are similar; technical prioritisation.

It should be noted that the MAS dimension exhibits a lower influence than those of PDI and IDV and is only evident towards the high or low poles.

Ambitious vs. Relaxed vs. Realistic

Most project professionals, including technical and senior stakeholders, have experienced various discussions as to whether a particular project plan is realistic, overly relaxed or overly ambitious. I myself cannot recall a single project that did not involve such discussions all the way from the technical to the most senior of stakeholders.

What then influences our planning approach in this context and should it not be based on accurate estimates involving technical experts and leveraging historical experiences? Yes, it should, but only when such expertise or historical data are available, which is not always the case; particularly for those types of projects that we have not attempted before. Nor is it uncommon for senior managers to disregard estimates and push for higher specifications with more challenging costs and delivery time; to the dismay and disapproval of the technical stakeholders.

* * *

Masculine cultures strive on challenge and competition and managers are particularly eager to cut timelines and push resources to meet them. Although this maybe stressful for some, in a high MAS culture many employees appreciate and are motivated by such a challenge, as rising to it will enrich their self-image and esteem. Managers therefore tend to prefer unrealistically strict timelines that may not be met to realistic but longer timelines. Interestingly, in a highly masculine culture such an approach works well, and often achieves a higher overall performance than would have been possible had they planned realistically. Furthermore, and contrary to expectations, a masculine culture is more accepting of delays than a feminine culture is. They even anticipate them.

A feminine culture favours a less aggressive approach, with deadlines being established on the basis of their true estimates rather than the challenge to meet them. This does not imply lower efficiency but simply an alternative approach that works for the culture. Planning in a feminine culture usually involves greater technical input, resulting in a more accurate plan and lower risk of time and cost overruns.

Both collective and sequential orientations influence the accuracy of project planning. In the case of collective cultures the reasons are the collaborative efforts that result in higher input for planning; while in the case of sequential cultures it is due to their preference and aptitude for structured project planning. However, it should be noted that there is no stopping a both 'masculine and sequential' culture from intentionally planning ambitiously.

In high uncertainty avoidance cultures, planning tends to be overly lax. A high UAI individual, be they a technical stakeholder or a manager, tend to exaggerate their estimates and the consequent certainty of meeting them. Likewise, but to a lesser extent, individuals within a high PDI culture tend to be generous with their estimates to avoid repercussions in the event of lower final specs, delays or cost overruns.

Procurement Planning

The autonomy to choose your own suppliers for a project depends on the organisation and its supplier policy. Yet, traditionally individualistic culture will chose from independent suppliers on the basis of best quotation and quality. A collective culture will follow the same line but with the difference that once a supplier has delivered efficiently and built a professional relationship with the client, they will become a 'preferred' supplier and given priority over their competition so long as the cost difference is not unreasonably high. While the establishment and use of 'preferred' suppliers is gaining strength today in individualistic cultures, where managers now acknowledge the value of supplier relations and reliability over relatively small savings, this practice lags behind those in collective cultures. A project manager in a collective culture will find working with their preferred suppliers easier and more reliable. In an individualistic culture more diligence is needed in supplier selection, especially if no list of 'tested and validated' preferred suppliers exists.

Table 12.2   Cultural influence on project planning

stronger influence	weaker influence

Planning and Tracking		Value vs. product oriented	Top-down vs. bottom-up	High level vs. details	Vertical vs. horizontal allocations	Technical vs. political vs. strategic prioritisation	Ambitious vs. lax vs. realistic
Dimension	**Orientation**						
Power Distance (PDI)	High Power Distance	Product	Top-Down	Details	Vertical	Political	Lax
	Low Power Distance	Value		High Level			
Individualism vs. Collectivism (IDV)	Individualistic	Product					
	Collective	Value	Top-Down			Strategic	Realistic
Masculinity vs. Femininity (MAS)	Masculine	Product			Horizontal	Technical	Ambitious
	Feminine	Value			Vertical	Technical	Realistic
Uncertainty Avoidance (UAI)	High Uncertainty Avoidance	Product	Top-Down	Details			Lax
	Low Uncertainty Avoidance	Value		High Level		Technical	
Specific vs. Diffuse (SDI)	Specific				Horizontal		
	Diffuse				Vertical		
Sequential vs. Synchronic (SST)	Sequential	Product					Realistic
	Synchronic			High Level			

Chapter 13
Risk Management

Risk management is the process of identifying, assessing and responding to risks that may compromise the projects' performance or outcome. It is an episodic process, in that the identified risks are reassessed from time to time and newly arising risks identified and added to the process.

Although some recent definitions of 'risk' include a possible event that may affect the project's outcome either negatively or positively; that is, as a threat or an opportunity, for our own purposes in this chapter we will resort to the more classic definition in which a risk represents the possibility of a threat.

Needless to say, for risk management to be effective it must involve the appropriate stakeholders throughout each step in the process. There are five major steps in project risk management:

1 – Identifying Risks

Identifying risks involves describing possible events that may compromise the project's overall performance or results should they materialise. These events can be either internal or external to the project's environment.

There are various types of risks which we will categorise as follows:

Project Risks – representing threats that may impact the time, cost or specifications of the project output, such as the possibility of falling short on resources with consequent increased costs, delays or impact on product specifications.

Process Risk – representing threats that may compromise the efficiency with which the project output is utilised; such as lack of user involvement and training, or other preparations of the department or function that will derive benefit from the project.

Strategic Risk – is characterised by internal or external events that may compromise the benefits that will be achieved through the deliverables; such as competitors announcing the release of related products, thus changing the market requirement and rendering invalid our current business case. For example, if during the development of a new mobile phone technology the competition released a similar or better technology, our original business case of 'prestigious brand' and 'higher market share' are strongly compromised.

2 – Assessing Risks

Assessing risks is the process of identifying the probability of the threat materialising and determining its impact in such an event. The higher the probability and impact, the more critical the risk is. A popular way of assessing risks is to assign an escalating value to the impact, say from one to five, and likewise to probability. The multiplication of impact and probability provides us with an indicator of how critical the risk is. Thus a risk with an impact of 4 (high) and probability 5 (very high) has an overall value of 20 (4 × 5) and is therefore highly critical; while a risk of a low impact of 2 and medium probability 3, has an overall value of 6 (2 × 3) which is far less critical. This process is referred to as 'quantifying risks'.

It is important to note that *quantifying risks is insufficient by itself* as proper assessment requires logical elaboration of the threat's nature and the area it may impact; as well as our own abilities to respond to such a threat materialising. However, quantifying risks is an excellent aid to assigning assessment priorities and for numerical and graphical reporting on overall risks status.

3 – Response Strategy

Once a risk is assessed, we need to decide what to do about it. Our options are:

Elimination – where the risk is unacceptable, we must act to remove it; this might involve providing users with comprehensive training on our product prior to its release, thus eliminating the process risk of their being unable to use it efficiently.

Mitigation – where the assessed risk is unacceptable and cannot be eliminated, we need to take action to either reduce its probability of occurring or reduce its impact should it occur, or both. An example is a dissatisfied technical stakeholder; a key engineer of who it has come to our attention, is searching for another job. Should our engineer abandon the project prior to its completion, there will be a significant impact on its time, costs and its output specifications. Given the risk, a mitigation strategy might involve an agreement on a sizable reward for successful project delivery, therefore reducing the chances of his early departure. Another option may be assigning a similar engineer to work closely with him, and consequently in the event of our engineer's early departure, the handover time to the replacement engineer is reduced along with the related chain of negative impacts.

Acceptance – either because there is nothing we can do about a risk, or because the overall impact of a risk materialising is too small to warrant an earlier response, and we are ready to accept the consequences in such an event, we may simply accept the risk. Where appropriate and possible, a contingency plan should be devised once a risk is accepted in order to be ready to act immediately should the risk materialise.

Sharing or transfer – the option of sharing or transferring a risk was introduced within the *Managing Successful Programmes* (MSP™) methodology of the Office of Government and Commerce in the UK. It involves an agreement with the client and/or the suppliers to share the cost of countering the risk should it materialise; alternatively purchasing an insurance policy against it. An example of such a risk could be severe weather conditions strongly impacting a construction project.

4 – Owner Allocation

Without official risk ownership, which involves an assigned owner who is given overall responsibility for monitoring, reassessing and addressing the risk should it materialise, the effectiveness of risk management is much reduced.

Risk owners should have expertise in their owned risks, and where such owners can be identified at an early stage, they should be involved in devising the risk response strategy.

5 – Risk Tracking and Update

Just as project plans should be tracked and updated periodically, so should the risks. This process is driven by the project manager and involves a review of the risks' progress and reassessment with their owners, as well as identifying newly arising risks.

Although the risk's *tracking and update cycle* may duplicate that of the project plan, some risks may present a need for more frequent tracking, and as such the cycle for each risk may be customised accordingly.

* * *

Two of our cultural dimensions significantly influence risk management. Namely, power distance and uncertainly avoidance.

Before we proceed to review their influence, I would like to remind my reader that 'uncertainty avoidance' is not 'risk avoidance', and therefore does not manifest in burying one's head in the sand nor in avoiding all risky situations. An uncertain situation is an ambiguous situation with no clear object, whereas a risky situation has an identifiable object that may materialise for which we can therefore devise a counter strategy.

How BIG is Big?

As in most elements of project control, risk management involves setting up escalation triggers that are related to the type of risk and their assessment. These triggers serve to determine the points at which they are to be escalated to the various levels of management and stakeholders as to devise an appropriate response strategy; and just as important, to avoid overloading senior stakeholders with risks that can be addressed without their involvement.

The higher the power distance, the less likely employees are allowed to make their own response decisions when facing a problem or a risk.

As a result, escalation triggers are lower and risks are escalated well before they would be in a lower PDI culture; this often results in increased timescales for the resolution of some less critical risks. It also requires senior managers to invest their valuable time to address such risks; which, in turn, influences the management approval decisions for internal proposed projects, with less being approved than would have been in lower PDI cultures.

Another influence of higher PDI is that strategic risks are far more likely to be escalated to higher management as the strategy is seldom shared with the employees; here however, the escalation is appropriate.

We had noted that a risk itself is not an uncertainty; however, every risk has an element of ambiguity and therefore uncertainty. Important to note that the uncertainty is not the object of the risk, but rather the probability or impact of that object materialising; the object itself is 'known' and not ambiguous. Using our earlier example of the dissatisfied engineer, the object of the risk is that the engineer may depart prior to completing his job on the project; the ambiguity of the risk is inherent in the chance that he will depart (probability) and the impact such departure would imply. Therefore, if we were reasonably confident (although not completely certain otherwise the risk would be an issue rather than a risk) that our engineer will depart, and we have a good understanding of the resulting impact thanks to our technical comprehension of his responsibilities, then the risk could be said to be of 'low' ambiguity. If on the other hand we are less certain of his departure (say about 50 per cent) and/or of the resulting impact should he depart, then the risk could be said to be of 'high' ambiguity.

Therefore, high uncertainty avoidance in risk management terms manifests in three ways:

1.   Projects with higher uncertainty in their identified risks are less likely to be approved.

2.   Risk tolerance is lower as managers feel uncomfortable delegating much of the risk management to their subordinates.

3.   When an uncertain risk is identified, the preferred response strategy is to reduce uncertainty; eliminate or vigorously mitigate.

With reference to the second and third points, a high UAI culture may invest a disproportionate effort analysing and devising responses to a bulk of risks the overall impact of which does not justify the effort.

The very opposite is true of low UAI cultures, but only towards the extreme low pole. As a result a low UAI culture may set the risk tolerance disproportionately high, causing many non-escalated risks to prove more detrimental than perceived.

So We Have a Big Risk! What Shall We Do about It?

Do we eliminate, mitigate, accept or share the risk? For escalated risks already delegated upwards to senior management, power distance has little influence on the decision. However, risks below the trigger points will need to be actively addressed by the technical stakeholders or members of the project team; and as the risk response is directly influenced by the anxiety experienced in anticipating that risk (and needless to say, the higher the PDI, the more distant the manager–employee relationship and the higher the anxiety), the result is a preference for elimination as opposed to mitigation or acceptance of non-escalated risks in high PDI cultures. This preference can result in lengthy and/or costly elimination of risks that do not warrant such an action. Risk sharing is not implicated in this trend as sharing decisions are made by the senior stakeholders.

We already noted the effect of high UAI being a preference for elimination or strong mitigation for high uncertainty risks. Again, using the example of our discontent engineer, the risk will probably lead to the organisation signing a binding contract with the discontent engineer that guarantees his stay until the end of the project. This will come at price no doubt, but it will be preferred to the uncertainties that may otherwise follow; even if the cost of addressing the uncertainties is likely to be lower than the bonus included in such contract.

Plan a Contingency or Face the Music?

Sequential or synchronic orientation has no significant influence on risk management overall. Nevertheless it can have an impact on risk response. Sequential cultures are more likely to plan risk contingencies in advance, while synchronic cultures have a tendency to delay contingency planning (if at all) until the risk materialises, at which point they will tackle it as it does.

Both approaches have their advantages and disadvantages. Sequential cultures are better prepared for risks but may tend to over anticipate risks before they happen. On the other hand, synchronic cultures are creatively equipped to manage inherently chaotic situations resulting from materialising risk; however, in deciding not to plan a contingency (as their sequential counterparts), they may face some significant risks materialising that cannot be creatively and synchronically addressed; in which case, they pay the price of being synchronic.

Table 13.1 Cultural influence on project risk management

stronger influence	weaker influence

Risk Management		How BIG is big?	Preferred Response Strategy	Plan a Contingency or Face the Music?
Dimension	**Orientation**			
Power Distance (PDI)	High Power Distance	Big	Elimination	
	Low Power Distance			
Individualism vs. Collectivism (IDV)	Individualistic			
	Collective			
Masculinity vs. Femininity (MAS)	Masculine			
	Feminine			
Uncertainty Avoidance (UAI)	High Uncertainty Avoidance	Big	Elimination (especially for highly uncertain risks)	
	Low Uncertainty Avoidance	Small	Acceptance	
Specific vs. Diffuse (SDI)	Specific			
	Diffuse			
Sequential vs. Synchronic (SST)	Sequential			Plan a contingency
	Synchronic			Face the music

Chapter 14

Project Communication and Reporting

As for any type of communication, project communication can be split into two parts: methodology and skill.

Methodology refers to the way the project communication plan is developed and implemented, and involves the process of:

- identifying all stakeholders and their various groups;

- identifying the stakeholders' impact on the project and the project's impact on them;

- identifying the stakeholders' interest in the project and the project's need for their input;

- devising a communication strategy that outlines the information sent and received to satisfy the stakeholders' interests and the project's needs;

- establishing the frequency and format of the information (format can be reports, emails, phone calls, meetings, seminars, publications).

This process will then be implemented throughout the project lifecycle with the communication plan changing, as needs change, with every phase of the project.

Without a clearly outlined and implemented communication plan, the entire project risks failure. Needless to say, the more complex the project, the bigger such a risk is. Lack of communication will directly result in lack of clarity about the project's objectives (outcomes and benefits), lower management support, low user involvement, lower team motivation, unmanaged customer and stakeholders expectations, unidentified interdependencies and a host of other detrimental factors. It is worthwhile noting that the first three noted results alone contribute over 50 per cent to the reasons behind failed technology projects in the United States (2011, The Standish Group International. The Chaos Manifesto).

A communication plan should be developed and implemented in all cultures, and its overall format would not differ much on the basis of culture. What would differ, are the *plan content* and its implementation *style*; and good implementation requires good communication skills.

Implementation style refers to how we present ourselves and therefore how our messages are perceived. 'Do we talk loudly or humbly?', 'Should we communicate authority or collaboration?', 'Is it better to demonstrate absolute confidence or allow our uncertainties to show?' The first option in each of these questions represent a culture or style that you might associate with the USA and the second, with the Dutch.

Until very recently, most Western countries following the American management style favoured loud extrovert type of communication and management. Today this style is being seriously questioned and is often blamed for giving disproportionate value to presentation over content.

Susan Cain, in her 2013 bestseller *Quiet: The Power of Introverts in a World That Can't Stop Talking* makes a fascinating argument into how this disproportionate preference for extroversion came to be, and the price we all had to pay as a result, including the 2008 recession. Of course this is not to say that introversion should be favoured over extroversion. Again, each style has its key values and plays a crucial role in balancing our lives.

The content of the communication plan is directly related to the persons, information and methods of communication that are appropriate to the project. This is strongly influenced by the culture and will be our main focus in this chapter. The project communication plan should answer the question:

- *Who* needs information from the project and who has information that the project needs?

- *What* is the nature of this information and what is its purpose?

- *When* is the information needed?

- *How* should the communication of this information take place?

As far as project schedule and resource allocation is concerned, much of the communication aspects were discussed in Chapter 12 'Planning and Tracking'. We will therefore place more emphasis on general project communication and reporting with regards to specifications, updates meetings and reports, and so on.

Who Knows Best?

It comes as no surprise, particularly when it comes to technical and specification planning, that knowing who to talk to to obtain the right information is a crucial element of the project's success. Talk to people who are not the 'go to' guys for technical context and your entire planning and all that is to follow may be very inaccurate. This may sound overly simplistic and obvious but it happens very frequently; for example, when specification planning takes place at management and development levels without sufficient involvement of the users in terms of their expert contribution on product practicality. According to the *Chaos Manifesto*, this one example is the reason behind 20 per cent of all unsuccessful IT projects in the US.

More tricky but less significant, talk to those who 'do know', such as the users or technical employees with a jealous or controlling boss, and you are unlikely to make many friends in high places, which can compromise the efficiency of your role.

With the last point in mind, in higher power distance, higher uncertainty avoidance and in diffuse cultures (low SDI) most bosses want the project manager to go through them and not directly approach their technical staff without their prior consent; and the staff themselves may feel uncomfortable and object if they are not approached on this basis. In the case of high PDI this issue mainly arises out of respect for bureaucracy and authority, while in the case of low SDI it comes from managers perceiving the horizontal information flow as infringing on their functional responsibility.

Remember what we outlined earlier; being 'diffuse' does not imply willingness and desire to participate and to be consulted outside of your specific area of responsibility, and likewise, being specific does not imply the opposite. Diffuse persons do not draw definite borders between various life and work spheres and expect behavioural codes and relationship patterns to be uniform throughout. A 'specific' person is the opposite, with clear borders between their life and work spheres so that relationship and behaviour codes do not diffuse. As a result, a seemingly contradictory but very logical outcome is that in a diffuse culture employees are less willing to participate outside their area of responsibility as they find it difficult to perceive this participation as confined to the project's context and perceive it as overstepping on others' responsibilities. On the other hand, in a specific culture they are happy to do so being naturally inclined to confine their participation to a specific context with no risk of being perceived as overstepping their mark.

The same situation applies for communication and reporting; at least, as far as projects are concerned.

Therefore, once the specific short-term nature of the project is explained and permissions asked and gained, both in the cases of high PDI and low SDI, the project manager may safely approach the technical team. However, in a high UAI culture this is by no means the case. High UAI will give rise to higher anxiety because of the perception of not being in control and not being perceived to be in control as a result; bosses may request that the project manager talk only to them for any information they need from their department and if the boss doesn't have the information to hand, they will request it from their staff and pass it to the project manager. The cost? Greater effort, longer timescales and a higher risk of inaccurate information.

Why, with hindsight, would senior stakeholders exclude users or others with product expertise from contributing to its specification and features? It is not as simple as that. The problem is that hindsight comes after the event (and the effort) and some cultures are more apt to learn only from their own mistakes rather than from others'; these are the more masculine cultures.

Feminine cultures in comparison have a significant advantage here for two reasons:

1.   Managers are more technically proficient than their masculine counterpart and are far less likely to oversee the importance of involving the technical experts including the users when developing the specifications.

2.   Even in the event of lacking contribution from technical experts, the damage is likely to be less than would be the case in a masculine culture; thanks to the manager's technical proficiency.

Consequently, in a masculine culture, involving technical experts is more crucial for success. If the culture is also one of high power distance and/or high uncertainly avoidance, that involvement becomes a real challenge that the project manager must face.

It should also be noted that collective cultures, with their emphasis on managers' technical meritocracy, also share some of the advantages of a feminine culture in this context.

Who Needs to Know?

Non-managers, including high-profile professionals such as doctors and academics, may respond to the question, 'Who needs to know?' with, 'Everyone, of course!' (that is, all, or at least all internal stakeholders). However, we managers and project managers know better that determining who needs to know is a little more complicated in practice. Efficient reporting and flow of information requires that those who 'need' to know are provided just the information they need. Other information may be available on a project portal, the project publications, newsletters or by request; however, stakeholders who need information to make a certain decision must receive precisely the information they need unlettered by other information, however interesting or however relevant to other stakeholders. Furthermore, and particularly with respect to external stakeholders in commercial projects, some information must be withheld if the organisation wants to retain their competitive advantage.

This is no surprise to any proficient project manager and is well imbedded in the various methodologies; however, culture plays a major role in making certain decisions about who needs to know, whether the news is good, bad or disastrous.

In low power distance cultures, there is a more open flow of information and specialists are both motivated and work better as a result of being given the full picture of 'what is going on'.

In high power distance cultures, managers may often ignore the need for subordinates to be better informed; and whilst it is true that the subordinates may be happier to have their manager make most of the decisions; to say that they do not desire to be in the wider picture would be incorrect (even in the highest PDI cultures).

I have worked with many team members in very high PDI cultures, such as the Middle East, and they often confided to me that they felt as if they are 'kept in the dark' and that their managers did not value them sufficiently to include them in the wider picture. They often complained that they receive information on a 'need to know basis' where 'need to know' refers only to the technical requirement for specific jobs. They therefore felt demotivated and separated from their organisation. Indeed, the culture of 'Us and Them' is very evident with employees and their managers in very high power distance environments.

This is not a contradiction to my earlier statement that stakeholders should be provided with only the information they need to know. Indeed the problem is that, in very high PDI cultures, managers often fail to acknowledge that their team does *need to know* much of the information currently withheld if they are to be motivated and work better; and in order to prioritise their own tasks on the basis of the wider picture and therefore the project outcome. My earlier statement is well illustrated by the example of the zealous, technically proficient, project manager who includes much of the technical detail in their management reporting; something they do out of pride and interest in the technical context; however, in doing so they often risk management ignoring their lengthy and detailed reports altogether, including the crucial data which may involve subtle nuances for them to make fully informed decisions.

There are always individuals who do not fit this scenario and prefer to be informed on a 'technical need to know basis', but they exist equally in both low and high PDI cultures which makes me inclined to believe that such preference is a personal trait rather than cultural. Clearly, a personal preference to know only what is needed to perform a specific task will be perceived as a negative trait in low PDI cultures, especially in a dynamic and open team environment. Such individuals are most fit for jobs of clear and well-defined scope that do not require them to know beyond their specific tasks; and it should be noted that contrary to popular belief (in low PDI and highly masculine cultures), such individuals in the right job can be extremely efficient. Some of the greatest minds in scientific research fit this description.

Senior managers in diffuse cultures often feel uncomfortable about sharing detailed information with those outside their functional area. This, again, arises from their difficulty in perceiving such sharing as 'specific' to the project context and duration, and therefore may hold the perception that, in doing so, they are losing autonomy over their area of responsibility. This is in contrast to managers in specific cultures that perceive this sharing as 'specific' to the project context with no influence otherwise over their functional role and responsibility.

Graphs vs. Figures

During the past two decades, we have witnessed the marvellous development of tools and software including spreadsheets and presentation tools, allowing us to better analyse complex data and present them in a logical and comprehensible format. As a result, we are able to process far more information and make more accurate decisions than ever before, and this was and still is of great value in all management contexts, including, project management.

However, such value has not come without a price; namely, the tendency to use the complex data and graphical presentations to impress rather than to inform.

There is no doubt that a colourful and well laid out presentation is more pleasant to the eye than a plain one. Yet, I continue to witness managers, including very senior managers, spending hours or days on end working on the format of their presentation to their own (even more senior) managers; adding animations, colours and diagrams, more often than not for cosmetic reasons. The result is a significant waste of effort and a shift of focus from technical content to presentation style. This is most often apparent in high power distance cultures.

In many cases, high PDI managers unconsciously seek to impress their own managers with style and complexity. Spreadsheets, project planning and presentation software have become the tool to do so. Furthermore, a shift from figures to graphs and diagrams can help conceal some of the lower performance figures and emphasise the higher ones.

Highly feminine cultures have the opposite preference to very high PDI cultures; letting go of most of the tools' graphical capabilities for detailed technical figures and data. This, in its own turn, can disproportionately shift communication away from the strategic perspectives provided by well-conceived graphs and diagrams.

In any culture, presentations should ideally use figures, graphs and diagrams to communicate the exact information needed for efficient and accurate decision making, and the project manager is always advised to follow a balanced approach.

How Frequently and How Much Detail?

As a result of the power distance effect on vertical communication, as well as on the level of trust between managers and their employees, a higher PDI manager will require more frequent and detailed reporting often down to activity level for their area of responsibility. On the other hand, a low PDI manager may be content with less frequent and higher-level reports without the need to go into the details of activities.

Both approaches are correct and appropriate for their own cultures and generally align with where most decisions need to be made.

Uncertainty avoidance also plays a significant role, with managers in high UAI cultures making more effort to introduce certainty through frequent and detailed controls; even when doing so doesn't improve oversight.

In extreme cases, and in very high UAI cultures, such reports can end up so complex and overcrowded with details that managers never read them. Yet, they insist on this level of detail in the belief that the project manager, having planned and then tracked progress in minute detail, should have avoided nasty surprises more effectively. In other words, they feel that detail reduces uncertainty. They may easily overlook the fact that controlling the details comes at a very high price; including reduced management involvement, lost time and effort wastage, loss of focus on the wider context and, worst of all, loss of focus from the final project outcome and benefits.

Meetings!

All professionals are aware of many of the reasons behind ineffective, inefficient and even counterproductive meetings; including issues with the purpose, process, participation and preparation of the meeting. Table 14.1 illustrates their most common problems.

Table 14.1   Common problems in project meetings

Purpose:	Preparation:
• No clear or shared objectives • Meeting not necessary	• Poor preparation on part of participants and leader • Wrong people present; right people absent
Process:	Participation:
• No agenda or plan • Getting off the subject • Habitual late starts • No record keeping • Meeting too long • No clear decision-making method	• Poor participation on part of participants and leader • Interruptions • Hidden agendas

In this section, we will focus on meeting issues that relate to culture.

Collectivism has many advantages that have proven its management effectiveness. However, when it comes to meetings, a collective culture fares less well on efficiency than their individualistic counterparts.

One typical approach to meetings in a collective culture is to invite all persons involved in all items to be discussed in the agenda. This comes naturally to a culture that values and respects the group over the individual and does not wish to single any member out. Nor do they wish to miss out on any members' input to the meeting. What if someone not present had something important to say or contribute?

This approach is undoubtedly noble and well intended. However, it does have serious drawbacks:

- *Loss of focus*: with a higher number of participants, it is easy to lose focus from the main objectives.

- *Longer meeting*: given the high number of participants and loss of focus, meetings take longer than they should.

- *Missing key participants*: given longer meetings and lower efficiency, key project members including more senior managers start to skip them.

- *Wasted time*: for all those who did attend but didn't need to, their time would have been better used elsewhere.

Synchronic cultures are highly prone to losing track of meeting agendas; bringing to the table any item that comes to a participant's mind and rarely achieving many of the meeting objectives. They are also prone to delays, missing participation and most of the problems outlined in Table 14.1. The good news is that synchronic cultures are under no illusions and are fully aware of their shortcoming in meeting management; therefore suggestions for improvement are well appreciated by synchronic managers.

Another mark of synchronic cultures are their frequent, unplanned yet highly significant meetings by the vending machines or in the smoking areas. This shouldn't be sneered at; it is often a highly efficient, less formal, more frequent and relaxed form of communication that significantly aids the synchronic creativity. When in Italy, half of my meetings with clients and sponsors are by the coffee vending machine. Therefore, the shortcomings are not the unofficial meetings themselves but rather failing to put actions down in writing and/or making sure those who need to know what was discussed are informed.

A Special Note on Communication and Synchronic Cultures

As we noted earlier, synchronic cultures are at an advantage when dealing with unforeseen events. We also noted how new and effective methodologies, such as those of programme management and agile project management, have borrowed much of the approach from synchronic cultures allowing them to better handle chaotic and turbulent environments.

However, when it comes to communication, a synchronic culture has much to learn from its sequential counterpart. Sequential cultures are ordered cultures and their communication plans are intricate and clear. Everyone gets the information they need and when they need it. Earlier in my career working with an American/British consultancy in London, I frequently had to interface on a project with the HQ in America and made a number of phone calls to the US every day. My manager, when he noted this, insisted that I follow calls with emails outlining what was discussed or agreed. He agreed with me that the phone was faster and more efficient for my purposes than emails but wanted a track of all project communication in writing should anyone need to refer to it at some point, either in the UK or the US. I therefore wrote a single email at the end of each working day outlining the earlier phone discussions. Later on during the project, this proved its value more than once, and I continue to summarise all conversations in emails to date.

A synchronic culture does not follow the same standards and guidelines of project communication and prefers to communicate organically at need. In a project with many stakeholders and involving various departments, this lack of standards in communication will result in data loss and repeated effort.

Therefore, the project manager in a synchronic culture should give particular emphasis to developing a comprehensive project communication plan and insist on it being followed rigorously. If there is one piece of advice I am to give to such a project manager, it is this one.

Table 14.2   Cultural influence on project communication

stronger influence	weaker influence

Communication		Who Knows Best?	Who Should I Talk To?	Who Needs to Know?	Frequency and Details	Graphs vs. Technical Data	Meetings ...
Dimension	Orientation						
Power Distance (PDI)	High Power Distance		The boss	Managers	High	Graphs	
	Low Power Distance			Everyone	Low		
Individualism vs. Collectivism (IDV)	Individualistic						
	Collective	Technical stakeholder and managers					Compromised
Masculinity vs. Femininity (MAS)	Maculine	Technical Stakeholders					
	Feminine	Technical stakeholder and managers				Technical data	
Uncertainty Avoidance (UAI)	High Uncertainty Avoidance		The boss		High	Technical data	
	Low Uncertainty Avoidance				Low		
Specific vs. Diffuse (SDI)	Specific						
	Diffuse		The boss				
Sequential vs. Synchronic (SST)	Sequential						Effective
	Synchronic						Compromised

Chapter 15

Delegation and Accountability

Delegation within the project context refers to delegating overall responsibility for the delivery of a work package (WP), a product or a specific result. This requires the person to whom the work is delegated to make their own judgement and decision as to the most appropriate tasks and activities to realise the delivery successfully. Delegation in this context does not mean assigning responsibility for a defined task or activity. Defining the tasks and activities for a delegated matter is the responsibility of the person doing the work.

Accountability implies holding someone as directly accountable for certain results, be they results from a delegated delivery or from their originally owned work.

Together, delegation and accountability are key to imbedding a sense of ownership and responsibility in anyone in charge of a delivery. Delegation and accountability are strongly correlated. Thus, if the environment encourages delegation then so it should accountability. Yet, as we will see, this is not always the case.

Delegation and accountability are strongly influenced by the culture; often to the extent that what might be a desirable approach in one culture is perceived as hostile in another.

Assigning Tasks vs. Delegating Deliverables

The opposite of delegation would be to assign specific tasks and activities to a specialist or team member; these are pre-defined tasks and activities which only require the assigned resource to implement them. If we were to consider preparing a one-hour project progress presentation to the sponsors of a new school, then a delegating manager (most likely to be the client) may ask one their team (most likely to be the project manager in this case) to prepare the presentation on the basis of the overall message they want to convey to the sponsors (for example, main features completed and still to be completed, their overall benefits, communication and feedback from interested communities, overall costs to date, expected further costs, major strategic issues and their resolution, expected completion date and so on). Exactly how to convey this message and how to present it are left to the team member to decide. A non-delegating manager on the other hand, would decide the exact type of content and means to present them; this includes the exact data such as, what specifications of which features to present, which benefits to highlight, what costs to emphasise and to what detail, and so on. They will also decide on the means of presentation including format, use of software and/or handouts, and then assign these specific activities to their team.

Delegation therefore requires that two main elements are present:

1.   Open vertical communication allowing employees to freely express their opinions and voice their concerns to their managers and by implication a manager who is aware and trusting of their employees' abilities.

2.   A relaxed environment and the willingness for managers to let go of some control, assigning the responsibility for important decisions to their employees; likewise, the employees need to feel relaxed and confident about taking such responsibilities.

The first point above implies lower power distance while the second, lower uncertainty avoidance.

Delegation and accountability works in similar ways in both masculine and feminine cultures. A feminine culture is neutral with regards to delegation and the team members would be happy to undertake the delegated job if they believe it fits their skills and capabilities.

Employees in masculine culture are even happier to be delegated a job even if it does not fully fit their skills and capabilities. Masculine cultures strive on achievement and challenges; and to a professional, being delegated an objective is nothing short of a challenge. A project manager can therefore expect more zeal for delegation in a masculine culture, but must also be aware that such zeal may not be justified. Masculine cultures tend to emphasise 'knowing how to manage' over 'knowing the technicalities' in the belief that by good management one can source the technical know-how from others.

The type of the project and the availability of supporting resources will help determine if technical know-how is a necessary attribute, or if good and resourceful management suffice.

In a feminine culture, the team member is likely to refuse a delegated task if they do not believe it to fit their technical capabilities. On the negative side, if the team member might efficiently source the requisite know-how from others, then an opportunity is lost.

Note that I did not identify the positive 'stimulating' (or interesting) aspects of making decisions as a motivator towards delegation in masculine cultures. This is because it applies as a motivator equally to all cultures apart from higher uncertainty avoidant cultures; in which the stimulating aspect is overridden by anxiety.

Who is Accountable?

Regardless of the tendency for higher PDI cultures to delegate less than lower PDI cultures, someone has to make the decisions on what to delegate and be accountable for it. Thus, for example, someone has to decide the structure, content and method of the sponsors' presentation; if not the team leader, then the senior manager or the client themselves.

From this perspective, high PDI employees have an advantage because their better-structured hierarchy, as well as their clearly defined managers' roles and responsibilities, makes accountability clearer and easier. Contrast this with low PDI cultures with less clear definitions of roles and responsibilities, as well as an acceptance of some overlapping responsibilities and working across horizontal functional lines. This message should reinforce the importance of clearly defined project roles and responsibilities, especially in low PDI cultures.

Who Takes the Credit?

Collective cultures share both rewards and punishment as a group and not as individuals. For example, a client may delegate all decisions on one of the project's products to the lead product engineer, including the choice of design, materials, suppliers and much of the specification, as well as implementation; the way that this delegation is perceived in a collective culture differs significantly from that of an individualistic culture.

In an individualistic culture such delegation is automatically taken as the responsibility of the lead engineer, and it is up to him or her to make use of their engineering team to deliver. The team members in turn are responsible to the lead engineer for the specific tasks or components that they in turn have been assigned or delegated. In case of failure, the lead engineer is held accountable. Thereafter, with their team, they may hold accountable those members whose tasks and subcomponents have failed and therefore contributed to the overall failure. Likewise, in the case of success the lead engineer will be congratulated and he or she may decide to congratulate their own team emphasising the achievement of the high-performing members.

In a collective culture, the client's delegation to the lead engineer is automatically understood as delegation to the whole engineering team, with the lead engineer being the 'leader' of the now responsible team. The team, as a whole, is therefore responsible to the delegator and a failure of one of their members is a failure of all of them. They would all accept being held accountable in such an eventuality. Likewise, success implies team success and they will expect to be acknowledged for it as a group.

Remember, collective thinking is not the sum of the group individuals' thinking. It is an *indivisible* collective thinking within each individual of the group.

A commonly made mistake by Western managers working in a collective culture is to make public acknowledgement of their appreciation of a team leader or a manager's achievement. Not only will their actions result in the group taking offence at being overlooked, but the team leader themselves will feel embarrassed and uncomfortable at being singled out from their own group; to be thanked for something that they did not do alone.

In a collective culture, acknowledgement and accountability goes to the group and not the individual.

Table 15.1   Cultural influence on project delegation and accountability

stronger influence	weaker influence

Delegation and Accountability		Assigning Tasks vs. Delegating Deliverables	Who is Accountable?	Who Takes the Credit?
Dimension	Orientation			
Power Distance (PDI)	High Power Distance	Assigning tasks	Clearer accountabilities	
	Low Power Distance	Delegating deliverables	Unclear accountabilities	
Individualism vs. Collectivism (IDV)	Individualistic			The individual
	Collective			The group
Masculinity vs. Femininity (MAS)	Masculine	Delegating deliverables		
	Feminine			
Uncertainty Avoidance (UAI)	High Uncertainty Avoidance	Assigning tasks		
	Low Uncertainty Avoidance	Delegating deliverables		
Specific vs. Diffuse (SDI)	Specific			
	Diffuse			
Sequential vs. Synchronic (SST)	Sequential			
	Synchronic			

Chapter 16

Project Leadership and Motivation

Part IV of this book is dedicated to managing the multicultural team from a people management perspective. Therefore, in this section we will briefly address the influences that specific cultural orientations may have on people management, beyond those addressed as part of earlier sections.

It is worth remembering that project teams and especially international project teams are not always acquainted with each other; some have never met before the project in question. Apart from the unfamiliar environment presenting a threat or an opportunity to most members of the team, this fact also implies that many of their initial practices and behaviours could easily be influenced by or be a direct outcome of, their consequent anxiety (or over excitement); and therefore their behaviour is likely to significantly change throughout the course of the project as they become familiar with each other.

Is the Project Manager a Boss?

In a high power distance culture, the project manager is more likely to be accepted as the manager in charge with authority over the project team; however, only if their role is officially communicated to the team by the senior management, which is often the case in a higher PDI culture.

In low power distance cultures, the project manager is not perceived as the boss but as the manager of the project who is in charge of coordinating all its aspects, including the project team, to reach the project objectives. Their relationship to the team is more of a responsible colleague rather than an authoritative boss. This does not imply that a team in a low PDI culture is any less cooperative with the project manager but rather the contrary. The lower PDI makes it less stressful for people to perform project roles alongside their standard functional role; something that often presents a project-process conflict in higher PDI cultures where project managers have to negotiate repeatedly with the functional managers for their project resources.

In a lower PDI culture, if a project-process conflict arises it is unlikely to be seen in the political light of higher PDI cultures, and it is the team members themselves who are more likely to discuss with their own functional managers the best options for their allocation of effort.

Doing Something Fun?

In all cultures, organising out-of-work events is an excellent means of team relationship building, communication and motivation; it also emphasises the group membership and demonstrates a management appreciation of the team's valuable contributions.

Events can vary from the most common after hours drinks, to dinners, sports, recreational weekends and boot camps whereby work and leisure are mixed together.

However, how the project manager and senior stakeholders may or may not behave in these events will vary tremendously depending on the culture being 'specific' or 'diffuse'.

During my early career in London with a project management consultancy, it was traditional on Friday after work for the entire company to mark the start of the weekend by going to the nearby pub. We would almost fill the entire space with all levels of the company staff; including secretarial, consultants, business unit managers and partners and owners. Rounds and rounds of drinks were purchased in turns (often at the company's expense) without reservation or constraint. The working week was over, and owners, bosses and employees were equal. Everyone was cheerful; joking, teasing and even cajoling sarcastically without any regard to status, seniority or authority were all acceptable and part of the fun.

Come Monday morning, each member of the staff took their appropriate position in the company giving the appropriate due respect and authority to their colleagues and managers as if Friday night had never happened.

This is because the UK is both a low power distance and a 'specific' (high SDI) culture, with the second orientation implying that behaviour in social or business situation is seen as 'specific' to that situation and does not extend (or diffuse) to other situations. We are therefore boss and employee at work and behave as such during work, while we are friends at the bar and behave as such during leisure.

If a British manager were to feel as relaxed and to let go of all formalities during a similar event in a diffuse culture (low SDI); or worse still, a high PDI and low SDI culture, such as in the Far East, they would lose respect and status, and would find it hard to re-establish their authority and standing back at work; because how their team, managers and colleagues perceived them during the event, 'diffused' to the workplace.

I frequently witnessed this with Western managers (especially British and Americans) in the highly diffuse Middle East. During out of work events they would feel entirely free and relaxed with their Middle Eastern teams; taking liberties, letting go of all formalities and indulging in unrestrained topics and discussions. Unnoticed by the Western managers, their team members maintained a sober and formal behaviour and were uncomfortable in their company. The next day, the story was always the same, with the Western managers making comments amongst themselves about the over formality and rigidness of their team, while the team members either complaining or joking amongst themselves about their managers inappropriate and 'humiliating' behaviour last night. The end result was that the managers lost much of their highly needed status and authority in the eyes of their diffuse team.

High power distance cultures also prefer to keep certain formalities between bosses and their employees during out of work events. However, in a specific culture the boss need not continue to play the role of the boss in a social event, but merely retain their formal code of behaviour and relationship patters with their team. In a high PDI culture it is continuing to be the boss that matters. Therefore in cultures that are simultaneously specific yet of high PDI, bosses may even become loudly drunk during the event, but they will never exchange jokes or tease their team members as equals, and vice versa. They are the boss being drunk and having fun just as their employees are – on the one and same table.

Prone to Conflict

Not all conflicts are unhealthy and some may even prove valuable as an efficient learning tool in the processes of identifying new and innovative solutions. In many cases, however, unmanaged and unresolved conflicts escalate and expand in scope, often significantly undermining the project's success.

Here again, some cultures are more prone to conflicts than others and, at the same time, some cultures are more open about conflicts than others; some cultures will avoid facing conflicts at any cost.

We have already addressed many drivers of project conflict arising from culture. In this brief section therefore, we will only review how culture may make us more prone to conflicts and the extent to which it makes us avoid it.

A highly political organisation, such as in a high PDI culture, will see more of its members prone to conflict, particularly at the middle–upper management levels where there is higher competition for status and position. Similar conflict is also present at non-management levels with employees competing for promotions.

Masculine and synchronic cultures are also prone to conflict, however for different reasons, and their conflicts are far less unhealthy than those influenced by higher PDI.

Members of masculine cultures enjoy competition and high proactivity and, as a result, are more likely to fall into conflict with their colleagues. This conflict, however, is also more likely to be addressed and resolved openly. Synchronic cultures, on the other hand, are more prone to conflict simply due to their poor organisation resulting in unintended conflict; such as failing to identify the over-allocation of resources across multiple projects, or failing to notify their functional managers that they have been co-opted by the project manager. Again, once the reasons behind the conflict are identified, the conflicting parties are likely to discuss viable solutions immediately. If this fails and matters escalate to a power struggle, then it is high PDI and not synchronism that is now influencing this conflict.

Collective cultures are the opposite. They are less prone to conflict than all other cultures. This is not because they are overly conflict avoidant (which they are), but rather, is simply due to their collective planning and decision making which leaves less space for conflict to arise. As a group, they are indeed more at harmony than individualistic cultures.

Conflict Avoidants

Why would anyone avoid facing a conflict if they believe it to exist and would benefit from its resolution? For two possible reasons:

1.   They believe the damage caused by facing the conflict to be higher than that arising from it.

2.   The individuals who identified the conflict do not care less about its resolution and therefore are entirely unmotivated to face it.

Does the second point sound disturbing? Unfortunately, and although this is not an uncommon reason amongst many employees in cultures that are moderate to highly individualistic and of very high power distance, the distance between managers and their subordinates has created a strong mistrust between them, and an 'us and them' culture amongst the employees has become prominent. Employees are therefore less concerned with the overall project benefits which they do not rate of value to their own career, and they will therefore avoid facing or resolving a conflict that means nothing to them.

The good news is that this scenario is particular to the noted culture combination. Most high PDI cultures tend to be collective, therefore they compensate for the manager–employees distance by a collective emphasis on the group and sharing decisions and information. The managers and senior managers are therefore not perceived as unconcerned about their employees' wellbeing but rather in an almost paternal light as guides and mentors.

Collective cultures *are* highly conflict avoidant, although not to the extent imagined by Western managers. The Western perception of collective cultures' conflict avoidance (especially Far Eastern cultures) is magnified because collective cultures particularly avoid facing conflicts in *the open and public way Western cultures often do.*

It is therefore highly significant to understand the source of the collective cultures' conflict avoidance as opposed to others. Collective cultures avoid conflicts because they perceive them to be a threat to their group harmony; and that harmony is one of their highest values. Indeed, in vast contrast to conflict avoidance due to purely higher PDI, in a collective culture, if a group member identifies an area that may cause conflict yet must be resolved, they will talk in confidence to their direct boss to identify the best way to address it without upsetting the group harmony. Rather than the 'us and them' attitude of the earlier example, here the direct manager is the person to whom you turn for help and advice.

Both higher uncertainty avoidance and more diffuse cultures also tend to avoid conflicts. In the first case this is due to the uncertainty around the possible reactions and outcome of the conflict. If the results are easily predictable and that uncertainly is minimised, the effect of high UAI on avoiding conflicts diminishes. For example, if the expected conflict involves a product designer who disagrees with one of his more envious colleagues on the choice of the product materials; and if our designer has already spoken to his boss who has agreed with his view, then he is assured that the conflict can only resolve with his choice of materials. Even though he is aware that his colleague will be upset by it, he will not avoid facing conflict on the basis of higher uncertainty avoidance. He may avoid the conflict on the basis of collectivism or personal sensitivity, but not uncertainty avoidance.

Diffuse cultures are more likely to avoid conflicts than their specific counterpart for the reason that they are less apt to perceive and accept a conflict as a conflict that is confined to its specific time and context. A specific culture is at an advantage here and feels comfortable with putting all issues on the table to be discussed, argued over, even fought over; and once the session is over, the conflict is over, until we meet again to re-discuss it.

This example I take from my own experience working with specific cultures. Indeed, in my admiration for this efficient approach which allows all conflicts within a team to be loudly voiced but not to diffuse beyond its context, I enthusiastically attempted to replicate it in a diffuse culture; big mistake!

Highly diffuse cultures require greater diplomacy and sensitivity on the part of the project manager. In extreme cases, it becomes very easy for even light or otherwise healthy criticism to be taken personally by its recipients who see it as impacting on their overall professionalism and even personal character. This is not an exaggeration. I repeatedly faced this unsettling response working with a team of local professionals for the European Commission in Syria before the current crises.

Rewarding Project Success

Collective cultures tend to be more long-term oriented than individualistic cultures. This has little influence on most of project methodology given that projects are relatively short-term initiatives, but it does have relevance for understanding project leadership and motivating a collective team. Long-term oriented cultures do not seek immediate rewards and are more at ease postponing any reward in favour of a more stable longer-term benefit. This means the project team are better motivated by the knowledge that their project performance provides them with an opportunity to learn and develop, as well as to contribute to their overall career progress; something that the project managers may point out to the senior stakeholders and the functional managers of the team.

Even within an individualistic short-term oriented culture, these rules also apply, albeit to a lesser extent and team members are more likely to be motivated by shorter-term rewards such as a bonus or small promotion. Still, a project manager who adopts a collective approach in an individualistic culture can still reap the benefits, as the prospect of long-term career development is always attractive and will contribute to overall team motivation. Be careful not to substitute the individualistic aspects of leadership and motivation by a collective management approach but rather use it to supplement a more traditional motivational style.

A Simpler Environment is a Happier Environment!

This is not the case for everyone. Especially not to very low uncertainty avoidant or very masculine teams and professionals who rather enjoy the uncertainty and challenge that lack of clarity can bring. However, these groups are the exception and, especially for high uncertainty avoidance cultures, this will almost certainly undermine the team's wellbeing and motivation.

We already addressed the need for clearer roles and responsibilities as well as detailed planning in a high UAI cultures. What it is also desirable is to establish clear and formal project management procedures such as the processes outlined in the Prince2™ methodology of the British Office of Government and Commerce.

However, we should be aware that Prince2™ and similar methodologies are comprehensive guides covering most projects situations and are not meant to be comprehensively applied to any type of project. Rather, the methodologies provide a reference from which only a selection of some of their 'processes' or 'components' should be applied as deemed necessary to the needs of the specific project in question.

A very high UAI culture risks applying all elements within a methodology indiscriminately resulting in overkill, highly decreased efficiency and lack of flexibility.

Table 16.1   Cultural influence on project leadership and motivation

Stronger influence	Weaker influence

| Motivation, team leadership and conflict resolution | | Is the Project Manager a boss? | Doing something fun ... | Prone to conflict? | Conflict avoidant? | Formal methodologies and procedures | Rewarding project success |
Dimension	Orientation						
Power Distance (PDI)	High Power Distance	Boss	Drinking with my boss	Yes	Yes		
	Low Power Distance	Colleague	We are all equal				
Individualism vs. Collectivism (IDV)	Individualism						Bonus or promotion
	Collectivism			No	Yes		Learning and overall career progress
Masculinity vs. Femininity (MAS)	Masculine			Yes		Demotivate	
	Feminine						
Uncertainty Avoidance (UAI)	High Uncertainty Avoidance				Yes	Motivator	
	Low Uncertainty Avoidance					Demotivate	
Specific vs. Diffuse	Specific		A boss is always a boss				
	Diffuse		This is a parallel universe		Yes		
Sequential vs. Synchronic (SST)	Sequential					Motivator	
	Synchronic			Yes		Demotivate	

Chapter 17

Managing Culture within the Project Environment

This part of the book is dedicated to cultural 'cause and effect' within the context of project management practices.

It is traversal and applicable to both culturally archetypical and non-archetypical situations. A note on archetypical situations; while it is true that they are becoming a rarer representation of today's international professionals, they still hold accurate when considering an organisation as a whole. That is, when considering the *norms and practices of the group* rather than the *beliefs and preferred practices of the individual*.

The project manager can therefore use this part of the book as a guide of 'what to expect' of projects in a cultural environment that is different to their own.

There are two main scenarios in which you can do this:

1.   *Archetypical*: If the environment is part of a distinct national group (that is, the project is in Holland within a business that has a predominantly Dutch management and therefore a Dutch culture) you can reference the latest statistics on the Dutch cultural orientations and compare them to the content of this part. You will be able to form an initial idea of what to expect in terms of project management practices, and therefore be prepared to make the best of the situation.

2.   *Non-Archetypical*: If the environment is largely independent of any distinct national group; for example, it involves an international project to be implemented across borders within a highly multinational organisation; one that has a highly multicultural mix of employees at any of their sites. In such a context, making reference to any national statistics is misleading since such an environment is a cultural melting

pot. However, unlike our single professional Culture Soup, these environments by virtue of being a group will have developed their own working culture alongside their values, norms and practices. It is therefore up to you to identify their cultural orientations by observing some of their practices. This will then allow you to make some calculated expectations of other project practices as noted in this part.

There is a third scenario in which the immediate project team that you will manage is made up of members of various organisations from different nations that have not as yet formed a working culture. Part IV of the book is dedicated to this increasingly common scenario and the strategy it outlines is equally applicable to the second scenario above.

Let's return to the first scenario in which I made a reference to statistical data on national cultural orientations; these orientations are widely and freely available through publications and websites. A simple query on any of the major web search engines will easily locate them. There are two items to remember when searching:

- Look for credible sources. Aim to obtain your information from the authors' original sources rather than secondary sites quoting from those originals. Many of the leading cultural researchers have either set up or sponsored an official website dedicated to publishing their and their collaborator's latest statistics. These are the most credible sources. Be wary of data from unknown sources or publications.

- Verify the dates of the latest update of any particular statistical information. Researchers are regularly repeating their surveys to keep up with cultural changes. The more recent the surveys, the more accurate the data. If there is no recent data on the nations that interest you, consider any changes that this nation may have gone through since the last survey and what that may imply with regards to their culture (see the note below on Greece). You may in some extreme cases opt to disregard the statistics altogether and resort to your own strategy of just using observation on the basis of the method outlined in the next part.

The Economic Crisis in Greece

Greece has traditionally scored the highest uncertainty avoidance orientation of all researched nations; an orientation that is strongly visible in their contemporary history. To non-Greeks, it manifests most evidently in the high average age of their government members and incredibly rigid and bureaucratic regulations and political system. From a Greek perspective, this orientation is also very apparent, and is complemented by a similarly very high UAI social and business attitude.

At the time of these earlier statistics and up to as little as ten years ago, these observations were accurate and representative, even if apparently not to visitors to the country, witnessing the modern and fashionable life of the younger Greek generations.

However, and as an outcome of the economic crises of the last decade, young Greeks have started to seriously question the values of their elders and ask themselves if these very values are not a major contributor to how Greece has fared in the crisis. Remember, many of the most influential government members represent the oldest generation in Greek society.

All of us around the world watched as young Greeks protested and fought against their government and system. In the end, there was no revolution but rather a form of extreme and visceral criticism which demonstrated a nation questioning and opposing its own values.

Can today's Greeks, as represented by the younger and middle-aged generations, and most of their private business be said to be the most uncertainty avoidant culture in the world? I doubt it. The post-crisis Greeks want the opposite to much of what many perceive as decadent and crumbling values as they face the uncertainty of the future.

Will this last or is it a mere phase in history? While there is little doubt that values crumbling under such visceral criticism will continue to hold sway longer than those expelled by revolution, there are no guarantees. Only time can tell.

Why did I opt to tell you this Greek story? As a warning to be careful whenever you consult statistics on a certain culture in an increasingly changing world.

* * *

When it comes to specific methods for *managing* the cultural influence within the project environment, I must disappoint some readers by emphasising that there are no absolute hard and fast rules. There are general strategies and guidelines; but to break them down into a generically applicable what and what not to do would be misleading.

Each project is different, as is each organisation, team, group of stakeholders, sector and economic era, and so on. Culture is one added element to the pot and not a factor that acts in isolation.

You will need to work out for yourself what to do to mitigate cultural influences with a negative impact on your project. For example, having noted that higher uncertainty avoidance implies overly low-risk escalation triggers and senior managers spending too much time resolving technical risks, you may want to suggest to your client that they increase the triggers to a more reasonable level.

Why would I not list such advice as a definite tool? Because in many situations, this suggestion will backfire on the project manager, the project team and the project overall. Here are two scenarios that illustrate the risk of getting it wrong:

- With the higher anxiety experienced by a high UAI culture, if senior stakeholders agree to the project manager suggestion (to raise the threshold for risk escalation), the technical team may feel threatened by the increased level of responsibility which, in turn, may cloud their judgement when assessing risks. Furthermore, such a suggestion is likely to reduce the technical team's willingness to collaborate with the project manager who was responsible for assigning them what they perceive as an unreasonable task.

- If the technical team fails to resolve any given risk that would normally have been escalated but is now in their hands (thanks to the higher escalation triggers), and if this has a serious impact on the project, the senior stakeholders may hold the project manager responsible and it may well further increase their lack of trust in their own technical team's abilities.

- The effect of these two scenarios, if they are accurate, will be a strongly compromised project performance.

Therefore, the decision to suggest higher risk triggers depends on the precise level of UAI in the environment, the cultural and personal traits of the client and sponsor, and the strength of trust and relationship that exists within the organisation. How much confidence do senior stakeholders have in the project manager to accept their suggestion when they know that certain risks will manifest themselves and not be resolved efficiently? Should it be the project manager, the client or the sponsor who initiates this suggestion?

These are the questions that only you can answer and on that basis you must decide if and how to vocally make the suggestion; how to handle any resulting anxiety; or if you choose not to make the suggestion, given the nature of the culture within which you are working, what may be the consequences and how best can you manage them?

On the other hand, some of the influences of culture are far less prone to conflict and can be more easily faced with direct open intervention from the project manager. For example, given that synchronic cultures hold many of their meetings informally by the vending machines and in the smoking areas, you might decide to join these meetings and then follow them up with an email to all relevant stakeholders elaborating the main points discussed. Similarly, when lower power distance cultures opt for very detailed reports, these reports may miss the bigger picture and risk not being read by the senior stakeholder. You may decide to introduce a one-page executive summary with high-level figures, graphs, critical flags and a roundup of progress at the beginning of the report. Another logical strategy is to place higher emphasis on planning and tracking of value in sequential cultures while emphasising deliverables and milestones in synchronic cultures. Such solutions are easily deducible from the culture and a critical awareness of what to expect from the environment is all you need to anticipate and then adapt them to the environment as you deem fit.

What follows are a few points of advice regarding situations *learnt through bitter experience* which illustrate how, when certain cultural solutions may seem both obvious and logical, if you implement them too hastily, they may easily backfire as in the example of the escalation triggers above.

The Powerful and the Powerless!

PLANNING

In a high power distance culture there is a greater risk of an exaggerated top-down approach to planning. This may lack crucial input from the technical team on the resources required or the feasibility of the project. You are strongly advised to involve all relevant technical staff in your planning, and not simply rely on their managers. This can be quite challenging given that higher PDI bosses are likely to be uneasy about you approaching their staff directly. However, if you have formal and visible sponsor support then this obstacle can be overcome and it is very much worth the effort. Nevertheless, even if you do have the sponsor's support, there are a few items you need to take into serious consideration:

1.   Regardless of the client and/or sponsor's support, make sure you request the approval from the various functional managers before you approach their staff; and ask these managers to communicate their approval to their staff.

     You may want to outline the format of information and collaboration that you will be seeking from their staff and agree the extent of your intervention 'without having to disturb the manager by asking permission every time'. The last phrase is very significant as it emphasises that your direct communication with the staff is not only for the benefit of the project but also for the benefit of the functional managers themselves who can do without frequent interruptions.

     You may further suggest that you send them a brief weekly memo outlining any significant communication or events that have taken place with their staff. This will reassure the manager that they remain aware of the activities of their staff, which is something that will be of high importance to a manager in high PDI culture.

     By being open with and respectful of the functional managers, not only will you reduce the risk of making enemies of important stakeholders but you have the opportunity of turning them into project supporters.

2.   Even if you obtain approval, do not immediately attempt to *rebalance the scales completely* if the planning culture is strongly top-down. Add the bottom-up element with moderation; otherwise, you may risk senior stakeholders losing confidence in the process.

3.   Now that you are in direct communication with the technical team, who are likely to be oblivious to the bigger picture, you may want to break the taboo of the 'need to know' bias. The team member will feel happy and motivated to be recognised as part of the project and not merely as a functional resource. A word of caution though: there is a good risk that sharing too much information with resources in a higher PDI culture would be perceived as weakness on the project manager's part. This is because of the long association the culture has developed between the managers' seniority and their distance from their employees.

I learnt this myself the hard way and it took me time to find a balance between sharing information with technical teams and retaining the minimum power distance necessary for effective high PDI management. Therefore, any information should be shared formally. Set aside a defined slot in your meetings with the employees concerned. Make it clear from the onset that the aim of sharing information is to help them better understand the purpose of, and therefore better manage, their project work. Some formality is important and sharing information on each new occurrence as it happens is best avoided if not requisite to the tasks at hand. Wait until your next planned meeting to share it.

4.   Be aware that the technical stakeholders may not be accustomed to making their own estimates and that, consequently, they are likely to exaggerate them in providing the *worst case scenario* to allow themselves a comfortable slack and avoid the risk of delays that might incur their manager's disapproval.

The reverse situation – a higher PDI project manager in a low PDI project environment – is simpler and less political, although it may prove more frustrating for the team. If this is the case, you may need to remind yourself that it is acceptable to talk to staff directly most of the time without offending their managers. I say most of the time because even in very low PDI cultures, functional managers are still protective of their areas, for technical and staff performance reasons, and may want to be kept informed of how their staff are being involved. Therefore, the earlier advice of agreeing your intervention tolerance with the bosses is equally applicable here and will help anticipate potential conflict. You may be pleasantly surprised by the ease with which you are given the go ahead without even being asked to keep the bosses informed of your activities, as their own staff will do so.

And remember, all stakeholders, including technical stakeholders and junior members of your team, expect you to share the wider picture with them. Your own team expects you to do so in your regular meetings, while the technical stakeholders will expect this when you approach them for technical information (planning, tracking, specification issues, and so on.). If you fail to adapt to this low power distance requirement you risk losing much of the stakeholders' cooperation and may even be accused of withholding information.

PRIORITISATION

When it comes to prioritising the specification of the products to be delivered, a discreet recommendation to the client and/or sponsor should be made to emphasise strategic prioritisation as a formal process to counter the political prioritisation common in higher PDI cultures. Care should be taken however not to be seen by jealous senior managers as compromising their decisions or suggestions. Therefore, if the client and/or sponsor accept your recommendation, ask them to communicate their decision without making overt reference to your role in the recommendation. This may sound insincere but it is not; indeed, you are sacrificing the opportunity to gain credit.

RISK ESCALATION TRIGGERS

While it is true that the project overall performance suffers as the results of overly low-risk escalation triggers, you have little influence in this context beyond your initial recommendations about the basis on which the triggers are set. Indeed, my advice is not to push for higher triggers unless you are a permanent member of the organisation with a solid relationship with the key stakeholders; otherwise, if indeed your suggestion is accepted, you run the risk of alienating some senior managers or being scapegoated if the new triggers prove problematic, as noted in a higher uncertainty avoidant culture noted earlier.

What would be a better approach with regards to risk management in high PDI cultures is to insist on formal validation of the chosen risk response against the risk's overall value. This is more likely to be appreciated as it leaves most risk decisions in the hands of senior management while providing them with an added tool to aid their decisions. As a result, the stronger tendency they may have to opt for in order to ensure risk elimination is balanced against the risk calculated validation.

In the reverse case, where you are a high PDI project manager in a low PDI environment, you will need to live with higher escalation triggers. This may cause you some discomfort but it should be remembered that, in a low PDI culture, employees have open communication with their managers and are more equipped to address higher risks strategically and politically; as well as being more aware when the risk should be escalated, thanks to their experience.

Facing the Collective

Whereas addressing conflicts openly, directly and freely in an individualistic culture is the norm, in a collective culture, conflict can be a terrifying experience for those involved. Individuals in a collective culture view conflict as a threat to the group harmony. Since they are part of the group, this makes it a threat to their own harmony and, worse still, if they are the cause of the conflict, they feel responsible for one of the most negative outcomes in a collective working culture. As a result, collective cultures are, by nature, conflict avoidant. Although this has its advantages in protecting group harmony, it has its disadvantages in making it difficult, particularly for an outsider, to know if they have group consensus or not. Most members of highly collective cultures would rather agree to something they do not believe in than risk creating a conflict.

There are two main issues you need to be particularly aware of:

1.   Given the collective culture, there may be covert conflict within your team which remains hidden and may not largely disrupt the group's harmony. However, hidden conflicts have an effect on an individual's motivation and they are very likely to diffuse negativity to other members of the team. The project manager should address the individuals concerned, who may be experiencing conflict, *on a one-to-one basis*. I cannot stress one-to-one enough and, remember, conflict discussions should take the form of advice, consultation and an offer of help. If you face resistance to your intervention, don't be dismayed but, on the other hand, don't insist. Having made the point of caring about the individual and the group's wellbeing, and having offered your help will, in itself, both raise individuals' and team motivation and boost their esteem for you; and you need to accept that some conflicts will remain hidden.

2.   When conflicts arise, seek your clients' advice before you intervene. Better still, ask them to act as the mediator to resolve the conflict. Regardless of how respected you may be, you are still new to the group and they will be far more comfortable with an insider's intervention than yours.

The Masculine Enthusiasm

DELEGATION

To a project manager from a feminine-oriented culture working in a masculine environment, the masculine zeal and enthusiasm for accepting or even soliciting delegated responsibilities is admirable, and so it should be.

But remember masculine culture values 'knowing how to source and manage' above 'knowing how to do it yourself'; especially when compared to the opposite preference of a feminine culture. This implies that you should not assume that anyone asking for or taking on new responsibility with enthusiasm is technically proficient to perform it themselves.

While this is not a problem in itself, it may become one if the person concerned fails to source the technical know-how from others.

Take a moment to check the technical proficiency of the candidate in terms of the delegated responsibility and, if they lack the requisite proficiency, ask them to spell out their strategy to make up for this lack.

They may have an excellent and very viable strategy already in hand; or they may not. As the project manager you want to make sure that no job is delegated without solid grounds supporting its delegation.

PLANNING

When it comes to project planning, while the natural tendency of the project manager from a feminine culture is to insist on technical details, in a masculine environment, this is less likely to add efficiency and may even demotivate the team who prefer to make their own decisions on how to approach details as and when they see fit.

This may prove stressful to a project manager unaccustomed to a masculine environment while frustrating for a masculine project manager in a feminine environment. The ability to moderate and follow the rhythm without losing your cool and to guide and motivate the team is key.

Beware! Diffusion ...

One of the most frustrating situations project managers may face is having colleagues or team members taking their professional comments personally.

During my work on various projects in the Middle East I often faced such a situation. On many occasions when I pointed out an error or a better way of working to a team member (often quite insignificant and perhaps something as simple as the format of a report), I would be struck by their emotional response. They would justify why they did it that way and how it was not their fault, when the idea of fault was never implied anywhere. Automatic defence mechanisms seemed to await me every time I had to make such a comment or request.

Taking things personally, as manifested in automatic defence mechanisms, is a mark of highly emotional diffuse cultures. While even more pointed comments on more serious shortcomings made to the more specific British managers are rightly perceived to reflect only on the context of their specific project dynamics; for the diffuse Middle Eastern, shortcomings in the project implies failure of character regardless of context. It reflects on their very person, self-esteem and ego. They will therefore jump to defend themselves.

Not all specific cultures make such emotional responses. According to the American sociologist Talcott Parsons, specific and diffuse cultures are divided into Neutral and Affective cultures. His model gives us four possible combinations being *Specific–Neutral, Specific–Affective, Diffuse–Neutral and Diffuse–Affective*. It is within *Diffuse–Affective* cultures, such as the Middle East and parts of Africa and South America, that you may face these defensive reactions. In Japan or Denmark, which are *Diffuse–Neutral* cultures this is unlikely to happen.

Taking things personally can be a tough issue to tackle given the emotions of the subject. Being very delicate and outlining issues in a positive way, noting that your comments do not reflect on the subject's general performance may help, although it may not completely eliminate the reaction.

PART IV
Culture and the Project Team

In Part III we reviewed how an organisation's culture, be it national, regional or any other working culture, will influence project management practices, and what options the project manager may have at hand to influence such practices for the benefit of the project's success and overall value.

In this part, we will address how the project manager can best manage the cultural diversity in a multicultural project team. This differs from the last part in two distinct ways:

1.   In this part we are concerned with the relationship that the project manager has with his or her direct team. That is, the direct stakeholders who report to them and for whom they are the project leader.

2.   Although a multicultural team can include archetypical members of the cultures involved, it can also include the zero archetype 'Culture Soup'; and as the last part concentrated mainly on the archetypical approach, we will be using the Culture Soup approach in this part.

A word of advice. When managing the individual members of a multicultural project team, start by assuming that each individual is a Culture Soup. There are two significant merits to this approach:

1.   There is a very thin line between archetyping and stereotyping. A project manager assigned to a project for an organisation that comes from a different national culture to their own is justified in managing their own expectations and approach by making an initial archetypical presupposition of what to expect of the organisation. But, they are not justified in applying this approach to any individuals. Individuals vary widely even within the most coherent of cultures and archetyping is more likely to be simple stereotyping.

2.   The Culture Soup approach works for Culture Soups and archetypes alike, and in being an approach that is open and free from any presupposition, the project manager is far more likely to objectively understand their team members' strengths and weaknesses. When this approach is applied to archetypical members of a culture, the team members will positively perceive this project manager's objectivity towards them.

Chapter 18

The Six Steps of Project Management Cultural Tuning

I can sense some of my readers wincing at this title. After all, it sounds like an instruction manual for something that is abstract and requires a soft rather than an elaborated step-by-step approach. I am also aware that the format of the title is rather 'clichéd'.

Please allow me to explain. The cultural tuning approach is far from a clear-cut step-by-step implementation guide, and is as you would rightly expect, a soft approach. When I wrote about this approach, which is something I have been informally implementing for over a decade, my main concern was the risk that readers misunderstood or misapplied it. Just as there is a thin line between archetyping and stereotyping, there is also a very thin line between an 'open minded objective approach to cultural tuning' and a deluded *'holier-than-thou psychoanalytical approach of cultural manipulation'*.

This is why I broke down a soft approach into *six sequentially* applicable areas that are crucial to keep the method open and objective.

Why the 'clichéd' language style of the title? To remind you that they are exactly *six* steps.

Step 1 – Awareness. You are Part of the Problem

A cultural conflict arises when individuals or groups from two or more cultures are unable to perceive each other's point of view; they do not see eye-to-eye.

The greatest error is to believe that we can naturally observe cultures 'objectively'. Culture resides in all of us and is as deep rooted as our oldest values and our identity. Whenever we observe a behaviour, we instinctively validate that behaviour against our own values. Our values are the subconscious filters through which we distinguish the desirable and the undesirable.

This process of filtering observations through our own values is key to our survival and wellbeing. We use our values subconsciously to determine who fits in our group and who does not, whom we would accept as friend and who we would not, who is fit to marry our daughter and who is not and who can we partner with for a new business venture and who we will not!

The cultural orientations we are addressing that sit on each pole of the cultural dimensions can neither be tagged as good nor bad. We had seen how the working context determines which culture works best. For example, lower uncertainty avoidance (UAI) in research and development while higher UAI in quality control.

Yet, our instinctive judgement will favour the practices of those who share our values. A high UAI manager would instinctively favour employees who avoid higher uncertainty initiatives and plan in intricate detail prior to any implementation. This has both pros and cons and it is where 'awareness' comes in.

Unless the manager is aware that they are highly UAI oriented, they will be unaware of the bias that this can create in their recruitment of others, their communication and their decision making. Once awareness kicks in, a good manager will set standards for recruitment that are objective to the job requirement and not subjectively shaped by their own cultural preference.

A multicultural project manager is unlikely to have the luxury of selecting his or her own team. More often than not, they will need to work with a pre-assigned team with whom they have never worked before. Awareness for the project manager is therefore not meant to serve in recruitment but rather in managing the multicultural team and allocating the right team member to the right job.

Let us illustrate this process. Using Table 18.1 below and scales from 1 to 5, rate yourself on each of the six dimensions. Do not rush; think about it in terms of your past experiences. Go back to the chapters that explain these dimensions and reread the end table with the opposing traits of each dimension. Take your time; this is a very worthwhile exercise.

Table 18.1   Cultural self-analysis

I – Very Low 2 – Low 3 – Neutral 4 – High 5 – Very High

Dimension	Acronym	High Orientation	Low Orientation	My Orientation
Power Distance	PDI	High power distance	Low power distance	
Uncertainty Avoidance	UAI	High uncertainty avoidance	Low uncertainty avoidance	
Individualism vs. Collectivism	IDV	Individualism	Collectivism	
Masculinity vs. Femininity	MAS	Masculine	Feminine	
Specific vs. Diffuse	SDI	Specific	Diffuse	
Sequential vs. Synchronous time	SST	Sequential	Synchronic	

Self-awareness of our own cultural orientation serves two prime purposes:

- Without self-awareness we cannot be objective and any judgement we make will be coloured by our own culture. We therefore must start by knowing ourselves before we proceed into the next five steps of cultural tuning, and we should remind ourselves of our own orientation each time we make an assumption.

- It helps you realise your cultural strengths and weaknesses with regards to your responsibilities. Project managers that identify themselves as highly synchronic and very low on uncertainty avoidance may decide to allocate the job of project planning and risk management to a team member who is highly sequential and of neutral UAI. This strength and weaknesses approach is not exclusive to culture of course and is already used by many good managers. However, in a multicultural environment, it adds an extra element to our advantage.

Step 2 – Observation. Free from Prejudice

Observe the way your team is working from the perspective of the cultural dimensions. Reflect on which observed behaviours are more masculine and which are more feminine. Who prefers doing things individually and who prefers working as a group, and so on. You may find this easier to do at the end of the working day by mentally recalling the days' events. Personally, I like to think of it as a movie playing back in my head with a challenge to identify cultural influences.

All you are doing is observing, trying to get some awareness of your new multicultural project team; nothing more. Make no assumptions at this point and, remember, if the team has never worked together before, it is likely that the members are adapting their behaviour and not working in their natural way. Your job, as the project proceeds, may involve allocating responsibilities to the appropriate team members that can perform them efficiently and without handholding; that is, allocating them tasks that fit their culture. For the moment just observe, do not judge, take notes and speculate but avoid assumptions.

To illustrate the six steps, let's use the following example. The narrator is the project manager:

> Newsmobile, an American luxury automotive manufacturer, is developing a new car model with a sophisticated computer control system and interface that will allow the driver to control various functions of their car with minimum distractions from the road. The computer system and interface project codenamed Seamless, involves the use of various hardware and software suppliers worldwide including Equipo, a Spanish auto computers manufacturer with long record of developing state of the art similar products in the industry.

> As most key project suppliers (including Equipo) are European, Newsmobile decided on Madrid as the location of the main project management and coordination office, with supporting staff in other key locations. The project manager was selected by both Newsmobile and Equipo on the basis of relevant experience.

Project manager's notes:

- *Clara, the lead project controller assigned by Newsmobile, mentioned that she will be working from home for the next couple of days to complete an analysis of resource requirements free from interruption in the office.*

- *Clara's first draft resource analysis has a very detailed breakdown of requirements. I wonder how realistic this is, given the duration of the project is over a year?*

- *Eduardo, the lead engineer at Equipo, has already started talking to our ICT suppliers although we have not completed the first draft of the technical specifications yet. He says this enables us to catch their interest and input suggestions in advance.*

- *Simon, the young man supporting the project planning and logistics supplied to the project by the British project resources consultancy ProSure, has voiced concerns to me in confidence that Eduardo is passing to him documents and notes from his meetings with the ICT suppliers, which are rather messy and confusing. He is also anxious that failure on his part to make sense of Eduardo's documents will compromise his role and may reflect badly on his reputation in the future. For this project he is reporting directly to Clara.*

- *Eduardo keeps going off track in meetings, bringing all kind of subjects into the discussion. I had to stop him on several occasions to get back to our agreed agenda.*

- *Clara suggested that we increase our tracking and update cycle frequency from bi-weekly to weekly.*

Such observations and note taking helps us formulate an idea of the working preferences of our team members.

Remember you need to remain an objective observer. Do not ask the members about their own orientation towards the cultural dimensions unless you know them well and have an existing working relationship with them; in which case, they are not the ideal target of the six steps approach as your perceptions are subjective to the existing relationship.

Asking the team about their cultural orientation will almost certainly result in some responses that represent what they'd like to be or what they think you want to hear. It will also colour your own observations. In the early days of the project team forming, probing them with questions about their psychology will feel intrusive to them and be unwelcome.

Step 3 – Association. Link to the Cultural Dimensions

As the project proceeds, certain issues and conflicts will arise. In a multicultural project, if these are not addressed immediately and efficiently, some of these conflicts risk becoming critical far faster than in a culturally homogeneous project. This is because, in a single culture there are more conflicts arising from differences in opinions or approach rather than an objection about what is believed to be appropriate or inappropriate. A multicultural environment holds an extra layer of complexity, and even the seemingly simplest of conflicts, left unresolved, can turn into an irreconcilable challenge of values.

The multicultural project manager needs to identify conflicts as soon as (if not before) they arise and, at that point, speculate if and how culture may have played a role. Use the cultural dimensions as your guide and keep in mind your own orientations throughout to counter any of your own subjective filters and be as objective as possible.

Do not force too much meaning into every element of behaviour, and do not attempt to map all the cultural dimensions to all your team at once. Do what is necessary at the time. Keep it simple.

A major factor behind large projects' failure is their sheer scale, which adds significant complexity to their management. Breaking down large projects into smaller chunks adds clarity, reduces complexity and increases chances of success. The same rules apply to the six steps. Break down each specific situation using past events as lessons learnt for the next.

Project manager's notes:

> Eduardo calls me asking to meet as soon as possible. He expresses concern and dissatisfaction with Clara's request for a weekly tracking and update meeting. Eduardo notes that he disagrees with Clara's detailed plan, believing it to be unrealistic in light of the relative ambiguity beyond the immediate future, especially given the innovative nature of the project's deliverables. Eduardo further notes that Clara's frequent interruptions with requests for yet unavailable information is causing delays and frustrations to him and his team. Now that she is requesting a more frequent tracking and update cycle, he felt he had to talk to me.

> What Eduardo is unaware of is that, a day earlier, Clara had come to see me to voice her own concerns about him. She had complained that Eduardo is disorganised and takes his own initiatives without consulting with her. She noted that he contacted various suppliers, bypassing her entirely and prior to the completion of formal requirements. Clara has no doubt that Eduardo is a brilliant engineer but her concern is that

the suppliers will not take us seriously if we make such unstructured 'requests for quotation', and that this lack of structure may set a standard with the suppliers we finally select. She is also displeased that Eduardo is not giving her his time to plan, claiming that it is 'too early to plan' and that he is 'too busy'. He even asked her not to approach his team without his knowledge and consent.

What am I to do? Both Clara and Eduardo's concerns have their weight in truth. After all, given that our project aims to deliver a new and innovative product does create ambiguity and detailed planning beyond the near future is unrealistic. Yet, it is also true that a complete lack of planning, even high-level planning, will only increase the complexity and ambiguity of this already ambitious project. Plus, Eduardo should have consulted with Clara prior to visiting the suppliers regardless of whether she was right or wrong; she is the project controller!

And why did Eduardo ask Clara not to approach his team without his knowledge? It is her job to do so.

Beyond personalities, could culture have a part to play?

Clara is planning in too much detail and has even taken time away at home to do so uninterrupted. She also requested a more frequent tracking and update cycle. There is no doubting her professionalism or conscientiousness, however, it seems that she is overly aiming to be in control of the situation. Is it because she is oriented towards higher uncertainty avoidance (UAI)? In light of earlier observations, Clara has no quarrels about working from home during the early days of this project, and she is happy to determine the planning and tracking approach independently based on her own experience, both of which could imply lower UAI and lower power distance (PDI). She also feels it to be appropriate to directly approach team members without having to go through the hierarchy, which also points towards lower PDI and lower UAI orientations.

Is she overly sequential? That could be a good clue. After all she is very organised and intricately plans her weekly activities in advance. To know what Clara is up to now or at anytime during the next week, you only need to view her visible calendar on the project portal.

What about Eduardo? He seems the opposite of Clara as far as being organised is concerned and his complete rejection of any planning is unreasonable. Indeed, he always arrives at meetings without reviewing the agenda and easily drifts off track. He is extremely clever and the best technically-equipped person his organisation could have selected to be the lead engineer for this particular project, but he surely needs to be managed. Is that going to be possible or will he take offence? After all, he asked Clara to go though him prior to approaching his team. Eduardo is perhaps synchronic with low UAI orientation, which is great for creativity but not so much for implementation; but is he of high power distance (PDI) orientation?

Whoever said engineers were overly organised … !

Clara and Eduardo could be a great team if I manage the situation well. I have made the following assumptions, but I must validate them first.

- *Clara: Very sequential and relatively low PDI orientation. Probably low UAI orientation.*

- *Eduardo: Low UAI orientation, synchronic and relatively high PDI orientation.*

And what about Simon? I can sense his anxiety and failing motivation. He is beginning to confine himself to mechanical documentation and taking meeting minutes. He also avoids any direct contact with the project team beyond the necessary minimum and prefers to request information and updates by email.

Noting his anxiety and avoidance of direct contact with the management, coupled with his preference for structure and organisation in his work, I believe that:

- *Simon is of relatively high PDI and UAI orientations, sequential and feminine (low MAS) orientation.*

Step 4 – Validation. Test Your Speculation

Having made your assumptions, the next step is to validate them. Validation is of prime importance for two key reasons:

1.   As self-aware and objective as one may try to be, your assumptions will still be coloured by your own orientation. A very masculine project manager who thrives on working late nights and weekends, may wrongly assume that reasonably masculine members of their team are feminine if they don't work the weekend and do no more than ten hours a day. The first of the six steps aims at reducing the subjectivity of such assumptions. However, and no matter how self-aware you try to be, complete objectivity is never possible.

2.   And, I dare say, as important as the above point is, the fact is that one and the same practice or behaviour can spring from different orientations. Both high UAI and being sequential result in the need to plan in detail; yet, the two dimensions show no evident correlation. You must therefore be sure of the dimension behind the practice prior to taking any action. And some unusual practices or behaviours may spring from neither culture nor personal trait. It could be that the specific situation has given rise to a specific practice. In our example, that may well have been the case behind Eduardo's apparently high PDI behaviour towards Clara.

Now back to our project manager:

One way or another, I must talk to both Clara and Eduardo and come up with a solution to their conflict. Should I call them to the same meeting and place all the cards on the table? My earlier speculation about Eduardo being of a high PDI orientation while Clara is the opposite may make this a bad idea. I note Clara's style of being admirably direct and to the point; however, if she and Eduardo have opposing values on PDI, then it is best that I talk to them one at a time to start with.

I need to get more clarity on Eduardo's thoughts and orientation so I will meet with him first.

(After the meeting):

That was interesting! I invited Eduardo to propose a structure to his work package (WP) with the corresponding interdependencies with the other stakeholders to enable them to manage their own structure accordingly. Eduardo acknowledged that he finds it particularly hard to organise his work and, usually, he relies on one of his team members to manage organisation. He then notes that given that engineering has to interface with external stakeholders beyond their organisation, his team may lack the skills to do the job efficiently. Then after a short pause he asked: 'But isn't this Clara's job?'

I pointed out that only a day earlier he had complained about Clara's interference and believed it to be too early to plan. I also let him know that I had the impression he did not approve of her approaching his team without passing through him. Eduardo did not need to reflect before responding, he immediately said:

'Clara is asking for first draft requirements which we are putting together. She cannot help us on that front, as it is technical and time consuming and we are already overloaded, and so she must wait until we have finished with it. Only then will we be able to provide our timeline and resource requirements for her to plan. I also asked Clara to go through me for the benefit of my team's morale. She is very persistent and they are getting quite annoyed by her!'

I promised Eduardo that I would talk to Clara and work on a mutually agreeable solution.

My meeting with Clara was less relaxed. Clara insisted that, regardless of what support she or others can give to Eduardo and regardless of his seniority, for this project he needed to be organised and plan his own activities. This took some discussion and I outlined three points:

1.   Creative people are often disorganised and being so can correlate to higher creativity.

2.   Is it realistic to expect a senior professional to change an approach that he's learned over many years for this project? Would this not present a risk rather than an added value?

3.   With all the uncertainties facing this highly innovative project, is she truly confident that detailed planning beyond the immediate future is appropriate?

Clara agreed that we have to find a suitable solution and made a comment that she admires Eduardo's designs. This last note I am sure she made to illustrate no ill feelings towards him and to assure me that she is not as inflexible as I may think. I left with a smile.

It's time to rethink my earlier speculations:

- *Clara is sequential and very low PDI oriented.*

- *Eduardo is synchronic, low PDI and low UAI oriented.*

This begins to look better ...

The next day, I asked for Clara and Eduardo to meet me after lunch.

But what about Simon?

Step 5 – Strategy. Plan Your Approach

As important as it may be to devise an effective strategy to address cultural conflicts immediately, it is much simpler than it seems once you have completed the previous four steps.

Having identified the cause and effect of cultural orientations within the context of a given conflict, we need to make a choice of one or more of the following four options:

CHANGE THE TEAM MEMBER'S WORKING CULTURE

This is not always a viable option, especially when it comes to more mature professionals and to cultural practices that arise from deep values. For example, a high PDI-oriented young professional may change to low PDI once they feel confident about their role and responsibility, and realise that the bosses are easily approachable and will listen to opinions and ideas that conflict with their own. On the other hand, it is particularly hard to get a masculine professional to become feminine and vice versa as this dimension has a much stronger link to personal preference than is the case with PDI. However, where possible, changing a person's working culture can lead to particularly satisfying results. The subject realises that they are capable of working effectively in different ways to those to which they were accustomed and this gives them higher confidence and motivation.

CHANGE THE TEAM MEMBER'S ROLE

Culture provides us with an indicator of strength and weakness which differ depending on our role and the context. A strength in a certain role or context can easily turn to a weakness in another, and vice versa. For example, high UAI orientation can impact negatively on planning projects that aim to deliver a new and innovative product involving uncertainly and low clarity beyond the immediate future's activities. Detailed planning of such projects will be unrealistic and mislead the stakeholders' expectations. Furthermore, as each new event proves itself at variance with the detailed plan, frequent replanning becomes a futile requirement and adds anxiety to the highly UAI-oriented person. On the other hand, the same high UAI orientation will prove useful in certain situations such as when planning the details of a well-defined deliverable.

SUBSTITUTE THE TEAM MEMBER

If, after considering these options, it becomes evident that a team member cannot function with the mix of cultures in the project, then substituting that member with another maybe an option. It is, however, not always possible to do so and depends directly on the project manager's authority and autonomy as well as the political implications for such substitution. Should you be considering this option you would be well advised to reflect on the impact it will have on the morale of the other team members.

ACCEPT AND PROVIDE SUPPORT TO THE TEAM MEMBER

If none of the above options apply, or as an alternative to substituting the person concerned, the project manager must accept the team member with their current abilities, identify the skills that are lacking for their role and provide support to compensate. This needs to be done discreetly and delicately and not be an open acknowledgement of shortcomings, which will only contribute to ill feelings and negative team dynamics.

The golden rule is always: if there is nothing you can do about a situation, accept it and make the best out of it.

> *Both Eduardo and Clara came to the meeting in good spirits with the objective of agreeing the best approach to communication, planning and control. After some healthy discussion in which both points of view were presented, we came to the following agreements:*

- *Clara will adopt high-level planning for the overall project duration. I will present the plan to our client as the only realistic option and explain that detailed activities with accurate timeline and resources are unrealistic at this point and that we will provide a detailed breakdown of the current plan as each emerging phase becomes clearer.*

- *Update and tracking will be increased to a weekly cycle since, regardless of the level of details in the plan or the readiness of any specifications, we need to be fully aware of our current status.*

- *Simon will be assigned three days a week as the project planner for Eduardo's department and will also assist in their documentation and reporting. Eduardo's design team are very casual and Simon should feel at ease working with them (while they in turn should feel less threatened by a young professional than an overly direct and persistent senior project controller. But this point, of course, I kept to myself).*

- *Both Simon and Clara can approach Eduardo's team directly as long as he is kept informed of any issues that need his direct attention.*

- *Eduardo will make sure he is better prepared for future project meetings; for the benefit of the other attendees and for his own efficiency and productivity.*

All clear then, but who should speak to Simon?

Step 6 – Act. Tune, Implement and Support

A good job involves two parts; 'doing the right thing' and 'doing it in the right way'.

While doing the right thing is perhaps more easily agreed upon, how to do it is not.

We had seen that, in collective cultures, group harmony comes before an individual's needs and that in high PDI cultures respecting hierarchy comes before faster communication. Thus, once we have identified the best strategy to reduce conflicts and make the best of our multicultural team's capabilities, we must give good thought to how to implement it.

Back to our story:

Simon, who's employer is likely to be of higher PDI orientation (given my observation of his own working culture), is unlikely to be comfortable in modifying his role without prior consent from his boss. Likewise, and if my speculation is correct, neither will his boss be happy. I am not sure if such speculation about his company's PDI orientation is totally correct. It may be that the high PDI orientation of Simon is an acquired culture from another environment (possibly his family or his national culture). This is, however, irrelevant and the good thing is that there is no harm speaking to Simon's boss to get his consent beforehand even if he is of low PDI orientation. It is appropriate to do so whatever the cultural context.

(After the call):

Simon's boss was pleased to have one of his employees exposed to an extended role from which he can learn. I have asked Clara if she minds that I speak to Simon about the role (he is less threatened by me than Clara, but then again, I kept this to myself).

*I have spoken to Simon who was nervous, at first, and probably feared that our meeting was about some shortcoming in his performance. He soon relaxed when I told him that we **need** him to help Eduardo and his team in planning their work; and to support them in documentation and reporting. He asked if this would be agreeable to Clara and when I told him that it was a joint proposal with her and that his own manager thought it a good opportunity for him to learn, he could not suppress a laugh of relief.*

Afterword

No professional text can ever be complete. However, there are three distinct areas where this book is evidently incomplete. The first is that it represents a mainly occidental perspective. This is a reflection of the author's professional background and the only way for this work to be relatively 'objective'.

Is this book then only of use to Western project managers? Not so, since the book contains two distinct elements common to all management – Content and Approach.

The approach to managing the cultural diversity and its influence on projects outlined in the last two parts is applicable across any culture, industry and type of business. The content, on the other hand, is written from the occidental perspective and therefore holds truer of the occidental managers who find themselves in similar situations to those described in the text. This however, adds a significant value to the non-occidental reader in providing them with a deeper understanding of the Western perspective.

The second way in which this book is incomplete is that it is not only a more occidental perspective, but more so the 'author's' perspective. I consider my cultural orientation to be of low power distance, moderate individuality, feminine, low uncertainty avoidance, very specific and moderately sequential.

One particular area where my own subjectivity has probably become apparent to the reader is my emphasis on the virtue of collective cultures; something that I myself only became aware of when finishing this book. In saying this, however, I am not taking back my positive observations on collectivism; instead, I am noting that I have given more emphasis to collective virtues as compared to individualistic virtues. In other words, in my efforts to be objective towards collectivism I became somewhat subjective towards individualism.

Finally, the third way in which this book is distinctly incomplete is that it makes use of existing 'culture and management' research, and these in their own turn are incomplete; as cultures continue to change and evolve, more rapidly today than ever in the history of humanity.

This research has identified three elements that constitute the foundations of multicultural management. These are: the cultural dimensions, the orientations that various nations hold on these dimensions, and how such orientations would impact management style and practices.

The cultural dimensions themselves do not change with time and globalisation, and form part of the fundamentals pillars of related current and future studies. This is not to say that we have identified all possible dimensions. There are more cultural dimensions yet to be discovered, and part of the researchers' job is to do so by involving the concerned cultures in structuring the very methods of such identifications; as did Michael Harris Bond with the Chinese Value Survey, which identified the dimension of long-term and short-term time orientations.

The second and third major contributions of the existing research is in identifying the various nations' orientations on the cultural dimension and the effects of these orientations on the various spheres of life including work. These orientations, which were identified mainly through surveys, have proven to be increasingly elusive with the rapid forces of globalisation; including economical and political crises resulting in sharing cultures, abandoning cultures, questioning cultures and for many social, ethical, political and professional groups to abandon or adapt their cultural values far more rapidly than would have been previously conceivable; and this last point is what is proving particularly challenging for the surveys to keep up with.

When we consider the above, coupled with, and not independent of, the growth of the international professional nomad which I refer to as the Culture Soup, and who hold values, beliefs and practices that have little resemblance to those of their cultures of genealogical and national origins, we come to understand that a new 'added' approach to culture and management is needed to cater for these forces and their significance.

This added approach, which I propose in Part IV of this book, through ignoring the culture of origin and adopting the illustrated 'here and now' six steps of cultural tuning, is far from complete and should be further examined and elaborated to make it more practical and efficient. However, it is the only approach today that a project manager or a 'temporary' manager can rely on in effectively addressing cultural diversity with the Culture Soups while lacking the cultural assimilation time. Furthermore, this approach can serve as a starting point even when addressing long-term initiatives that cater for assimilation time; by achieving higher harmony and efficiency during the initial periods and prior to assimilation and stabilisation of a long-term working culture.

A final word of advice; caution should be made not to fall into the trap of unconsciously categorising our colleagues and team members on the basis of brief and initial observations. Therefore, following all the six steps in their order is crucial to avoid such a trap which undoubtedly will prove counterproductive should one fall into it.

Without cultural self-awareness and maturity, which allows us a relative objectivity, flexibility and adaptability, no existing or future approach to cultural harmony works.

In managing a multicultural mix, the starting point is always the managers themselves.

Appendix I

The Relationship between Individualism and Collectivism

Although most cultural studies place individualism and collectivism on a single scale with one being the opposite of the other, it is important to understand the relationship between the two opposites, as neither is perceived as an absolute virtue by any society. This is because of the very nature of individual and collective thinking.

For most of the cultural dimensions, a society's orientation towards one pole or another is usually perceived by that society as generally beneficial (for example, being feminine rather than masculine and thus placing emphasis on the work–life balance; preferring lower to higher power distance be it in the family, in politics or in the workplace); with individualism and collectivism this is rarely the case.

If you ask a colleague a series of questions to determine their IDV orientation you will most likely find that context rather than culture will be the main source of variation. This is not unusual and it is common in some cultures to find a simultaneous preference for strong collectivism in the family and strong individualism in the workplace or politics. In the Middle East, where this is often the case, it is probably an outcome of the changes experienced by the region following the First World War. The political and economical structures that gave wealth and power to the few over the many, and finally resulted in the revolution we call today the Arab Spring, were felt and resented throughout this period by the majority of the population. Citizens of these countries lost trust in the government and their monopolised economies, and broke the collective ties with them. The family, on the other hand, became even more collective as, along with close friends, they remained the only group whom you can trust and rely on for support in the absence of an honest economical and political system.

On the other hand, during the era of the Soviet Union, a child or a young man renouncing his *capitalist* parents to the mother state was not an uncommon occurrence. The emotional orientation for many was the exact opposite of that of the Middle East. Absolute collective thinking when it comes to society and state as a whole (including the state's economic machinery) left little collectivism to spare to family and friends. Indeed, at its extreme the communist state perceived strong family ties as a threat.

In Plato's *Republic*, the philosopher represented his ideal of the perfect state, which was of significant influence to the development of later communist states; children are separated from their parents at birth so as to prevent family ties from compromising loyalty to the state. The only exception was for the producer classes, such as rural farmers who had little to do with politics and city life and could not therefore, through their imbalanced loyalty between family and state, cause damage to the perfect state harmony.

This makes it inappropriate to set expectations in one context (for example, the workplace) based on an observed behaviour in another (for example, family and friends). The various studies on individualism and collectivism and their published results are an average across the various contexts; often producing a meaningless score in terms of useful application.

> It could easily be the case that two countries which scored similarly on the IDV index are exact opposites when you consider the dimension in a specific context, such as the workplace and therefore project management.

Consequently, and apart from one or two exceptions, most collective cultures do not see collectivism as a virtue *per se*. They see it as a virtue in a specific context (and a vice in another).

Understanding this special relation between the two poles of this dimension and their often independent play in different contexts explains many of the various research contradictions for one and the same country. It also explains why some of the countries that scored high in collectivism have few collective values at work (or vice versa). Consider the differences in orientation towards the state, work and family in China, Bangladesh, Singapore and West Africa, all of which have scored exactly the same on the IDV index (20).

Finally, we should not shy from asking whether collectivism/individualism is not more than a single cultural dimension. If it should not be divided into the main spheres that are political, social, family and the workplace?

The first criticism I can imagine to this suggestion would be that each dimension manifests itself differently in different spheres, but this fact does not mean that it is more than a single dimension. However, I argue that power distance, which research has shown to be closely correlated to the IDV index, is approached as a different dimension due to its different implications in different life spheres from that of IDV. In other words, expanding the scope of IDV further would make it encompass the PDI, yet this would make it difficult to study its practical applications.

One thing is for sure: social psychologists have only touched the surface of this most powerful of dimensions and we still have much to learn.

Individualism and Collectivism vs. Universalism and Particularism

Amongst Fons Trompenaars's cultural dimensions is Talcott Parsons's *Universalism vs. Particularism* social dimension.

We had noted earlier that a universalist culture views rules and regulations as universally significant with people in such cultures sharing the belief that general rules, codes, values and standards take priority over particular needs and claims of friendship and family relations. In a particularist culture, far more attention is given to the obligation of relationship and particular circumstances. Exceptions are often made for friends and family and rules are regularly undermined by the particular needs and certain situations within a relationship.

Although this dimension differs in its dynamics and effects from the IDV dimension, there is a strong correlation between the two.

A collective society will tend to be more particularist whereas an individualistic society will favour universalism. Each of these societies will frown at the other's preference. The individualistic–universalist sees the collective's particularism as *corrupt* and standing in the way of meritocracy while the collective–particularist will see the individualistic's universalism as unreasonably cold and lacking of consideration to particular needs.

Yet, and at the extreme poles, the opposite can sometimes be true. Consider the early Soviet Union's orientation towards *Universalism vs. Particularism*. As far as family and social circles are considered, the orientation was highly Universalist. Any exceptions or preferred treatments provided on a basis other than state benefits were seen as corrupt or even criminal; that is, within the family and social context they were simultaneously highly collective and highly universalists. This observation further re-enforces my argument for splitting the IDV index into the main life spheres.

Individualism and Egoism

One of the most commonly made mistakes is to associate individualism with egoism and consequently believe that members of an individualistic society are more selfish.

Although such belief is not without some visible evidence, the correlation made between individualism and egoism is incorrect.

Culture is developed by the group, which in turn forms a moral circle, and even the most individualistic of cultures is a culture that is developed by a group.

Four centuries ago, the English poet John Donne wrote:

No man is an island, entire of itself, every man is a piece of the continent.

What distinguishes an individualistic from a collective culture is not in the strength of the desire to contribute to the group, but in the belief of *how* such contribution can be best achieved for the overall benefit of the group.

A collective culture believes this to be best achieved by retaining tightly cohesive group dynamics in which all individuals should participate; with individuals never acting independently and the group providing each individual appropriate support and protection, society as a whole will flourish. The benefits of collective initiatives are therefore seen as both morally and practically higher than the total sum of its otherwise separate individual's initiative.

On the other hand, an individualistic culture believes that the overall group benefit is best achieved by liberating its members' individualistic potential. In many situations collectivism is believed to be oppressive to the individual's initiative both morally and practically. Therefore, the sum of the society individuals' initiatives is seen as, overall, more beneficial to the group than those of the collective initiatives.

Having said that, evidence shows, beyond any doubt, that members within individualistic societies are more likely to act egotistically and with less consideration *to their group* than their collective counterpart. Yet, the very fact that individualistic societies have less rigid values and norms makes them more open, tolerant and considerate to other societies and groups which do not form part of their moral circle.

One can deduce that from a perspective that is within-the-group, members of an individualistic society are more egotistic than members of a collective society, whereas from the perspective of those outside-the-group, members of a collective society are more egotistic than members of an individualistic society.

If you have travelled to, or worked with, organisations from countries towards the poles of this dimension then you would have surely experienced this. It is far easier for an outsider to be accepted into an individualistic culture than a collective one.

A point that is frequently quoted in support of collectivism against individualism, is that members of a collective society are expected to take care of their parents in their old age while this is rarely the case in an individualistic culture. It is important to note that *not being expected to look after one's parent in their old age* is not a mark of egotism. This independence in individualistic societies is valued by the young and elderly alike. Old members of a high IDV society value their own independence and would feel a great loss of dignity if others (including their own children) have to be *hampered* by their needs. Indeed, pensions, formal social systems and both state and private institutions are developed by individualistic societies to help guarantee their members' independence throughout their life.

I am not naive to the evident reality that not caring for one's parents during old age and preferring to leave them to their own devices or state care is a far more prominent tendency in individualistic societies; indeed, in socially collective societies this would be unthinkable. However, this egotism or selfishness is not an outcome of individualism but rather a negative tendency that flourishes in highly individualistic societies while very rarely in collective ones. Children in a socially collective society who, for whatever just or unjust reason, grow to detach emotionally from, or even hate, their own parents, will still look after their wellbeing until their very last days; it is a revered value in the culture and failure to adhere to it will result in expulsion from the group.

Individualism and Modernisation

For decades, the West believed with good reason that modernisation was best achieved though individualism. At the very peak of this belief today is the US. Tocqueville, the 19th-century French aristocrat, described Americans as exhibiting *a strong confidence in self, or reliance upon one's own exertion and resources*. The 'Commission of National Goals' reporting to President Eisenhower claimed that *the possibility of individual self-realisation was the central goal of American civilisation*.

At the very heart of the Renaissance, the Age of Exploration, the Netherlands' Golden Age, the French Enlightenment and the industrial revolutions of Britain and the US was a move from a more collective to more individualistic thinking. This unleashed the individuals' potential which fostered creativity and faster results. The results of the above were not only enjoyed by the creative individuals but by the society as a whole. Today's Western modernisation, creativity and technology have much of their thanks to give to their earlier shift to individualism.

As a result, for many years the West frowned at the East and considered their collective values to be counter to modernisation. This, however, became a questionable point of view given the rapid and impressive rise of the collective East in the past few decades. Indeed we now know that collectivism does contribute to economic growth and the question being asked is: which part of which pole (individualism and collectivism) leads to which development (early wealth vs. economical growth)?

In other words, it is not the values of individualism as opposing collectivism that are being questioned, but rather the extent of, and the role each of individualism and collectivism in a society's growth.

Circle of Friends

During my earlier career acting as an interim manager for a sub-programme of the European Commission in Syria, I spent approximately 15 weeks a year in the country, split over a number of visits of two to three weeks each.

In the first year, and then throughout, I came to befriend two highly intelligent Syrian professionals. My friends in turn introduced me to their social group (they both are members of the same social group) and I was delighted to be accepted and integrated so rapidly into the group – no doubt thanks to my Syrian, or more specifically Damascene, origins. Indeed, in no time I was treated as any lifelong member and was invited daily to join the group in their social activities, which I did.

These activities, as in many parts of the Middle East, were composed in great part of getting together in cafes or popular restaurants, and passing a good part of the evening eating, drinking fresh fruit juice or tea, smoking narghile (the Turkish habit of smoking tobacco through a bubble pipe), and chatting away pleasantly. Not all members of the group would be present throughout the evening which started about 7pm, but at one time or another in the evening, almost each member (totalling about 15) would pass by at least for an hour; and rarely if ever, would any of them miss more than a day or two in a row.

A few years following my assignment I began to miss out on many of these pleasant outings, reducing my attendance to no more than once a week. Not for any other reason than that I wished to spend some of my free time reading, exploring the local culture or spending some social time with my European colleagues who were also managers and consultants on the same programme. What I never realised at the time is that when I turned down social invitations repeatedly from various members of the group, and was then spotted a number of times socialising with other groups, this was perceived as snubbing the group that had so kindly opened their doors to me few years back. Indeed, they sadly never invited or informed me again of their plans. Some avoided my phone calls and never called back. I realised later that social membership of collective groups has its obligations on all members and these include *exclusivity* and regular attendance.

Governments, Laws and Regulations

Government, laws and regulations are built to reflect the needs of the culture. As such, and especially with regards to IDV and power distance, the impact of culture is striking.

There are, however, many nations where the state does not reflect its national culture but has instead imposed its norms through the governing elites in the belief that the national culture does not hold appropriate values for the overall wellbeing of the country. The USSR is a classic example. The crumbling of the USSR was in part due to the contradiction between the state-imposed norms and the cultural values of the nation. Trompenaars noted that a group with norms that do not reflect its members' values is unstable. More recently, we have witnessed this very instability between state and nation in the Arab Spring.

However, and most interestingly, the second wave of the Arab Spring (the overthrow of the Muslim Brotherhood's democratically elected president by the Egyptian Army in 2013), has shown that this instability can exist even within democratic societies. Up until that and other recent events, it was commonly believed that democracy would eliminate such instability through equal voting rights; the state's norms and the nation's values effectively reflecting each other closely.

Few were so naïve as to believe that democracy is a perfect system but even fewer would have ever perceived that a democratic society does not necessarily reflect or serve the national interests.

One crucial factor is becoming apparent. Consciously or unconsciously, it is the fact that many individualistic cultures have invited very little (or no) collective contribution into their socio-political science that has limited their own understanding of the collective state in modern times.

I can confidently make an exception to the above conscious or unconscious and say mostly consciously of the USA not long ago. In the early 1990s I applied for a visiting visa to the US. Here are some of the questions to be answered on the application form:

- Have you ever been arrested or convicted for any offence or crime, even through subject of a pardon, amnesty or other similar legal action?

- Have you ever unlawfully distributed or sold a controlled substance (drug)?

- Are you a member or representative of a terrorist organisation as currently designated by the US Secretary of State?

- Have you ever participated in persecutions directed by the Nazi government of Germany; or have you ever participated in genocide?

•   Are you a communist or have you ever been a member of a communist party?

The last of which has now been removed from the application form.

Not that political collectivism is necessarily manifested in communism, but communism is a possible manifestation of strong collectivism and holds many social values adapted and practised in many democratic societies today. Rejecting any association with communism outright, to the extent of placing it in a list of exclusions including terrorism, genocide, drug dealing and other hideous crimes, illustrates strong unwillingness to see or hear the point of view from other nations or cultures.

Appendix 2

Sex, Age, Sexism and Masculinity

A Masculine She and a Feminine He?

A major factor that distinguished the masculine–feminine dimension from the others considered in this book is that the masculinity (MAS) orientation differs between men and women. Understandably.

The original Geert Hofstede IBM survey found that, on average, men and women gave different answers when it came to measuring MAS orientation. This was not the case for any of the other dimensions where, on average, within any single society, men and women gave similar answers.

For the majority of cultures measured (and apart from the very poles), men stressed the importance of high earning, competitiveness and achievement (masculine pole), whereas women stressed the importance of the working environment and relationship with colleagues, managers and subordinates (feminine pole).

Interestingly, and on closer observation of the survey answers, women's MAS orientation was more consistent than men's across cultures. Women's scores of the MAS values ranged from very feminine in highly feminine cultures (for example, Sweden and Norway), to moderately masculine in the most masculine cultures (for example, Japan). Men, on the other hand, scored very feminine in highly feminine cultures and very masculine in highly masculine cultures.

The difference between a masculine and a feminine society is therefore more noted in the values of its male members rather than its female members.

The graph in Figure A2.1 shows this difference between men and women on this MAS scale.

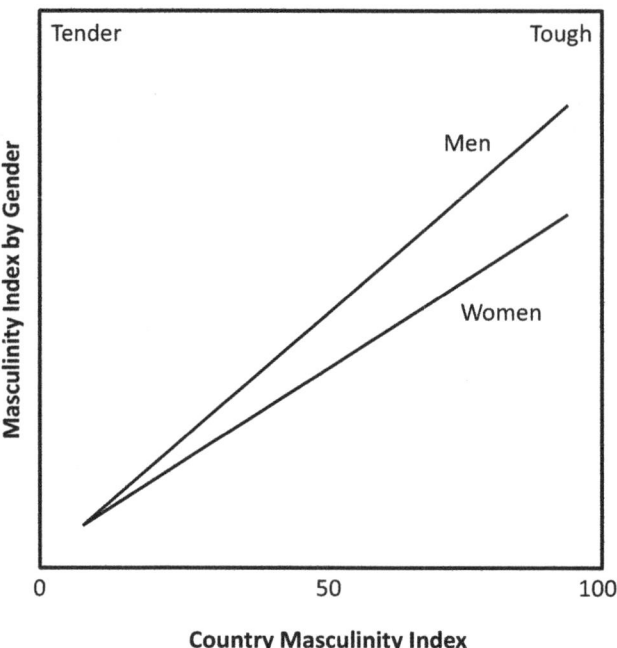

Figure A2.1   Country masculinity score by gender

Source: Geert Hofstede, Gert Jan Hofstede, Michael Minkov, 'Cultures and Organizations, Software of the Mind', Third Revised Edition, McGrawHill 2010, ISBN 0–07–166418–1. © Geert Hofstede B.V. quoted with permission.

Age and Masculinity

Another well-noted aspect of the MAS orientation is age.

As we get older we become more relaxed with regards to achievements, the need to be competitive and face constant new challenges. We have already been through it all (if we are masculine) and now we can relax into the older age of wisdom wishing to enjoy what life has to offer. We therefore become more feminine.

Note that this older age does not start at retirement but sometime in our late 30s (Figure A2.2). It is the period of our life whereby we have already accepted and settled into what we have achieved and can now help the younger generation in their turn. This is one reason why older managers can be better people managers than younger ones.

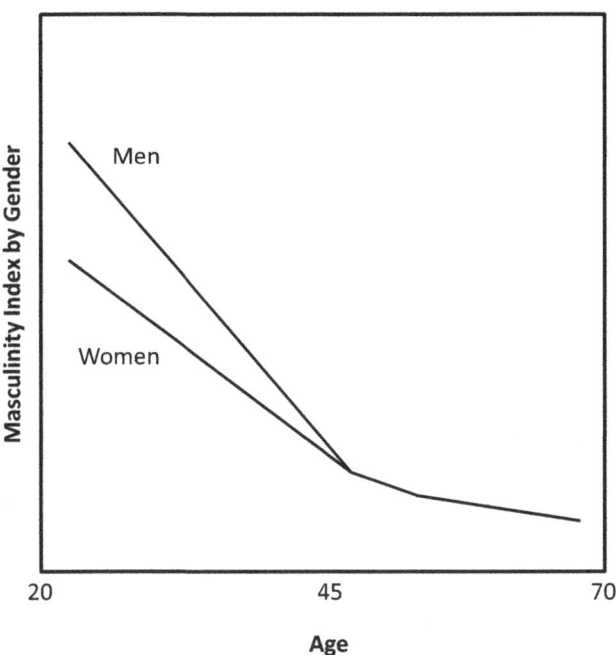

Figure A2.2   MAS score by gender and age

Source: Geert Hofstede, Gert Jan Hofstede, Michael Minkov, 'Cultures and Organizations, Software of the Mind', Third Revised Edition, McGrawHill 2010, ISBN 0–07–166418–1. © Geert Hofstede B.V. quoted with permission.

This age tendency towards femininity at older age is naturally far more marked in masculine societies. It can also be clearly noted in the better harmony enjoyed by couples as they get older.

Men Rule!

Unfortunately but very largely true, even in modern societies, men still rule!

As we have noted in the context of masculinity and femininity, modern societies offer the opportunity of crossing pre-modern gender roles, and choosing not to do so (as in the US and Britain), is *mostly* a matter of choice.

I do not wish to contradict myself within the same chapter but I must highlight the significance of the word *mostly*.

Modern society has stressed equal opportunities for men and women within its rules and regulations, especially in the workplace. This is indeed the case for the US and Britain and most of the European Union. Yet, we have to ask why is it then that many women in these societies continue to fight for equal opportunities and claim the society to be unfairly male-oriented?

Depending on the society in question, the answer could be any or a mix of the following:

- *Sexism* – Equal opportunity rules and regulations are in place, but the male-dominated economy does not adhere to them and still favours employing men to women.

- *Taboo* – Equal opportunity rules and regulations are in place, but the male-dominated society, still imposes the norms which places the woman's role mainly at home, making it socially harder for them to break taboo.

- *Choice* – Equal opportunity rules and regulations are in place, the economy adheres to them and the society accepts them. Most women still play a traditional role by choice. Arguments claiming otherwise are mainly by a misled minority who perceive their own ideal of women sharing men's role at work as superior to those of others; that is, the traditional women role.

The arguments and justifications behind each of the above scenarios are numerous and will not be discussed here. Suffice it to note that not every modern society truly provides women with equal opportunities to men.

We should also note that a modern society may not necessarily have equal opportunities within their rules and regulations. This could arguably be the case for Kuwait whereby:

> Rules and regulations do not present equal opportunities for men and women in each of the various life spheres, still, they do represent what the society at large including both men and women believe to be the correct opportunities for each of the sexes.

Normally, such a society will give higher advantages to women in one sphere while to men in another. All in all, and as far as such a society is concerned, both men and women agree that the system represents their wishes of how their society should be.

To refute this as an example of a modern society on the basis of our differing views is both naive and arrogant. Just as it would be naive not to accept that, in numerous instances, this argument is used by males to justify social inequality when, in truth, women do not share their argument and are indeed at an unfair disadvantage.

Appendix 3

On Time Orientation

Perception of time is not an abstract concept. Social psychologists and anthropologists have split time into well-defined elements. Still, contemporary occidental studies into culture and management, including the pioneering work of Geert Hofstede's IBM research, have failed to identify time as one of the cultural dimensions. It was not until Michael Harris Bond's Chinese Value Survey (CVS) that the significance of time orientation gained prominence.

There is an important lesson to learn from this. Not a new lesson but one well noted by the researchers and that is: a questionnaire or survey constructed by a specific culture will hold questions relating to issues and elements that are *visible* to that constructing culture and can therefore never be objective. Michael Bond understood this limitation when he sought the help of his Chinese students in constructing the very questions and structure of the CVS. Interestingly, while the answers to the CVS identified *time orientation* as a significant cultural dimension, they completely missed out on *uncertainty avoidance*.

As we know, this does not imply that time orientation does not exist in the West or that uncertainty avoidance does not exist in the East. On the contrary, the fact that the occident failed to identify *time orientation* highlights how deeply the concept is imbedded in us. It is so much the norm that even researchers failed to see it! The same applies to uncertainty avoidance in the East.

It is for these reasons that constructing future cultural surveys should have the input, as far as possible, of all the various cultures represented to make them less subjective.

The Origins of Time Orientation

LONG-TERM VS. SHORT-TERM ORIENTATION

Necessity is the mother of invention. In this case, the lack of natural wealth forcing the group to plan long term.

If we return to the case of early societies, settlements were either fortunate to have a stable, habitable, generous and fertile land; or less fortunate in having to work harder for their survival.

Most African and South American countries, which enjoyed being in the first group, sit closer to the pole of short-term orientation. Historically, and prior to the more recent desertification and global economy reducing agricultural wealth to unsustainable levels, early African settlers enjoyed a relatively easy life with sustenance being available in abundance. Even the climate was favourable, requiring little protection from the elements. There was no need for organising and planning long-term expeditions and hunts to maintain a safe and stable society and, as a result, long-term orientation made little sense.

As we move towards colder climates and harsher lands, without social planning and coordination to amass winter provisions and build stronger shelters, the settlement would be threatened. These settlers learned to plan ahead and long-term orientation was born.

Most of the Far East and much of Eastern Europe are long-term oriented.

It is probable that the same factors played a role in making a culture sequential and, indeed, there is a correlation between LTO and sequential cultures as well as between STO and synchronic cultures.

Quality vs. Punctuality Orientation

On this subcomponent of time for which little historical information is available, our research group suggested that STO cultures favour punctuality while LTO cultures favour quality. There is definitely a good logic behind this argument given that faster time to market will achieve profits quicker although not sustainably if quality has been compromised. On the other hand, taking a little longer to get to the market in order to provide better quality often pays off in the longer term.

Our excitement at noting this was short lived when we compared countries' data on the LTO/STO and quality vs. punctuality orientations. They demonstrated no such link.

The only conclusion we can derive is that prior to the industrial revolution and the development of mass manufacturing, our speculation was probably true. It was as industries developed rapidly and good quality became a required feature of acceptable products that STO cultures no longer gave priority to punctuality over quality.

Although this is not a certain conclusion, it does correspond to the fact that projects in STO cultures which deliver a product to be used internally by the organisation (and not to be released to the market against the competition), still compromise quality for the sake of punctuality. This is very often the case of the US and Britain but not in the Far East.

References

Adler, Nancy J. (2007). *International Dimensions*, 5th Edition, South-Western College Publication.

Bond, Michael Harris (2002). Reclaiming the Individual from Hofstede's Ecological Analysis – A 20 Year Odyssey: Comment on Oyserman et al. (2002), *Psychological Bulletin*, 128(1): 73–7.

Bridge, William (2003). *Managing Transition*, 2nd Edition, Nicholas Brealey Publishing.

Cain, Susan (2012). *Quiet: The Power of Introverts in a World That Can't Stop Talking*, Penguin.

De Mascia, Sharon (2012). *Project Psychology*, Gower Publishing.

d'Iribarne, Philippe (1998). *Cultures et mondialisation: gérer par- delà les frontières*, Seuil.

Downes, James F. (1971). *Culture in Crises*, Glencoe Press.

Hofstede, Geert (1980). Motivation, Leadership and Organisation: Do American Theories Apply Abroad?, *Organisational Dynamics*, Summer 1980.

Hofstede, Geert (2003). *Culture's Consequences: Comparing Values, Behaviors, Institutions and Organizations Across Nations*, 2nd Edition, SAGE Publications.

Hofstede, Geert and Michael Harris Bond (1988). The Confucius Connection: From Cultural Roots to Economic Growth, *Organizational Dynamics*, 16(4): 5–21.

Hofstede, Geert, Gert Jan Hofstede and Micheal Minkov (2010). *Cultures and Organizations: Software of the Mind*, 3rd Edition, McGraw-Hill Professional.

Lewis, Richard D. (2006). *When Cultures Collide*, 3rd Edition, Nicholas Brealey Publishing

McClelland, David C. (2010). *The Achieving Society*, Martino Fine Books.

Miknov, Michael (2011). *Cultural Differences in a Globalizing World*, Emerald Group Publishing Limited.

OGC (2007). *Managing Successful Programmes*, 4th Edition, Stationery Office.

Parsons, Talcott (1951). *The Social Systems*, Glencoe Press.

Pollock, David C. and Ruth E. Van Reken (2001). *Third Culture Kids, The Experience of Growing Up among Worlds*, Nicholas Brealey Publishing.

Sadler, Philip (2001). *Management Consultancy*, 2nd Edition, Kogan Page.

Scott Shane, Shekhar Venkataraman and Ian MacMillan (1995). Cultural Differences in Innovation Championing Strategies, *Journal of Management*, 21(5): 931–52.

Shane, Scott (1993). Cultural Influences on National Rates on Innovation, *Journal of Business Venturing*, 8(1): 59–73.

Smith, Peter B., Ronald Fischer, Vivian L. Vignoles and Michael Harris Bond (2013). *Understanding Social Psychology across Cultures*, 2nd Edition, Sage.

The Standish Group International (2011). *The Chaos Manifesto*.

Thiry, Michel (2010). *Program Management*, Gower Publishing.

Triandis, Harry Charalambos (1977). *Interpersonal Behavior*, Brooks/Cole Monterey.

Trompenaars, Fons and Charles Hampden-Turner (2012). *Riding the Waves of Culture*, 3rd Edition, Nicholas Brealey Publishing.

Young, Trevor (2005). *The Handbook of Project Management*, Kogan Page.

Zein, Omar (1994). British Operations in Saudi Arabia: A Cultural/Managerial Conflict (Thesis: International Management MBA, University of Exeter).

Zein, Omar (2010). Roles and Responsibilities in Programme Management. Originally published as a part of 2010 PMI Global Congress Proceedings.

Zein, Omar (2012). Cultural Complexities in International Projects. Originally published as a part of 2012 PMI Global Congress Proceedings.

Zein, Omar (2013). A Borninian Project Manager in Ausmania. Originally published as a part of 2013 PMI Global Congress Proceedings.

Index

References to figures are shown in *italics*. References to tables are shown in **bold**.

If you have found this book useful you may be interested in other titles from Gower

Bridging the Business-Project Divide
Techniques for Reconciling Business-as-Usual
and Project Cultures
John Brinkworth
Hardback: 978-1-4094-6517-1
e-book PDF: 978-1-4094-6518-8
e-book ePUB: 978-1-4094-6519-5

Communicating Projects
An End-to-End Guide to Planning, Implementing and
Evaluating Effective Communication
Ann Pilkington
Hardback: 978-1-4094-5319-2
e-book PDF: 978-1-4094-5320-8
e-book ePUB: 978-1-4724-0832-7

Customer-Centric Project Management
Elizabeth Harrin and Phil Peplow
Paperback: 978-1-4094-4312-4
e-book PDF: 978-1-4094-4313-1
e-book ePUB: 978-1-4094-8379-3

Gower Handbook of People in Project Management
Edited by Dennis Lock and Lindsay Scott
Hardback: 978-1-4094-3785-7
e-book PDF: 978-1-4094-3786-4
e-book ePUB: 978-1-4724-0299-8

GOWER

Leading Complex Projects
Kaye Remington
Hardback: 978-1-4094-1905-1
e-book PDF: 978-1-4094-1906-8
e-book ePUB: 978-1-4094-5923-1

Naked Project Management
The Bare Facts
Dennis Lock
Paperback: 978-1-4094-6105-0
e-book PDF: 978-1-4094-6106-7
e-book ePUB: 978-1-4094-6107-4

Project Success
Critical Factors and Behaviours
Emanuel Camilleri
Hardback: 978-0-566-09228-2
e-book PDF: 978-0-566-09229-9
e-book ePUB: 978-1-4094-5896-8

Reinventing Communication
How to Design, Lead and Manage High Performing Projects
Mark Phillips
Hardback: 978-1-4724-1100-6
e-book PDF: 978-1-4724-1101-3
e-book ePUB: 978-1-4724-1102-0

Visit **www.gowerpublishing.com** and

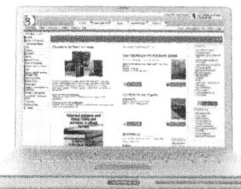

- search the entire catalogue of Gower books in print
- order titles online at 10% discount
- take advantage of special offers
- sign up for our monthly e-mail update service
- download free sample chapters from all recent titles
- download or order our catalogue